Many sensible things get said in this book . . . Kipnis and Herron take up different themes on popular distinctions between the genders . . . and offer a picture of what a complete or thoughtful men's movement would look like.
— Robert Bly, author of *Iron John*

This is a powerful, engaging work. Perceptive and useful, it is also graceful and lyrical. Herron and Kipnis have given a gift to us all.
— Ralph Blum, author of *The Runes Book*

What I loved about this book is, that unlike so many others in the realm of self-exploration, I never felt that I "needed" to finish the read because it was "good" for me. Rather, it moves with a narrative thrust that kept me interested . . . enthralled in fact, while incidentally offering—not teaching—insights into male-female relationships that are profound.
— Bob Chartoff, Academy Award-winning producer
of *The Right Stuff, Rocky,* and *Raging Bull*

What Women and Men Really Want takes us on an important journey into discovery. We learn that the soul-destroying war between the sexes can be won in a way that heals the broken spirit of men and women alike.
— Susan Jeffers Ph.D., author of *Opening Our Hearts to Men,*
Feel the Fear and Do It Anyway, and *Dare To Connect*

Aaron Kipnis and Elizabeth Herron have added another important and encouraging step on the journey of reconciling the sexes.
— Daphne Rose Kingma, author of *The Men We Never Knew*

This is more than a masterful book about relationships. It is the best kind of adventure story, a passionate journey into the heart of the deepest mysteries and bonds which connect men and women. Please read and study its wisdom.
— Gay and Kathlyn Hendricks, authors of *Conscious Loving*

This wonderful book is a bridge over the chasm that has separated the sexes for centuries. A must read that explains men to women; women to men in a way that is personal, poignant, psychological, and passionate.

—**John Lee, author of** *The Flying Boy*

Kipnis and Herron have concluded that women and men do not derive from separate species—that we can be friends and lovers, not foe—and for this I applaud them and their new book.

—**Karen De Crow, former president of NOW**

In its celebration of what's good about gender differences, this book deals a well-deserved blow to the battle between the sexes.

—**Susan Estrich, USC Law Professor and author of** *Real Rape*

This is the book that tackles the topic for the 90s; friendship between the sexes. Male or female, you can only gain from its wisdom.

— **Susan Deitz, nationally syndicated columnist**
and author of *Single File*

Provocative, exciting and immensely useful! This book is a rare gift. Where *Backlash* and *The Myth of Male Power* end, *What Women and Men Really Want* begins. With grace and the force of truth, it propels our culture into the healing phase of gender relationships.

—**Michael Gurian, author of** *The Prince and the King*
and *Mothers, Sons and Lovers*

Aaron Kipnis and Elizabeth Herron are pioneers in this culture, and we need them. *In What Women and Men Really Want*, they move into uncharted territory with grace and determination, and they wind up—both men and women—in a better place. I honor their work in gender reconciliation, and I hope we hear a lot more from them.

—**Asa Baber, columnist for** *Playboy*
and author of *Naked at Gender Gap*

Just as *The Feminine Mystique* heralded the women's movement and *Iron John* catalyzed the men's movement, so does *What Women and Men Really Want* signal the beginning of a third great movement toward gender reconciliation. May both women and men heed the call!

> —Mark Gerzon, author of *A Choice of Heroes*
> and *Coming into Our Own*

Kipnis and Herron walk us into the woods of male-female misunderstandings and prove to be gentle, thoughtful and balanced guides whose leadership will allow us to set up one camp with love rather than two camps of hate.

> —Warren Farrell Ph.D., author of *The Myth of Male Power*
> and *Why Men Are The Way They Are*

This fresh, intelligent, and reader-friendly book demonstrates that understanding, compassion, and justice between the sexes is indeed possible. Kipnis and Herron help us to see the futility of the "war" and the beauty of peace.

> —Marvin Allen, M.A., author of *In the Company of Men:*
> *A New Approach to Healing for Husbands,*
> *Fathers, and Friends*

Aaron Kipnis and Elizabeth Herron are a great storytelling team. *What Women and Men Really Want* reads like an exciting novel. It captures the drama between men and women and has the authority, power and clarity to help revolutionize their relations.

> —Dr. Shepherd Bliss, Psychology Department, JFK University
> and coauthor of *A Quiet Strength: Meditations on Men*
> *and Masculinity*

What Women and Men Really Want is absolutely MUST reading for men and women who are tired of the endless battles and are ready for peace, joy, passion and intimacy now and forever.

> —Jed Diamond, author of *Looking for Love in All the Wrong Places* and *The Warrior's Journey Home*

A well-written book about a timely, important subject. Aaron Kipnis and Liz Herron skillfully combine interesting narrative with useful insights. Both women and men will benefit greatly from reading *What Women and Men Really Want*.

> —Riki Robbins Jones, Ph.D., author of *The Empowered Woman* and *Negotiating Love*

An entertaining adventure tale, a storehouse of interesting facts, and Kipnis and Herron's experienced counsel are skillfully combined to make *What Women and Men Really Want* THE road map for honest and compassionate woman-man dialogue.

> —Joel Edelman, author of *The Tao of Negotiation*

At last we have a book that successfully reframes the polarized dialogue between men and women. This is an extraordinary accomplishment, intelligent and wise, and a good read to boot. Kipnis and Herron are heralds of a new era of reconciliation between the sexes.

> —Jeremiah Abrams, editor of *Meeting the Shadow* and *The Shadow in America*

Aiming to explore the differences between the sexes and facilitate some kind of understanding, two psychotherapists married to each other take some men and women into the woods for an eight-day retreat. . . . we see some genuine breakthroughs and hear some valuable insights. . . . as a model for similar groups on a gender discussions, [*What Women and Men Really Want*] is excellent.

> —*Booklist*

WHAT WOMEN AND MEN REALLY WANT

WHAT WOMEN AND MEN REALLY WANT

*Creating Deeper Understanding
and Love in Our Relationships*

AARON KIPNIS PH.D. AND ELIZABETH HERRON M.A.

NATARAJ PUBLISHING

NOVATO, CALIFORNIA

Published by
Nataraj Publishing
1561 South Novato Blvd.
Novato, CA 94947

Edited by Hal Zina Bennett
Cover art and design by Greg Wittrock
Cover photo by Jerry Bauer
Typography by T·HTypecast, Inc.

The authors of this book do not dispense medical advice nor prescribe the use of any technique as a form of treatment for physical or mental problems without the advice of a physician either directly or indirectly. In the event you use any of the information in this book neither the authors nor the publisher can assume any responsibility for your actions. The intent of the authors is only to offer information of a general nature to help you in your quest for personal growth.

Library of Congress Cataloging-in-Publication Data
Kipnis, Aaron R.
     What women and men really want : creating deeper understanding and
  love in our relationships / by Aaron Kipnis & Elizabeth Herron. —
  Rev. ed.
        p.   cm.
     Rev. ed. of: Gender war, gender peace. c1994.
     Includes bibliographical references.
     ISBN 1-882591-24-0 (alk. paper)
     1. Sex role.   2. Sex differences (Psychology)   3. Communication—
  Sex differences.   4. Man-woman relationships.   I. Herron,
  Elizabeth.   II. Kipnis, Aaron R.   Gender war, gender peace.
  III. Title.
  HQ1075.K573   1995
  305.dc20   95-16835
                                                                   CIP

This book was originally published in 1994 as *Gender War, Gender Peace: The Quest for Love and Justice Between Women and Men* by William Morrow and Company, Inc., New York.

Original hardcover edition, 1994
Revised edition, First printing, September 1995

ISBN 1-882591-24-0

Printed in the U.S.A.
10 9 8 7 6 5 4 3 2

For the children,
with hope for the rebuilding of families
and the renewal of kinship between women and men

CONTENTS

ACKNOWLEDGMENTS

W E WISH TO THANK the following persons who made significant contributions to our ongoing conversation on gender issues: Professor Robert Greenway, who more than twenty years ago, created the first Men, Women, and Nature programs at Sonoma State University and planted many seeds that have borne fruit; Dr. Shepherd Bliss of J.F.K. University for his enthusiastic personal support; Robert Bly for various kindnesses along the way; Helen Starkweather and Dr. Judith Sherven for validating our views on the feminist shadow as they emerged; Dr. John Gray for many discussions deep into the night, in years past; and Dr. Aftab Omar and his wife, Dr. Melissa Swartz, who provoked many in-depth conversations on our topics.

Our parents, Kip and Joey Kipnis, validated our work from the perspective of an older generation, and our daughter, Noelani, kept us in touch with teen culture while being very patient about our long hours locked away in the study. Men's movement pioneer Dr. Warren Farrell was very generous with his research, time, and good will, as was Dr. Dianne Skafte. Alan Rinzler was insightful in helping us sort out our ideas for the initial book proposal and has provided important personal support along the way. Our part-time staff of one, Dona Haber, was a fantastic personal and professional assistant during the many times we just had more to do than was humanly possible.

Dr. Sara Stark provided enormous friendship, many jokes, roller-blading companionship, and teen care. Tory Pyle Becker also provided unwavering emotional support. The women of the Fierce Beauty Society, the men of the Knights Without Armor, and the Malibu gang have all been part of the web of life that sustains us.

Our editor for this paperback edition, Hal Bennett, was a joy to work with. His sensitivity to the story, deep understanding of the material, and gentle yet fierce guidance pulled many diamonds out of the dust. The rest of the team at Nataraj have been great, exemplifying the highest professionalism combined with a deep sensitivity to authors' needs and a commitment to bringing exciting new ideas to the public.

We also want to deeply thank each other for the patience, commitment, trust, playfulness, genuine risk, and love it took to finish this book. We are indebted to the many people who have educated us while attending our workshops and trainings over the years. Most of all, we are grateful to the courageous women and men whose voices fill these pages for granting us the permission to share their private experiences, hopes, fears, and insights with the world.

INTRODUCTION

THIS BOOK GREW from in-depth conversations and experiences with thousands of women and men who have attended our Gender Diplomacy™ workshops, trainings, and conferences around the nation. Most of our workshops are conducted in auditoriums and lecture halls. And we've been impressed by the extent to which women and men can discover a new openness with each other, in a very short time, given the opportunity to do so.

To more deeply explore the material for this book, however, we decided to lead a group of women and men on a one-week trip into the wilderness where we could relax in an environment without the interruptions of preordained meals, starting and stopping times, and the ever-present hum of urban life. We wanted to see if we could deepen the level of intimacy and honest communication within a group by living together as an experimental village. Against the backdrop of nature, and collectively facing the challenge of wilderness survival, the women and men were inspired to open their hearts and minds to new perspectives. The length of time allowed for in-depth dialogues also afforded us an opportunity to take a closer look at many contemporary gender issues such as dating practices; sex discrimination toward women and men; emotional, physical, and sexual abuse; female nurturing power versus male economic power; parenting and relationship conflicts; divorce inequities for both sexes; different communication styles; and differing spiritual and philosophical ideals.

At this point in the evolution of societies throughout the world, many of us are looking for ways to better understand and communicate with the other sex and thus create more fulfilling relationships. That is a primary objective of this book. Incidentally, we intentionally use the word "other" sex, one that begs inquiry, instead of "opposite" sex, a word that for centuries has promoted an adversarial stance between the sexes. This is a small change in language, but it implies one of our basic beliefs: that women and men are different but not intrinsically opposite to one another. When our differences are better understood, we can experience our often mysterious otherness as complementary, rather than as a never-ending source of conflict.

It's apparent to most of us by now that the social contracts between women and men are rapidly changing, offering new hope for expanded freedoms for both. Yet, in our experience, contemporary women and men still remain divided on many issues. Some things we hear as we teach around the nation are that:

Men fear women's power to wound them emotionally; women fear men's power to wound them physically.

Women feel sexually harassed; men feel sexually manipulated and that their courting behavior is often misunderstood.

Women resent it that men won't take no for an answer; in men's experience, however, no often does in fact mean yes.

Men say that women are too emotional; women say men don't feel enough.

Women say that men don't do their fair share of housework and child care; men feel that women don't do an equal share of providing income and home maintenance.

Men feel that they no longer have regular opportunities to meet in private; women insist on their right to women-only clubs and schools.

Many women say that God and nature are female; many men believe the opposite.

Many women feel morally superior to men; many men feel they are more logical and just.

Women say that men have destroyed the environment; men say that the women's movement has destroyed the family.

Men are often afraid to speak about their own vulnerability and victimization; women frequently deny their real power and capacity for abuse.

Women feel that men don't listen; men feel that women talk too much.

> Many men believe that they must become more like women to be whole; many women are trying to be more like men.
>
> Both women and men have lost connection with a powerful, sacred image of masculinity and femininity that is in balance with the other sex.

One of our major beliefs is that there are usually two equally valid points of view toward all gender conflicts. In most books and the media, however, we generally hear about these issues only from a woman's point of view or from a man's. In this book we hear equally from both as we propose new directions that can help resolve our age-old conflicts, directions that have the power to create deeper love and understanding in our relationships.

The stories we are about to tell about the courageous people who joined us for a week in the wilderness give readers a deeply revealing glimpse into ways we might all improve our relationships, institutions, and communities. But make no mistake, as the authors we come to this work waist-deep in our own personal biographies. We therefore include our own experiences as we discover more about the deep concerns of gender. We recognized early on that we were not just experts in this field, but were as deeply immersed in these issues in our personal lives as anyone else on that trip.

Both of us struggled with the risk of being looked upon as traitors to our individual women's and men's camps as we, of necessity, departed from old orthodoxies and party lines to begin building a new kind of relationship between women and men. Readers will also find expressed the drama of the struggles we all face as women and men searching for more intimate, satisfying relationships. Through exploring our feelings about our often polarized roles we can also find the genuine common ground between them.

The wound between women and men is deep in our collective souls, wedded to our bones and a constant theme in both our ancient and contemporary mythology. The need of men and women to find more harmonious ways to communicate with one another touches each of us deeply. If we have had a single mission in writing this book, it is the belief that our efforts might make a contribution toward a deep healing with the other sex. Our hope is that our personal stories, as well as the research and anecdotal information we have gathered, will be useful to all our readers as together we seek more peaceful and fulfilling relationships with our spouses, parents, coworkers, and, perhaps most important of all, our children, who represent the future.

We hope you enjoy the book, and we look forward to hearing from you when you have completed it.

—Aaron Kipnis, Ph.D., and Elizabeth Herron, M.A.

Revised: September 1995
The Gender Relations Institute
Box 4782
Santa Barbara, California 93140

CHAPTER ONE

A Gathering of Women and Men

If you don't know the kind of person I am
and I don't know the kind of person you are
a pattern that others have made may prevail in the world
and following the wrong god home we may miss our star.
— WILLIAM STAFFORD

WHY ARE YOU BRINGING MAKEUP and jewelry on a wilderness trip? Nobody really cares what you look like in the woods, do they?" I asked, instantly regretting the words as they came out of my mouth.

"I care," replied Liz. "And I'm bringing a pretty scarf and skirt as well," she said firmly. "Just because you're content to spend eight days in the same pair of jeans and your old flannel shirts, don't expect me to live by the same standard. Anyway, what about this pile of fishing gear? Last time you brought all these lures and gizmos and never caught a thing until you started using grasshoppers. And how about the huge knife your father gave you? You never slay any bears with it. It just hangs there on your hip adding another pound to your load. So who's being frivolous about what they're taking along?"

It was already past midnight. We were preparing to leave at first light in quest of another plank for the bridge we were attempting to build across the gender gap. As is often the case before a gathering, we were a little testy with each other.

As we packed for our trip, I observed how differently Aaron and I regarded the importance of various things. I was more focused on aesthetics: packing spices and teas, an extra foam pad for comfort, an attractive cloth for us to set our meals upon. Aaron was more vigilant about survival stuff. Along with his already maligned big knife was a folding leathermaker's tool, sort of like a Swiss army knife with pliers and other mini-tools. He also packed extra twine, snakebite and medical kits, a waterproof match container, and an extra, large ground cloth for building shelters.

Thinking back over the years, I recalled that as our camping trips progressed we usually came to appreciate what the other person brought along. For example, I delight in the fish he catches, and he is frequently pleased that I remembered to bring some "nonessential" item for comfort like hot chocolate or tea. Often the sum product of our individual aesthetic and practical differences makes a much better whole. But like many couples, we often don't initially see the whole picture.

As I mentally reviewed the many one- and two-day workshops and trainings for women and men that Aaron and I had conducted over the last few years, I was suddenly aware that we had upped the ante on our gender reconciliation work. Were we really prepared to spend eight days in the wilderness with twelve acquaintances and strangers who, like us, wanted to explore more deeply the conflicts and truces between the sexes? Honestly? Not really. But we needed a vacation and we wanted to do a summer workshop, so we had hit upon a plan to combine both. And now it was upon us.

As Liz and I continued packing, we considered discarding more items to keep our pack weight down. I was continually reminded of how different we really are. Items that were essential to Liz seemed incidental to me and vice versa. I wondered, as I often do, Can women and men really understand one another?

As we challenged each other about this or that item, I asked myself, Can't we simply work together without attempting to control each other? It was time to stop, to take a deep breath. We had to reconnect with what we knew to be true: We love each other. And we're very different. We respect each other. And we're very different. We admire each other's ability to teach. And we're very different. We're a great team. And we're very different. Every time we've taught together it's been great. Yet, every time we embark on a new adventure, we go through the same old anxieties.

"Why do you think it's still so hard for us to trust each other at times?" I asked.

"Because," Liz replied, "I think we're afraid that the other person's way of doing things will somehow harm us or inhibit our power or make us look foolish. And at the heart of things, we each think our own way is best."

"Yeah, all that's true," I replied. "But even after these years of working well together, without dominating each other, we still have that fear deep in our bones."

"Yes," said Liz. "It's as if some of our fear is rooted in something much deeper than our personal experience. There seems to be some sort of fundamental fear between women and men that's gone on since the beginning of time."

❧ WHY WILDERNESS?

Liz and I got a late start on the morning of departure. We overslept. Each time we tried to make it out the door, the phone kept ringing. People were calling with last-minute queries. As we finally drove from the city toward the mountains, I was filled with delight. All the myriad details were handled. We had a ten-hour drive ahead and at last we were on our way. It had been almost two years since we were in the wilderness. Too long.

Our plan was to get to the first camp a day before the rest of the group to have some time to rest, tune in to our new surroundings, and decompress a little before beginning the trip. Toward the late afternoon we were driving alongside a cascading creek that fed into Lake Shasta. It was a hot day and we were tired. Liz said, "Hey, let's stop and check out the creek."

"No way, Liz," I replied. "We're already late. I want to get to the camp before nightfall."

"Aw, come on, Aaron, just for a moment. Let's take a break," Liz playfully implored.

"I don't want to have to hunt for the trailhead in the dark and it's already unlikely that we'll make it before sunset. I just want to keep going," I said irritably. Liz, however, was insistent about stopping.

"I've gotta pee anyway," she said.

So we pulled off, down a gravel road till we were out of sight of the highway. Liz immediately stripped off her clothes and hit the water. How could I resist? I joined her. The water was cold, clear, and refreshing. We splashed each other, laughed, and tumbled in the water. It felt great. It was as if, in addition to cleansing my body, the creek water was washing the dust off my senses as well. I suddenly became aware of the play of sunlight on the leaves fluttering in the warm afternoon breeze. I began to smell the pungent verdancy of the woods and the river vegetation. Birdcalls, the chuckling of the creek, and the swish of air flowing through the branches filled my ears. "Okay, Liz, this was great. Good idea."

As a man, I was trained to focus on the goal. The problem with this training, however, is that sometimes I miss the pleasure of the journey along the way. As a woman, Liz is often more process oriented. She reminds us to jump into creeks. But for me, it presents a problem at times. It was getting dark and we were still a long way from the trailhead where we would meet the group—our goal.

By the time we passed through Shasta, it was well past dark. We stopped at a cafe for dinner, and Liz suggested that because it was still several hours to the trailhead, we should just spend the night in a motel. But there was Mount Shasta, its glacial peaks glistening in the moonlight. I was still determined to spend the night in the wilderness. I persuaded Liz to forgo a hot shower, and she reluctantly agreed to find a place to camp nearby for the night.

Less than an hour later we were in our sleeping bags in Panther Meadows on the flanks of Mount Shasta, breathing the sweet night air and feasting on the complex beauty of moonlight and shadows on the tumbled moraine. Liz looked over at me as I snuggled deep in my sleeping bag and said,

"Thanks for getting us here, Aaron. I love your capacity to say 'The hell with the flow' and push on for something you know is worthwhile."

I lay there looking up at the huge face of Mount Shasta and thought about all the old stories about the mountain being a sacred spot for native Americans in this area. It certainly felt special. Although I had heard for many years that the earth is our mother, this mountain felt to me like a giant male god sleeping in the earth. I yawned, secure and at peace. It was good to be here, an auspicious beginning for our journey. Although I had many doubts at first, I was beginning to think that we had made a good decision to hold the council in the wilderness instead of at a conference center or other facility as we usually do.

I thought about how so much of what we know about ourselves is culture-specific. Who are we underneath the thin veneer of civilization, I wondered. Some people fear monsters. Others suggest angels may lie there, too. In his book *Journey of the Heart*, psychologist John Welwood says,

> Our deepest sense of being male or female comes
> from the body, as our direct inheritance from the
> energies of earth and sky. . . . Unfortunately, however,
> many of us have lost touch with the powers of nature
> that nourish the essential male or female within. So,
> to find our genuine, powerful male or female ener-
> gies, we need to reconnect with the wild, elemental
> spirit that lives in us.

Liz and I were hoping that through being in the wilderness the members of our group would become more connected to their instinctual bodies. We were curious about whether this connection could lead us into a deeper experience of our intrinsic gender identity, if such a thing actually exists.

🎼 FIRST CAMP

Aaron and I were the first to arrive at the campsite the next day. Several hours of highway driving preceded another hour on the dusty, rutted dirt road that led to the trailhead. We were exhilarated to be done with driving at last and ready to begin our group. We lugged our gear to a battered redwood picnic table. Yellowjackets were buzzing angrily over some discarded chicken bones, and flies were swarming around a horse trailer. Several cowboys were preparing for a journey. Much to our dismay, they were packing in large amounts of beer, canned goods, and hunting gear. It was somewhat inconsistent with our Rousseau-like fantasy of idyllic nature undisturbed by the trappings of civilization.

I said, "I'm outta here, Aaron," and proceeded to walk toward the sound of a nearby creek.

I returned in a few minutes. "There's a much better spot upstream," I told him. "It's clean, right by the water, and there's more privacy."

"But who's going to wait in the parking lot for the others?" asked Aaron.

"We'll take turns," I replied. "We'll all enjoy ourselves more if we camp in a pleasant spot."

Aaron suddenly realized I had a good point. The campground was a drag. It definitely lacked the wilderness aesthetic that we were hoping to experience, so we agreed to take turns walking back to the trailhead every hour or so. We picked up our gear and headed upstream. Just as we started to leave, however, the first carload of fellow adventurers arrived.

Marie and Larry had carpooled with Joel and Lisa. In the course of organizing the trip, we had put them in touch with one another because they were all from the San Francisco Bay Area.

"Yeah!" cried Marie. "We made it!"

Larry was strangely silent, seemingly a little dazed. Joel and Lisa piled out of the back of the car. Lisa looked at the cowboys standing around, smoking and drinking beer in the shade of a magnificent red fir. She glanced at us with a slight wince that seemed to say, "What have you gotten me into?"

Lisa was a thirty-five-year-old professor of psychology at a community college, and her husband, Joel, was a forty-two-year-old professor of sociology at a major university. They had one child who was left in the care of Joel's mother for the week. Over the years Joel has invited Aaron, with whom he shares an interest in male psychology, to address several of his classes. Through their acquaintance Lisa and I met socially. The four of us had already had some lively conversations on gender issues. Both Aaron and I were happy they had decided to join our trip and that they had already hooked up with Larry and Marie. For them, the group experience had already begun.

Like most of the others who were about to arrive, we'd never met Marie and Larry. Marie was thirty-seven years old. She was a lawyer and the main provider for their family, which included two girls aged four and ten. Marie was active in women's politics and women's rights advocacy. Larry was a thirty-four-year-old self-employed software developer who works at home, providing most of the child care. Larry walked over to us and said, "Wow! This place is great. When's dinner? We jammed all the way from San Francisco without stopping for lunch. Marie can happily live on just trail bars and fruit, but I need a real meal, now!"

The six of us moved up to the creekside camping spot. Larry immediately began gathering firewood, intent on a hot meal. The spot I had found was surrounded by tall, majestic cedar trees. Blue Water Creek rushed by, cool, clear, and sweet. The slanting rays of fading sunlight reflected on the water, dancing in the swirling currents like a cascade of diamonds.

While Aaron and the others set up camp, I walked back to the parking area to check on other participants. When I got there, four more members of our tribe had arrived. Gloria introduced herself and her companion, Jerry. Gloria was a forty-eight-year-old businesswoman who runs an art gallery with several other women. Jerry, a thin, gentle-looking man also in his late forties, was a sculptor and an activist involved in a variety of social and environmental issues. He and Gloria have been living together for five years.

Also, there was Andy, a single twenty-seven-year-old man. Andy was a counselor at a home for disturbed adolescents who had attended a workshop we had presented for their staff. He was six feet three, looked like a linebacker, yet was very grounded, humble, and genuine. During our training I was impressed by his practical insights about how to heal the lives of wounded boys.

Dave, another single man, was a stockbroker, divorced, with an avid interest in mountaineering and other out-on-the-edge sports. He had attended one of Aaron's workshops for men and was interested in the possibility of bringing this material into his highly competitive work environment. Both these men had told us in our preinterviews that they were frustrated with their relationships with women and were hoping to learn more about how to get along with them during our encounters. Gloria and several other women who were increasingly perplexed about how to relate to men also held this view.

I led the tired, dusty crew along the trail on the edge of the creek. After brief introductions, everyone set about unpacking, pitching tents, and beginning preparations for sharing our first meal together. Then Aaron and I went back to the parking area to wait for the others.

Doris arrived on her own toward sundown. As she climbed out of her car, she had a look of awe. "It's beautiful here," she said. "It feels so good to be out of the city." Doris, a single woman in her early fifties, was the director of a family service agency. She had been fascinated by the differences between women and men for many years and had been involved in one of my empowerment workshops for women.

After dark our last couple, Alan and Merle arrived. They were obviously not happy campers. Merle spotted the three of us sitting at the battered picnic bench, huddled around our Coleman lantern. As she stepped out of the car, we could hear her exclaim to Alan, "See, I told you this was the right road. We would have been here three hours ago if you had just listened to me and asked for directions at the ranger station. But no," she said sarcastically, "you had to be the great Pathfinder."

"It's all right, really," I said, ambling over to the car. "We're just glad you made it," I added as Alan climbed out, looking tense. We led the last arrivals up the creek by flashlight to the camp, which by now had a cheery fire going. Larry was gleefully in self-appointed charge of preparations for a communal meal.

We introduced everyone informally. With no other agenda but to let everyone settle down, we ate and chatted by the fire. Aaron looked around at our crew and asked jokingly, "Well, are you all ready for this?" This was met by various grunts and some laughter. "I don't know," said Marie, "but you couldn't have picked a prettier setting for this gathering." As we ate, we relaxed and talked about our backgrounds and why we had decided to join the group. We were beginning the process of making connections that would help us in the deep work we hoped to do together in the days ahead.

It was hard, however, for Aaron and me as the trip leaders to relax completely. We were still short one member, Susan. Throughout the evening we took turns hiking back to the parking area, but to no avail. Susan did not arrive. Finally everyone was comfortably settled for the night, and we decided to give up. We zipped our sleeping bags together, and after briefly admiring the stars and successfully locating the polestar and a few other constellations, we kissed each other good night and were instantly asleep.

Dawn arrived. Aaron's quick hike to the parking area revealed that Susan, a thirty-two-year-old manager in a large corporation who had attended one of my workshops for women, had not come in during the night. I had talked to her the day before and everything seemed fine. What should we do, we wondered. Our first group decision was at hand. We gathered on the gravel beach, sat in a circle, and discussed it. Aaron suggested that one of us drive to the Klamath National Forest Service headquarters and leave a note while he drove to Happy Camp to call her to find out what had happened. But that would take three hours round-trip. It would mean we would be starting for the second camp in the heat of the day. Some of the group felt we should go on without her.

"She's already a day late," said Dave.

"Let's not let it hang us up any longer," said Alan.

Lisa then said, "Hey, what's the hurry, guys? We're short one lady and I think we should just wait here until we figure out what happened to her."

Already some differences were apparent. Some women had an investment in trying to keep the group together while some men were attached to keeping to the agenda. We had five or six uphill miles to hike that day to get to the second camp. The men felt it was time to go. Their sentiment was that she blew it, for whatever reason, and it wasn't fair for the rest of us to be hung up on her account.

Fortunately, we did not have to resolve this conflict. (Many others lay ahead, however, as we would soon discover.) While we were still sitting on the beach, Susan wandered into camp.

"There you are," she cried with relief. "Why weren't you in the parking area like we agreed?" she asked accusingly. "I was beginning to think you'd abandoned me or something."

She explained that she had left home without the map we had sent to everyone and had driven to three trailheads in search of us. She finally arrived at the designated campground late in the night. One of the cowboys, awakened by her, assured her that this was in fact the base for Blue Water Creek trail. Aaron had missed her in his dawn perusal of the campground. It never occurred to him that she would be camped with the cowboys. Later in the morning, when none of us showed up to meet her, the cowboys pointed her upstream in the direction they had seen us take the day before.

"They were awfully nice," she told us. "They fed me some dinner and let me camp by their fire. And two of them are super cute," she added with a playful leer and a chuckle.

Gloria then commented snidely, "Yeah, cute macho jerks if you ask me." A few of the men winced at this comment, but nothing was said in response. It sort of lay in the air for a while like a sour smell.

Aaron then called the group together for our first meeting.

OUR HOPES AND FEARS

All together at last, we sat in the first of many circles and officially began our quest. Liz and I spoke about the intent of the trip and some of the ground rules we thought would help to make it safe for everyone:

1. There's no such thing as an accident. People generally are injured because they, or others, have been careless. So we all need to make a commitment not to get hurt on this trip and not to hurt each other.

2. We want everyone to stay together unless we agree otherwise. No one should run too far ahead of the group, and we'll keep a pace that doesn't cause anyone to lag too far behind.

3. We will respect one another's personal boundaries in all matters.
4. Each member needs to be responsible for his or her physical and emotional well-being and should look out for the safety and comfort of others as well.

I asked if anyone disagreed with these rules. There was no dissent, so we went on. Liz picked up a gray stone, rounded smooth by the stream's waters. With a white stone, she chalked upon it the universal symbols used to represent women and men. I asked each person to hold the "talking stone" in turn and name his or her hopes and fears about the trip, as a more intimate introduction to the group. I also asked that we respect whoever holds the talking stone by listening without interrupting. "We've found it best to try not to rehearse what you are going to say when it's your turn. Rather, we suggest that everyone just pay attention to each speaker as it goes around the circle."

Liz began. "I feel honored to be here with all of you. This work is the realization of a lifelong dream for me. I have really big hopes for this trip. I'd like to come away from our time together with a deeper understanding about men. And I'd like to find out more of what it means to be an authentic woman in community with other women as well as with men. I also hope that we can build a safe container together, where we can tell the real truth to each other. And I know that the truth can be uncomfortable and scary sometimes. I guess that's my greatest fear, that I'll be confronted with something that I don't want to hear."

She passed the talking stone to Larry on her left. He held the stone thoughtfully for a moment and said, "I've been looking forward to this trip for months. Marie and I have had many talks, arguments, and even a few pretty hairy fights about our roles in our relationship, and the roles of women and men in general. In many ways we're an unconventional couple. She makes more money than me and I do more home care. But I don't feel we've figured it out any better than any other couple.

"I'm interested to hear about how others are working stuff out, and my hope is that we will all have a good time together while we're at it. My fear is that Marie will bond with all the women, as she usually does, and that I'll feel a little like the odd man out with most of the men." He glanced at me as if he were looking for some affirmation that he would not be abandoned by the men. I offered him a reassuring nod.

Marie, who was sitting to the left of her husband, Larry, spoke next. "Well, I'm already having a great time. I love this little creek and I'm looking forward to getting to know the group better. These days I'm struggling with a lot of issues around being a working mother. In the last few years our daughters seem a lot closer to their dad than to me. I also feel that I'm losing touch with my femininity in some way. I'm getting more brittle at work. I'm pissed off much of the time. I don't know, I guess mostly what I'm hoping for out of this week is some personal renewal and healing.

"The gender stuff is genuinely interesting to me, but I also want lots of time to play and rest. That brings me to my fear: my fear is that everything will be too structured. My whole life is already way too structured. So I want to have the freedom to sort of drift in and out of the group as need be and to not feel that I have to be focused all the time."

"My sentiments exactly," said Doris, as Marie passed the stone to her. "I want to learn more about the dance between women and men, and I want to play and rest and soak up some of the beauty that we've placed ourselves in. I'm also hoping to learn things which will be useful in my social services work with women and men. My main fear is that I won't be able to keep up with the hiking. I like moving through nature at a slow, savoring pace. I'm afraid I'll be an anchor at times and that will breed resentment from men who want to hike faster."

"Why do you think it will be the men?" interrupted Susan. Little did we know she was an accomplished long-distance runner and competition cyclist who, as we would discover, could easily hike every one of us into the ground.

"Well, that's just been my experience in the past," Doris replied. "In any case, like Marie here, I need the freedom to be able to just move at my own pace."

Alan looked uncomfortable as the stone was passed to him. "I'm not sure what to say," he said hesitantly. "Merle basically talked me into this trip. Her therapist thought it would be a good idea for us. I'm not so sure. I used to be in the Boy Scouts when I was a kid, though, and those were some of the happiest times of my life. So at least I know I have the capacity to have fun in the woods. Fears? I don't know. Maybe spending too much time sitting around yakking about heavy stuff. I'm eager to get on the trail now."

As he passed the stone to Merle, she said nervously, "I hope that Alan and I can gain some insight into some of the problems that come up in our relationship. And I hope this trip will help Alan to calm down a little. He really needs a vacation. He works so hard all the time. So I hope this week will help restore his spirit. My fear," she said, giving Alan a darting glance, "is that Alan will be unhappy all week and that will make the whole time miserable for me as well."

I noticed that Merle didn't say much about herself, what she wanted, hoped for, or feared. Her relationship with Alan seemed to fill the whole focus of her attention. After she spoke there was an awkward silence. This exercise was perhaps a little more deeply personal than some people had expected at the outset. But then Dave broke the ice by vigorously exclaiming, "I'm praying for fish. If there's one thing I fear about this week it's that I won't catch any." Several people laughed and a few acknowledged their encouragement for Dave's aspirations. He then passed the stone to Andy, who commented, "I've been thinking a lot about this trip over the last few weeks. One thing that's become real clear to me, from working with adolescent boys and girls, is that men and women are really different. I hope to learn more about that, and I have a lot of questions that I want to ask women. So I'm hoping that there will be a real opportunity for us to have some honest talk. What I fear is that if I'm really given the opportunity to explore the truth between men and women I'll be afraid to speak honestly about the issues that disturb me the most. I'm afraid I'll just chicken out."

Gloria's turn was next. As she took the stone and looked around the circle, she said, "I feel more fear than anything else. The only groups I've been in for many years now have only had women in them. Quite honestly, I don't have much trust or respect for men anymore. It seems like you guys are ruining everything. But I trust Liz and am intrigued by the vision she is trying to create with Aaron. So . . . I'm here."

I glanced at Jerry, curious to see how he reacted to Gloria's comment. I was surprised to see no visible response. Although Liz and I are encountering more couples like them—outspoken women with slightly apologetic men—I wondered what he was doing with a woman who disliked men and, for that matter, how she could be in relationship with a man, feeling the way that she did about men as a group.

Gloria handed the stone to Jerry, who said, "I'm really glad to be sitting here on the earth. I want to learn more about what women want and I hope that the men will respect the women and listen to what they have to say. My fears? I guess I'm afraid of people's anger getting out of hand, especially the men."

He handed the stone to Joel, who looked at him and said, "Well, I'm more afraid of the women's anger than the men's. I know when my wife, Lisa, gets pissed off, she can totally waste me with her words. So I can imagine all of you. . . ." He trailed off, looking at the women. "But I hope that we can have a good adventure together that gives birth to a better understanding between men and women."

Lisa followed. Looking thoughtful, she commented, "Wow, this rock is getting hot. There's a lot of energy in this group. I feel excited and scared at the same time. I haven't done anything like this in a long time. Over the last decade my life has been all about my career and Joel's career and taking care of our son in between. I hardly have any time for myself. And we don't have time for each other," she said, looking fondly at Joel.

"I feel like men and women really need to start working together to make some big changes in the world. We both work and Gabe goes to school and child care. It's such a push all the time. I guess what I need from this trip is to slow down and have time to be with myself and with you, Joel."

Susan took the stone next. I remembered Liz telling me that she was kind of a wild woman who had a good heart but was unpredictable at times. As Susan fondled the stone, she looked at the other members of our circle, meeting each person's eyes before she spoke. "I'm really interested in all of you. Hearing you all speak, I relate to a lot of what's already been said. I guess I'm here because I feel confused about my relationships with men right now. I love men, but every one of my relationships seems to end up with a lot of hurt, frustration, and blame.

"For a long time I always thought it was the man's fault. Now I'm not so sure. I see myself and other women doing some pretty shitty things, too. I hope I can learn something new on this trip that I can use in my personal life. My fear is that we might all just be hopelessly and eternally stuck in the war. How depressing."

I was the last to speak. "My hope is that we will work the edge of our truth together without backing off. I also hope that we will dive deeply into the pleasure of our shared mysteries. That is, I hope that we won't try to figure everything out, but rather give room for some of the deeper feelings within us to find some path to expression. Some of my fears are that my leadership will be inadequate to the task, my weak ankle will give out, and my sleeping bag will get wet."

With some of our hopes and fears now out in the open, we gathered our gear. We headed up Blue Water Creek trail toward the clearing we hoped to occupy for our second camp and the first of several encounters we had planned between the women and the men.

We were off to a good start. There were many common interests and good intentions in the group. There was clearly some tension as well—more than was visible on the surface, apparently. We were to find that fireworks awaited us at second camp.

CHAPTER TWO

THE FIRST
SUMMIT MEETING
OF THE SEXES

That which you resist, persists.
Conflict seeks resolution
Just as a discordant note in a melody seeks resolution.

— DANAAN PERRY

WE QUICKLY CLEANED UP the first camp, picked up our packs, and headed up Cedar Trail. Starting at about one thousand feet elevation, we climbed steadily throughout the morning. When we rounded a sharp bend in the trail and came to a point that looked over a vast expanse of forest, most of us were unprepared for the sight.

Where unbroken miles of forest should have been were ragged checkerboards of devastation. Entire tracts of land had been clear-cut, with only a few trees left standing in each square-mile section. Adjacent to these sections, in sharp contrast, were areas of towering, undisturbed trees, glistening and vibrant in the sunlight now breaking through the overcast morning.

"This is grotesque!" cried Gloria. "How can they get away with this in a national forest?"

I wondered the same thing. A look at Aaron's topographical map told the tale. Within this outer portion of the government preserve, every other section of land was a privately owned inholding. That was why the logging was done in a checkerboard fashion. Every other square mile of land had been logged. Not just logged—the forest had been raped.

"This is the work of men who've lost their souls," cried Lisa. Others joined in, nodding their heads and vigorously agreeing.

"Wait a minute," said Dave. "What about the women who send them off to work each day? Do they retain their souls by simply keeping their hands clean?" A good question, for which there was no simple answer.

This brief encounter was typical of many disputes between the sexes. Like most of our conflicts, the issue is complex. Only the most superficial analysis of our environmental crisis could hold that the destruction of the wilderness is caused solely by men who have gone berserk, with women merely representing the innocent bystanders. In this case, men are identified as the perpetrators while the women's role in the destruction of the environment is more covert. In actuality, as Dave tried to point out, not only do women collude with men in their acquisition of wealth, but also they are primary consumers of manufactured goods. Women live in wooden houses and use paper goods. Women own stock in many corporations that are exploiting our natural resources.

By the same token, many men are fiercely committed to environmental activism. But because men are the ones who actually cut the trees, they easily become identified as the sole implementers of a destructive industry. And, as we will see, men often make the same knee-jerk responses to the overt roles of women while neglecting to account for their own part in helping to create those roles.

After this encounter with disaster, we walked on another mile or so, leaving the destruction behind us and penetrating deeper into the undisturbed dignity of the old-growth forest. We stopped for lunch at the site of a giant windfall. The tree, more than one hundred feet long, was lying across the ground like a toppled silo. Much of it was jutting out, dramatically cantilevered over the canyon. Some of us climbed on it and ate lunch while enjoying a spectacular if slightly unnerving view of the canyon and creek far below.

After lunch we continued climbing through a virgin cedar grove that became variegated with bull pine and huge white firs as the elevation increased. The sweet smell of incense cedar, warmed by the midday sun, pervaded the still summer air. In the distance I heard the cry of a hawk. Nearby, however, the forest was evocatively silent, there being little bird life at these higher elevations.

I looked over my shoulder at the group trailing behind me. As she had predicted, Doris was bringing up the rear. I was grateful for her presence and her pace that allowed us to enjoy our surroundings more fully. Doris was chatting with Jerry, who was also more of an ambler than a vigorous hiker. They made a picturesque pair: she with a Panama hat and Guatemalan vest, he with a bright red bandanna tied around his forehead and a six-foot-long carved hardwood walking staff. The rest were spread along the trail in various groups.

❧ SUGAR AND SPICE; SNAKES AND SNAILS

As the day grew hotter, we shucked the heavier clothing we had donned in the overcast morning. For a time I walked alone, ahead of Liz, until I found myself hiking directly behind Susan, who was then in the lead. We were on a narrow portion of the trail that required us to go in single file. I could not help noticing, after she stripped off her baggy Wellesley College sweatshirt, that Susan was wearing very little. Her halter top was quite skimpy and she was braless. Her shorts were jeans that were so high-cut that a significant portion of her bare buttocks protruded below the frayed hem.

Although I make a committed effort to be respectful toward women, it was difficult for me not to glance occasionally at her rear when she was scrabbling up rocks or steeper portions of the trail ahead of me. As the day wore on, and positions changed in the group, I noticed several men casting distracted glances in her direction. Consequently, I was not surprised when the issue came up later that evening in our first conflict council.

In the late afternoon, we arrived at the clearing that we intended to use for our second camp. We were now only slightly above the creek; through the afternoon we had descended from the higher trail along the canyon wall. A gurgling spring flowed out of the hillside, cutting a tiny elf-sized creek into the earth at the edge of the clearing. Shooting stars, wild iris, blue-eyed grass, Indian paintbrush, and other wildflowers abounded in the meadow.

Merle was in the lead at that time and was the first to enter the clearing. She was about twenty yards ahead of me when I saw her suddenly stop and visibly stiffen. She slowly backed up and looked over her shoulder imploringly at her husband, Alan, who was a few steps behind her. She gestured with her eyes and a turn of her head toward a large, flat sandstone rock, low to the ground alongside the trail leading into the clearing.

Alan advanced and I came up behind him. There, regally sunning itself with little concern for us, was a large, dusty brown western timber rattlesnake. It was almost three feet long and almost as thick as my wrist. As Alan came alongside Merle, the snake was suddenly startled and gave a warning shake. Agh! The hair on my arms stood straight up. This sound caught everyone else's attention as well. We all stopped in our tracks, and Liz, who was behind me, shushed the rest as they arrived, one by one, at the edge of the clearing.

Alan, Merle, and I all slowly backed away. The snake, though clearly agitated and alert now, held its ground. This surprised me because snakes usually tend to slither off when startled. Perhaps it had babies nearby. Maybe it was just ornery or irritated about having its nap interrupted. Who knows? What was known was that there was no way we were walking past that stone into the clearing ahead.

A brief discussion ensued about what to do. Alan, the former Boy Scout, decided to take command. He borrowed Jerry's hiking staff and held it in front of him, poking at the snake. Instead of backing away, the snake repeatedly struck at the stick and seemed intent on reaching Alan if it could. In apparent frustration or perhaps just abject terror, Alan took a step back, swung the stick over his head, and bashed the snake on its head.

Dave yelled, "Hey, just leave it alone! We can go back down the trail a way and walk down along the creek to the other side of the clearing."

But it was too late. Alan smashed it again. After that stroke the snake twitched for a little while and then lay still. It was obviously dead.

I felt totally ticked off. Liz and I had brought these people to the woods in the hope that they would live together in relative peace for a week, and the first day out one of the men starts slaughtering the local wildlife. Also, I wanted the women to feel safe, to begin to extricate themselves from the blame game with men, and here was Alan making fuel for the fire. Liz and I had assured some of the more cautious women that these men were more enlightened than the average male. Now I felt put on the spot, embarrassed, set up somehow, betrayed. I saw our hopes for a peace council crashing on the hard rocks of compulsive male heroics.

"That was completely unnecessary," declared Marie. "Just what the hell are you trying to prove?"

"Oh, did you want that thing hanging around camp?" asked Alan sarcastically and perhaps a bit defensively as well. "Maybe you'd like to wake up with it crawling into your sleeping bag?"

"No, I wouldn't," Marie replied firmly. "But you didn't have to kill it!"

"I didn't see you, or anyone else for that matter, willing to do anything about it. Look," he said more gently, "I was concerned for Merle's safety. I grew up in the Southwest and we generally just kill vipers that come too close to the house or the yard. We don't usually invite them to stick around for dinner."

Merle jumped in to her husband's defense. She said, "Listen, a rattler killed my dog when I was nine. And I loved that mutt. Alan has heard this story and he knows that I'm genuinely terrified of snakes. He was just being protective. Personally, I think he was very brave. We should be thanking him, not chastising him."

Alan continued. "Look, I'm genuinely sorry if it upset you. Honestly, I was just trying to do what seemed to be the right thing at the moment."

I was touched by what he said and instantly let go of my anger. Right or wrong, he had acted quite courageously to do what he thought was his duty as a man: to protect his wife, and the rest of us as well, from danger. I thought about how frequently men's good intentions are negatively interpreted, and I did not want to be yet another voice in the rising chorus that is bashing male behavior these days. I still thought it was unnecessary for him to kill the snake, but I gave him a reassuring slap on the shoulder and said, "All right, what's done is done. Let's make camp." We all proceeded into the clearing. But we had not yet heard the last word about that snake.

SECOND CAMP

Gratefully we slipped off our heavy packs and began to set up camp in the lush meadow. There was a great deal to be done, and many of us hoped to take a dip in the creek before dusk.

Aaron and I started putting up our tent. A few feet away, Joel and Andy were rigging a line in a tree to hang our food away from bears and other critters.

Doris said, "If someone collects some wood, I'll start the fire." Wood was abundant. Within minutes Jerry and Alan created a large pile of kindling and larger branches. As Doris started to build the fire, Dave came over and said, "It'll work better if you arrange the twigs like this." He started to show her how to build a kind of square-shaped structure.

"Thanks," Doris replied, clearly attempting to be polite, "but I have my own way of doing it that's always worked before."

"Okay," said Dave, looking doubtful as he moved away.

Andy finished his rigging and then walked back over to the edge of the clearing where we had seen the snake. He spent some time there. I assumed he was burying the snake. But he had other plans, as we were to discover a few days later.

Susan finished with her tent and strolled over to a heap of rocks left from previous campers. "Hey, Merle," she called. "Come help me set up a kitchen. This is a great spot to make a work area for preparing dinner."

They began to arrange some rocks and a flattish piece of driftwood into some semblance of a makeshift kitchen. I whipped out the tablecloth I had packed under Aaron's protest, and Marie began gathering flowers to decorate our dinner site. Larry approached, offering to help, but Merle quickly said, "That's all right, we've already got things under control here." Larry shrugged, then picked up the folding shovel and strolled into the woods with Andy, looking for a good place to dig a privy.

Many of us in this group were not living traditional gender roles in our everyday lives. We had our share of career-oriented women and care-oriented men. However, for all our self-appraisals as "new" women and men who already had had our own consciousnesses somewhat raised about sex roles, most of us still tended to fall quickly into traditional, habitual division-of-labor roles.

With the exception of Doris, the women were tending to food preparation and to aesthetics. The men were doing the construction and the safety preparations. And even Doris's crossing of the lines, taking on the job of fire-builder, was challenged by a man, just as Larry was shooed off kitchen duty lest he invade Susan's and Merle's domain. It was both funny and tragic to watch. We were all such a mixed-up blend of old habits and new aspirations.

After making camp and dinner, we gathered around the fire to begin our first council. Aaron and I had already decided that we should start by expressing some of the major conflicts between the sexes. We invited the women and men to inform one another honestly and directly about what they disliked and resented the most about the other sex. As with all our exercises, we offered some safe space ground rules:

1. Listen to the other person without interruption or commentary. We will all have an equal chance to speak.
2. Of course, there can be no violence of any kind, toward anyone, for any reason.
3. We must all make a commitment to stay in the circle and see the process through. Nobody should

get up and leave the council (aside from pee
breaks) without discussing it with one of us.

4. Try to speak for yourself and avoid pointing your
finger at others; instead, simply let others know
how they make you feel.

"And finally," I said, "Aaron and I want you to grant us a
special power. If either one of us raises our hand straight above
our heads, it means 'Just a minute, whoa, time out.' We want
everyone to agree that if we give this signal, whoever is talking
will stop, everyone will go back to their corners, and we will
talk about what just happened before going on."

"So, if anybody here can't live with these agreements, let's
hear it now," Aaron said. No one objected, so we continued
with an opening talk that we felt would give some good back-
ground understanding and help create a foundation for the
work ahead.

✗ CREATING A COOL SPACE FOR HOT WORK

Aaron and I wanted to create an atmosphere in which it was
safe for people to express their deepest truths and hurts about
the other sex without further alienating the participants. Yet,
at the same time we did not want to be so nice, so politically
correct, careful, and afraid of giving offense that we avoided
the conflicts altogether. Conflict avoided does not go away. It
merely festers underground, like fires in long-abandoned
coal mines that unexpectedly erupt to the surface in great
conflagrations.

Danaan Perry, an international conflict mediator, suggests that some human beings are like volcanoes plugged at the top. Internal pressures build, then things blow, causing vast devastation as a consequence. However, when the lava is allowed to flow a bit at a time, sure, it burns a few trees. But it also makes new land upon which new life can grow. By letting the lava of our conflict flow, we hope it will create solid fresh ground upon which a new alliance between the sexes can take place.

A few years ago, Aaron and I attended a gathering in a spiritual community. The purpose of the encounter was to bring healing to the wounds between the sexes. Before meeting together we gathered separately in our same-sex groups. Aaron later told me that he asked the men how the weekend was going to address conflict between the sexes. The reply he got from every man was that, essentially, there was no need to engage in conflict. They were just going to come together with the women, exchange gifts, and meet one another with love and sincerity. They believed that goodwill alone would bring healing to the age-old war between the sexes.

Well, on the surface that was a great idea. But it seemed rather naive to me. As it turned out, all the conflicts were swept under the lovely Indian blankets that were covered with flowers, crystals, and baskets of fruit. There they festered and rotted. Over the next three years, several individuals in that community were shamed, blamed, and named as the source of all the bad energy coming up in the group. They were scapegoated and, in some cases, subsequently barred from attending the group's meetings. Because the shadow—the real anger, fear, and resentment that most women and men feel on some level—was never addressed, it took over the collective consciousness of that group.

After a time few people came to the meetings. More and more diverse voices left the dialogue. In the end only a small group of radically feminist women and apologetic men was left. Little healing between the larger men's groups and the women's groups ever occurred.

If you don't invite the shadow to the party, it comes when you least expect it. So Aaron and I told our group, "We're not going to start out with the sonnets and psalms. Rather, we are going to begin our council with an invitation for everyone to tell the other sex what it is that really bugs them.

"Some of what will be said will fit. Let's try to take it in and learn from that information. Much of what will be said may not fit. So, let's take that information for what it is: the other's distorted picture of us. That information is useful also, if we don't get too caught up in reacting to it defensively, but rather try to gain understanding about how these personal projections color our thinking.

"All that said, we encourage you to tell the truth. That's why we came here, isn't it, to speak and hear the truth? So, we don't have to be politically correct or claim our feelings as our own projections, even though we've just suggested that's the truth much of the time. Nor should we fall into the self-deprecating trap of qualifying or diminishing our statements as 'just my feelings.' No! Now's the time to let it rip. Our feelings represent a major aspect of our deepest truth. They're not right or wrong. They're vital expressions of our realities. We hope we are creating a safe environment here that can hold the truth in all its beauty, wonder, and pain."

At this stage of our discussion, the point was not so much to create a lot of direct confrontation or debate on specific issues as it was to provide a forum for the lively exchange of information and differing perspectives in an atmosphere that guaranteed we would be heard. So often in public debate we are shouted down, shamed, or subjected to attempts to convince us emotionally or intellectually that our position is not valid. This is one of the reasons women and men so rarely come into direct communication with one another over their issues. We were ready to begin, but first we wanted to set the stage a little more dramatically than we usually do.

✣ MEETING ON SACRED GROUND

There is more to relationships than conversation. There is energy, feeling, and a something quite mysterious generated among us that some call soul, spirit, or even magic. In order to honor any spirits of healing that could help us in our work, Liz began by creating a ritual space that invited the unknown, the unexpected, and the unseen to be a part of our process.

Liz took a small abalone shell from her pack. She filled it with some dried cedar she had collected on the trail and lit it with a hot coal. The air was quickly filled with the sweet and pungent smell of incense. She held up the shell and walked around the circle, stopping at each of the four cardinal directions, welcoming the elemental powers—Earth, Air, Fire, and Water. In the shadowy light of the campfire, with the flames dancing and sparking toward the dark night sky, she looked quite mythical, like a priestess or shaman from some other time. For a moment I couldn't help thinking about what a far cry this was from the last seminar we taught to a group of executives from a multinational corporation. We were all wearing suits, twenty-four floors above the ground in Manhattan. I smiled to myself as Liz's invocation brought me back.

"I invite the ancestors into our circle, those who have gone before us, the grandfathers and the grandmothers," Liz cried. "Come, share your ancient wisdom with us. There is room for you here."

She moved to the center of the circle, lifted the shell of burning cedar high into the air and called, "I invite in the spirit of partnership and the spirit of honorable conflict and sacred battle. We know so little about how to fight with each other in a clean way. We invite you to teach us how men and women can be together in a new and better way."

As Liz prayed, I felt as if our circle was being joined by a host of benevolent beings. She continued, "I call to all that is Feminine and sacred, and all that is Masculine and holy. We honor these great polarities of the universe in ourselves and in the natural world. We open ourselves to learn more of these mysteries.

"And last, but not least," Liz said, looking around at the dark silhouettes of the trees and up at the stars, "we honor and give thanks for this beautiful place that we are in. We ask the spirits of this land to watch over us and guide us as we do this work together." She walked around the circle, fanning the cedar smoke over all the participants. We had both studied with native American healers, who advised us that this was a traditional method for purifying people who were about to participate in a ceremony.

We then invited the men to sit on one side of the fire and the women on the other. And we suggested that they attempt to direct the energy of their comments into the fire, rather than hurl them across the fire at the other sex.

We suggested that each speaker not go on for much longer than a few minutes, and that we keep going around the circle until the moon begins to set behind the ridge to the west of us. To determine who would go first, we flipped a Chinese coin that Lisa carried as a good luck charm. The women won.

THE MEN FACE THE WOMEN'S FIRE

I took my place with the women and sat next to Gloria, who was the first to speak. She said into the fire, "What I'm most angry at men about is how physically and sexually violent they are toward women. I don't know any woman who feels safe on the streets anymore. I work as a volunteer at a battered women's shelter. Every day I see women who come in with the shit beat out of them. Not only that, half the time they've been raped by their boyfriend or husband as well.

"Well over a hundred thousand women were raped last year and the numbers just keep going up. What is it with men, anyway?" she said, looking accusingly at the men sitting across the fire. "Men are so used to having vastly more privilege than women that they feel they have the God-given right to abuse us as some sort of lesser species. You can tell me all you like about the new male sensitivity. But more and more, as time goes on, I am coming to believe that men are just fundamentally abusive, brutal, insensitive, and uncaring!

"I know we're not supposed to get personal in this first round, but I just have to say that I'm still very angry and upset about Alan killing the snake. I don't buy any of the bullshit rationalizations you gave this afternoon," she said, looking up from the fire again, directly at Alan. "The snake is an ancient symbol of the Great Goddess. And I think it's no coincidence that a man killed it the day of this council. It was just another blatant attempt by a man to prove his dominance over women and nature. If we weren't all the way out here in the middle of nowhere together, I'd already be gone. You think you can just take whatever you want by force? Well, not anymore. Not anymore!"

As Gloria passionately concluded, affirming cries of agreement were raised by several women. Alan started to respond but Aaron intervened, saying, "It's all right. This can be hard, but let's just stick to the process without interrupting the women. We'll get our turn."

Lisa then reached for the talking stone and said, "I'm really tired of how disconnected men are from their children in this culture. Joel and I both work, but it always seems to be me who ends up having to alter my schedule when Gabe, our son, has a doctor's appointment, a teacher conference, is sick at home, or has to be picked up from an after-school activity. It's simply taken for granted that in most cases, because I make less money in my career, my time is less important than his.

"I know Joel tries really hard to be an engaged father. But the truth is that I feel I'm always on the front line when it comes to the responsibilities of parenting and keeping the home together. I mean, when I go to do the shopping, Joel never hesitates to ask me to take care of various errands for him. But if I ask him to pick something up on the way home from work, he always makes me feel that it's some sort of imposition. It's just not fair."

Marie jumped in next. "I'm really angry about the way men systematically deny women equal political and economic power," she said. "Yeah, I know women are now running for Congress and moving up corporate ladders, but the reality is that most women still struggle against a deeply held male prejudice that they are inefficient and unreasonable. Many men clearly still believe that we can't handle the stress and responsibility of executive positions, that we will crack under pressure and are just too emotional to be trusted. I can't believe the condescending crap some male lawyers still dish out in the courtroom.

"Last year I handled over thirty different lawsuits on behalf of women who were denied promotion or advancement either through outright sexual harassment or through more covert discrimination. Male managers habitually pass over qualified women in attempts to keep the power in the men's club. This has got to stop."

Merle then said, "What bothers me the most these days is that men don't seem to know how to connect and be intimate with women. I want to know why men never ask for feedback from women. I'm also frustrated that men don't open up and share what they are really feeling. It's as if I have to pry every piece of information out of them, just to know what's going on in any given situation. When Alan comes home from work he just reads the paper and watches TV. He never asks me about what I've been doing or how I feel. Most of my girlfriends complain about the same thing.

"No matter what we do to try to get their attention with new hairdos or new negligees they just don't seem to be very interested. Whatever happened to the guy who used to bring me flowers and take me dancing? He died about the time Mary Jo, our daughter, was born, and hasn't been seen since. Sometimes I feel so lonely. . . ." Her voice cracked, she looked away and was silent. Because I was sitting to her right, she then passed the stone to me.

Whenever Aaron and I conduct these groups, we feel that it is important for us to participate fully as well. And I always have many issues that I am still working through, even after years of full-time gender-reconciliation work. What was affecting me most at this time was feeling the collective wound all women bear about their physical appearance. This theme had come up a lot in my women's groups lately, so I needed to express to the men some of my anger about the issue.

I said, "I don't like how men only seem to value and appreciate one kind of beauty in this culture. Men seem to only want women who are thin and young and look like the models in the magazines. This image is almost impossible for most women to attain. We're killing and maiming ourselves through diets and surgery to transform ourselves into something that will please you. It's dehumanizing.

"I don't know a single woman who genuinely feels good about her body. Even my gorgeous, totally knockout thirteen-year-old worries about her looks. She didn't get that anxiety entirely from me. She picked it up from television and the print ads and all the other media that are constantly informing her that she isn't enough, doesn't have enough, and needs a bunch of makeup and lots of other stuff to look okay. This beauty trip is killing us and men just keep right on trading in their older wives for younger women."

Doris then said, "I'm tired of always winding up being mom whenever I'm in a relationship with a man. I'm strong and self-sufficient. Why is it all the men I meet wind up being dependent on me emotionally or even financially? Men just don't seem to be able to care for themselves. They act like dependent little boys, or worse, like babies. They want us to act like patient mothers when they're hurting, but when we're hurting, then they're busy with other things. Then, they lecture us about how we need to learn how to carry our own pain. It seems as if to stay connected to a man we have to give and give and give, and then just be grateful for what crumbs come our way.

"In my experience as a single person, men don't want a strong, independent woman. They're more comfortable with the helpless, dependent girls. When we're assertive about our desires, men head for the hills and demean us as being too aggressive."

Then Susan said, "I'm flat-out, totally tired of being regarded as a sex object by men! Why do men always stare at your tits instead of looking you in the eye? At work, when I walk by the executive offices, I can feel their eyes on me. And sometimes I even hear them making snide comments that they are afraid to say to my face. When I go out with guys, I can practically hear the wheels turning in their heads as they try to figure out how to separate me from my panties while pretending to be genuinely interested in what I have to say and who I am as a person.

"Even here on this trip it angered me that several men were touching me with their eyes today. I don't feel safe! Why do men always have to cruise us? Can't we just be free to dress and walk the way we want without feeling that we are going to be ogled and harassed? Then we're accused of being teases if we make ourselves attractive but don't want to be intimate."

Susan was the last women to speak. But before she could pass the talking stone across to the men, Dave jumped right in.

✥ THE WOMEN FACE THE MEN'S FIRE

"Well, I have to respond directly to that one," he said. "Just what are we supposed to do when your behind is practically jumping out of your shorts? I mean there it was, right there in our faces on the trail, as impossible to ignore as a luminous full moon in the center of the midnight sky. If you don't want to be looked at, why don't you keep your ass in your pants?" I glanced at Liz as I prepared to say something to Dave, but just then he appeared to realize that he was "crossing the fire." He stopped confronting Susan and continued in a more general way.

"I feel like I'm in a double bind with women much of the time," he exclaimed. "I've only been single again for about a year and all the rules I learned as a kid are changing. Women put all this energy into looking sexy—not just attractive—but sexually provocative. Just look at the women's magazine ads and articles. They say 'Dominate the boardroom with your sheer panty hose, your wet glossy lips, or your celebrity perfume.' Women consciously try to get our attention by finely honing their sexual appeal. But then when men respond, they're labeled as aggressive jerks if they come on too strong or wimps if they don't come on strong enough.

"I feel that most women these days are dishonest about the ways in which they covertly manipulate men, and most of the men I talk to these days are angry about it. I wish women would become truly liberated and start being more up front about their desires, and stop playing this covert game with men having to do all the guessing and making all the overt moves. It gives women all the power. It's men who get all the blame when they don't advance according to the women's often secret, or at best unclear, rules."

Dave then took the stone from Susan, having neglected to do so before he spoke, and passed it to Alan, who said, "I'm also angry about the double standards men face. But my issue isn't so much about sex, it's more about work and sharing responsibilities. Most women don't make as much money as men, but more and more they expect men to equally share work in the home.

"Ever since Merle joined her women's group, she's been complaining that I don't do enough around the home or enough child care. Her new girlfriends tell her that she's an oppressed housewife. Shit, I work over fifty hours a week. I'm already stretched so thin I'm about to snap. She's got time for her women's group, her soap operas, her art class, and her health club. After work, I'm so exhausted I just want to be taken care of a little. But now she says she's too tired from dealing with the home and the kids all day.

"Well, I understand that it's hard, but I don't feel that it's as hard as doing construction ten hours a day. I look around on the job at the guys with bad backs and missing fingers, and I don't feel that being a housewife is as dangerous or demoralizing as performing hard labor every day. I feel that I should get a little respect for putting my body on the line every day to pay the bills. Merle has more free time than me, and I think she should cut me some slack around the house. Or maybe she should go to work full time and see how it feels. Then we can hire someone to deal with all the housework."

Larry then said, "What bothers me the most about women is that they are always putting men down. They act like we're responsible for every single bad thing in the world. Women are especially down on fathers these days. You know, Deadbeat Dads who abandon their families and won't pay child support. And every man is a potential child molester, rapist, or wife beater just waiting for a chance to screw up some woman's life. Women rarely acknowledge the great dedication, honor, commitment, courage, and responsibility displayed by most fathers. I'm really tired of men getting a bad rap all the time. I'm a full-time dad and when I go to PTA meetings, I get a lot of weird attitude from some of the mothers. They act like I'm some sort of pervert for being so involved with my kids."

Then it was Jerry's turn. He said, "I'm not angry at women about anything. Women have taken enough abuse from men, and I'm not going to contribute to it by saying anything against them here. I'm angry at the men for complaining so much and clearly not understanding how women in this society are much more oppressed then they are. I think women and men would get along a lot better if the men acknowledged that they are more privileged than the women and put their minds to figuring out how to right the wrongs we men have done to women for centuries. I think this whole exercise is disgusting. We should be asking women how we can support their just quest for equality rather than expressing our anger toward them."

This report brought groans of disapproval from several of the men and applause from Gloria and Marie on the other side of the circle. Liz admonished the women to honor our agreement and let the men speak freely without any potentially inhibiting commentary.

Then Joel took the stone from Jerry and blurted out, "Women don't want equality anymore, they want dominance and control. At the university where I work, political correctness and affirmative action have created an anti-male climate in almost every department. Recently a highly qualified friend of mine applied for a position in my department. He was turned down. A less qualified woman was hired instead. The chairman of the department candidly told me that we can't hire another man here for the next five years, there's just too much pressure to hire women regardless of who is the most qualified.

"I understand that there's been discrimination in the past. But now the discrimination against men is even more blatant and conspiratorial than any prejudice ever was against women. Everywhere I turn, anti-male policies are displaying the same sorts of sexism and unfairness that the old, male-dominated institutions did. Now it's in reverse. Does that make it right? I don't think so. I'm interested in figuring out how to create real equality between men and women, not just turning the tables to give women power over men."

Andy then told us, "Women are always complaining about men's violence, as if they themselves are blame free. They act as if they have the high moral ground. But every day at the group home I see the damage women have done to their children. It's not very pretty. In fact, according to the government statistics I've seen at work, women represent the majority of childbatterers. They also assault their spouses at about the same frequency as men. I agree that we men need to become accountable for the amount of violence we put in the world and that we should be attempting to heal the lives of violent men. But I'm also really sick of women not copping to their own violence. And it's not just physical. Women are emotionally abusive, too. That kind of violence doesn't leave any bruises or visible scars, but I can assure you its wounds last a long, long time."

I was the last man to speak. "What's been bothering me the most these days is the women's movement's attacks against the men's movement. I think it's true that there is a backlash against feminism, just as there's one against men's attempts to change their own roles. And some of the backlash against the women's movement is unfair and sexist. It's based on men's fear of change and their fear of women's power. But some of the backlash is deserved. It is in reaction to a lack of balance around gender issues and unfairness against men in general,

as well as the shaming of women who choose to be homemak-
ers. Even so, almost all of the men in the men's movement
that I've talked to around the country fully support women's
initiatives for full equality and self-determination.

"Men are just beginning to find their own voice and to
realize the extent of their own wounds. We're also rediscovering the depth of our masculine spirituality and beauty. But the
women's movement, for the most part, has made a concerted
attempt to undermine that work. Rather than let men struggle
with their own liberation, many feminists are attempting to
define men and masculinity according to women's perspectives. They celebrate the soft, obedient male who serves the
Goddess, carries women's pain, and has no autonomy, needs,
or wounds of his own for women to contend with. Yuck! That's
like men saying, 'We want women to be passionate, empowered, and equal as long as they still do whatever we tell them.'

"Most feminist writers seem to fear that anything men do
which is not controlled by women must be inherently bad for
women. For the most part, feminist reviewers of the men's
movement come across as mean-spirited, manipulative, dis-
torting of the truth, and, worst of all, woefully misinformed.
There are many excellent teachers attempting to heal men's
wounds and redefine masculinity in a life-affirming way.
There are dozens of books which thoughtfully and insightfully
probe the depths of the masculine psyche. These perspectives,
however, are rarely referenced in feminist critiques.

"Certainly there is room for dynamic criticism of the
men's movement. We have much to learn. But before I commented on feminism in my last book, I read over a hundred

books on the topic and interviewed many feminists. I hope before any more women comment upon or attempt to predetermine our course, that they will do the same."

I realized that I was beginning to lecture the group and that I had exceeded my allotted time, thus doing something that women justifiably resent men for—taking up too much space. I apologized for not keeping to the time, and I sat down.

We shared a lot of heat with one another in this council. But the evening was not complete until we informed each other about what we had just heard. We went around the circle, and we simply repeated something we had heard a member of the other sex say. It continued until we agreed that our issues had been heard by the other side. Thus, a lot of conflict was aired. But at every step we all were assured that at least one member of the other sex had heard our issue, even if there was no agreement.

Simply knowing that you have been heard is very healing. It softens the atmosphere. It helps create an atmosphere of empathy and trust in which there is at least the possibility for some real agreement to emerge eventually.

THE WOMEN CROSS THE RIVER AND THE MEN HIKE UP THE RIDGE

After our initial encounter, it was obvious to everyone that there was a great deal that had to be faced together; we had a lot of anger, mistrust, and misunderstanding between us. One of our initial agreements was to stay with the process. That's one of the safety factors in our work: We have to keep our commitment to continue moving along, to keep putting our faces in the fire until something changes. So, before we broke up for the evening, we all agreed that we felt okay about stopping for the night and would continue our council in the morning right after breakfast.

Conversation was subdued that night. There wasn't the lively joking and boisterousness we had experienced the night before. Everyone was clearly shaken, disturbed, or at least provoked to deep and quiet reflection on what had transpired.

Liz and I made our way around the camp, checking in with people, making sure everyone was really all right. From our conversations we learned that for most of them, this was the first time they had been directly confronted with the collective anger of the other sex. We have all heard it in the media and in our one-to-one relationships. But hearing the collective outrage of an entire group that is facing you across the fire and is still going to be there in the morning is a powerful and transforming experience for most people.

For the most part, the war between the sexes has been a covert operation to date, with each side sniping at the other from hidden vantages. We were trying to create a peace conference that was safe enough for people to bring their weapons into the open, for all to see, without actually firing them at one another.

Of course, the ultimate goal is to disarm altogether. However, mutual disarmament will come about only in a measure equal to the demonstrated capacity to offer mutual solidarity, understanding, and support. Before we can experience our potentials for alliance, we must acknowledge our wounds. The first step toward that acknowledgment is to uncover the wounds in front of everyone and know that the other sex has borne witness to them. Then in our following meetings we can take the next steps toward healing by becoming accountable for the pain we may have inflicted on the other sex during our lives.

As Liz and I settled in for the night, we heard the hoofbeats of horses on the trail at the edge of the clearing where we had encountered the snake that afternoon. It must be those cowboys, I thought, but it seemed odd to me they would be traveling at night. "I hope they aren't going to camp here," whispered Liz. They must have spotted the remains of our fire or simply had other plans. In any case, they moved on. There was no trace of them the next day.

When we gathered in the morning, several men suggested that before another council was called we should hike up the trail another three miles or so to get to a glacial cirque named Summit Lake. Andy thought it might make a better long-term camp because we could go swimming there and have a more secluded camp away from the trail and cowboys passing in the night.

Dave and Larry were obviously eager to go fishing. Secretly, so was I. They were making a lobbying effort by appealing to our stomachs with the promise of German brown trout, hard to reach at the creek still far below us, but easily accessible from a campsite next to a lake. It sounded very sensible to me, and I gave a covert nod to Liz, indicating to her in the silent language every couple learns to speak over time that I thought this was a good plan. But several women and Jerry wanted to slow the pace of our journey. They wanted to spend a day resting and lingering by the natural beauty of the creek before hiking higher into the mountains.

Liz and I had previously discussed the possibility of separating the women and men at some point during the trip. It's standard in our gender-reconciliation councils. There are many good reasons, which we will elaborate on later, why each sex benefits from having some time alone with their same-sex group. Apparently, without our mentioning our hidden agenda, the group spontaneously decided to split over this issue. So we proposed that the women and men spend some time alone in their separate groups.

Thus, the women decided to remain at the camp and the men, including a reluctant Jerry, hiked up the canyon. Before leaving, Liz and I asked both groups to ponder the following questions while they were apart: How have you been fueling the war between the sexes? What is your part?

We agreed that the women would follow the men to Summit Lake the next day, but as it turned out, like many things on this trip, our plans were destined to change.

CHAPTER THREE

IN THE WOMEN'S CAMP

In the Primordial Age Woman Was Once the Sun.
—JAPANESE FEMINIST SLOGAN

THE CAMP SUDDENLY BECAME very quiet as we watched the men move up the trail and over the ridge until, one by one, they were all out of sight.

"Well, what now?" asked Merle, looking a little uncomfortable.

"Let's pack up our stuff and move down nearer the creek," suggested Susan.

"That sounds like a good plan," I said. "I'd really like to be further away from the trail. Did you hear the horses that passed through after we went to bed last night?"

"Yeah, I did," said Doris. "After our council last night, I was too disturbed to go to sleep. So I went and sat by the coals of the fire for a while and saw them ride through like dark shadows against the night."

"God, I hope they don't come back this way while the guys are away," Merle spoke up. "I've never been alone in the woods without Alan before. Cowboys make me nervous."

"Not me," said Susan. "You're safe with us, Merle, and besides we could have some fun with them. Really, a couple of those guys are pretty cool."

"Yuck, Susan, how could you think like that?" cried Gloria.

"I know, I know . . . that's not what we're here for." Susan sighed. "But I wouldn't mind finding a little romance in the woods with a 'real' man while we're so busy solving all the world's problems."

Several women laughed, and Lisa said, "Well, let's solve ours by going to the creek. My immediate problem is feeling grubby and I want to wash my hair."

We packed our gear and moved it all down to the new spot.

❧ THE WOMEN CROSS THE RIVER TO LIVE WITHOUT THE MEN

"This is great," said Marie as we began to get settled. "It's much more private and it feels refreshing to be right by the creek."

We set up our new camp quickly and efficiently. Doris, our designated fire-builder, started a fire so that we could heat some water. By midmorning we were sitting around our new hearth, relaxing with steaming cups of tea. We started discussing feelings about the council from the night before.

"How are you feeling now, Doris?" I asked. "You said earlier that you felt disturbed last night."

She was silent for a minute before she answered. "I feel discouraged, I guess. There is so much hurt and anger between us and them," she said, gesturing toward the direction in which the men had headed. "I don't know how we're going to come back from this place." There were several nods from the other women, obviously in agreement with that sentiment.

"I feel angry," said Lisa, "and misunderstood by the men in our group. It was really hard to sit and listen to all that stuff they said last night. I kept vacillating between wanting to yell at them for being pigs and then feeling ashamed when some of their complaints rang true."

"You think these guys are bad, you should see the jerks I work with," said Susan. "There are very few women in my department. I feel alienated and isolated from my coworkers most of the time. I have to be very careful that I don't behave like an 'emotional' female, and God forbid I should disagree with some of the male executives who have seniority. Then, instead of being seen as assertive or capable I'm just written off as a bitch."

"I feel resentful and confused," said Marie, continuing with this theme.

"About what?" asked Lisa.

"Well, the more I try to make it in a man's world, the angrier I get. I've made an enormous effort to become the kind of woman who could be successful and climb the corporate ladder. I've wanted independence ever since I was a kid. Now I've achieved some success. But I still feel frustrated about my life. It seems somehow empty and devoid of

meaning. I'm beginning to feel dried up and bitter. I feel isolated from my family and most of my friends now because I
never have time to connect with them. Sometimes I'm no
longer sure of what it is I'm trying to accomplish or even who
I am as a woman."

"That helps me get clearer about what I'm feeling right
now," said Doris. She took the red bandanna from her neck
and wiped off the sweat that was starting to run down her face.
"I think both men and women are more confused than ever
about who we are and what we want from the other sex. We
could argue the issues endlessly. And we all have valid points.
But I believe that the healing will come from someplace
deeper in us all, someplace that maybe nature knows more
about than we do.

"I was just thinking about my grandma. We used to go visit
her on the reservation when we were kids. The house was
barely more than a shack, but we loved it there. She was full of
earthy wisdom. When my brothers and I used to squabble,
she'd make us stop, go outside, and sit by a tree. We weren't
allowed to come back until the tree had 'spoken' to us, and
then we had to share whatever the tree said with one other. We
always went off resentfully to sit by the tree, it felt so hokey.
But it never failed to work. Somehow we would come back in
a much clearer place."

"That's a great story," said Gloria. "I like the image of your
grandmother. She sounds like a great lady. But I didn't know
you were a native American."

"Well, only a quarter. But I did have the opportunity to
learn a lot about her culture."

"So, maybe we're like those kids who need to go sit by the tree? Is that what you are saying?" asked Merle.

"I think so," replied Doris.

"Would pure melted snow and big white boulders work, too?" Merle asked playfully. "It's getting pretty hot."

"Look at us here, sitting around drinking tea in the middle of nowhere," Susan said, laughing. "We could be any group of women, anywhere, doing what women have always done together—sitting around yakking, trying to figure it all out."

"Maybe we will," said Lisa. "All things are possible. But do you think the men are worrying about this right now?"

"I doubt it, they're probably baiting their tackle and getting ready to be the Great Hunters," Gloria said in her usual sarcastic tone.

"Well, if that's the case, maybe they've got the right idea," said Susan, starting to strip off her clothes. "Let's go swimming."

It was a relief to spend some time without the men and good to have this time to relax and get better connected with one another. We had a lot to think about after the previous night's meeting. It's difficult to communicate what we want from men if we don't even know ourselves. What we want is often better discovered when we spend some time without the men. Most of us, however, don't want to be with only women. We get enormous benefit and pleasure from men. The separatism touted by some feminists is not a practical option for most of us. And yet, as I looked at the women washing and combing their hair and lying in the sun, it seemed impossible that we could ever have been this relaxed and at ease if men were present.

56 ✣ WOMEN
AT THE CROSSROADS

As I listened to the women chatting amiably by the creek, I thought about how many women I know who often feel confused about their sense of feminine identity. There are parts of us that are still deeply embedded in traditional roles and habitual patterns of behavior. Yet, in the midst of these changing times, many of us are struggling to find a powerful new identity. At this time, in this society, we are reaching for a new understanding of what it means to be feminine as well as powerful. And there are many obstacles along this journey of self-discovery.

One of the ways we resolve some of these inner conflicts is through getting together with other women and pooling our resources. Jungian therapist Naomi Lowinsky calls this experience of collective female wisdom the "Motherline." She describes the Motherline as the embodied experience of the female mysteries. Unfortunately, many of us have become disconnected from our Motherlines, from the essence of deep femininity itself—the feminine soul.

It seems that women's loss of soul has some of its roots in the cultural drift over the last hundred years toward abstract thinking, logic, and individuality—all values traditionally emphasized in the socialization of men. We live in a culture that judges many areas of human behavior by male standards, particularly in our religious, political, economic, and legal systems. This trend has created problems in self-esteem for many of us. More recently, this loss of self-esteem has been compounded by our attempts to become equal with men by attempting to become the same as they are.

I reflected that in the past, gender differences have been used to discriminate against women. How many of us were told as children that we could never become the president of the United States because we might make bad decisions under the influence of PMS? Unfortunately, assuming that we are the same as men creates a new set of problems. We are increasingly expected to deny the needs of our bodies, our emotional expressions, our own styles of leadership, and our need for connection to our families. Women in the workplace have been a cultural minority whose voice has been drowned out by the louder, more established tones of traditional male culture. In these arenas, there is an emphasis on doing things the way men have always done them rather than recognizing that we bring a unique and valuable perspective to the workplace.

In the workplace there is often a superhuman expectation for female employees that exceeds the natural limits of our bodies, hearts, and souls. Consequently, the prestigious gains we make in the workplace are frequently offset by a cultural message that says, "You don't do enough, you don't have enough, and (essentially) you are not enough." Marie and some of the other women were expressing the alienation this message breeds as we sat by the creek talking about our lives.

Increasingly, many of us feel that we have to be superwomen. We try to maintain our roles as wives, mothers, and lovers while trying to access our creative, political, and economic power. Our primary relationship, if we have one, is often under stress from these extreme pressures in a rapidly changing culture. Divorce rates are at an all-time high, and more women now find themselves the sole head of a household. Not surprisingly, according to government statistics, working women's rates of alcoholism, depression, smoking, hypertension, and divorce all appear to be rising.

Perhaps, I thought as I dipped my feet in the icy cold mountain stream, these ominous trends are indicators that the problems we face have been only partially solved. The first step was breaking through the prison bars of old stereotypes and making entry into new areas of self-expression. But perhaps the next step we need to take is to learn how to move into the world with our feet firmly rooted in female culture instead of rejecting it as either being nonexistent or of no value.

Some female scholars have suggested that a healthy and integrated adult woman has biological, psychological, and psychic realities that are fundamentally different from those of a man. Many of us, for example, still feel that our female identity and self-worth are based more on the quality of our relationships than on our performance in the world. We have been brought up to think of ourselves as caregivers. And although this role has become limiting for many of us, it also continues to represent a deep cultural theme—the primary matrix in which the female identity arises.

I think that connection with the deep feminine, however, should not be confused with the "new traditionalism" often touted by religious conservatives. The answer is not to go backward, but rather to move forward in a manner consistent with feminine values and in harmony with women's needs. Just as some traditionalists are embedded in an outdated model of femininity, some of us went to the other extreme and embraced an outmoded, toxic, heroic male model of empowerment. What we need is a new vision of women being fully and powerfully engaged in the world without sacrificing the vitality, passion, and nurturing pleasure of deep femininity.

One way we can reconnect with female culture is by simply meeting with one another and talking about the daily challenges and pleasures of being female. Through honest conversation and deep connection with one another, we can begin to understand the uniqueness of our situation. Through being in the energetic field of other women, the character of the feminine soul begins to be felt on many levels. This is what was happening as we spent time together, bitching and moaning, soaking up the sun, sighing, drinking tea, and just hanging out by Blue Water Creek.

IN THE MOON LODGE

"Oh, damn," cried Merle as she returned from a dip in the creek. "I've started my period, and I didn't bring anything with me. What a hassle."

"I've got some extra pads in my pack," Susan said. "I started mine yesterday."

"I feel so embarrassed," said Merle. "I wasn't due for a week. I can't imagine a worse time."

"It couldn't be a better time," I suggested. "I can't remember how many times I've wished that I was in the company of other women when I started to bleed. I've always wondered what it would have been like to be in a traditional menstrual lodge. In many cultures women have a special house—a moon lodge—where they could go and have lots of restful, quiet time. Other women would make restorative teas, play music, and bring them pillows. When do we ever have the opportunity to just surrender to our cycles without the constant distractions of work, children, and partners?"

"I always want to be alone during this time," said Marie. "Yet, the way my life is set up, it's next to impossible. I'm at work all day. And then when I get home, Larry and the girls really need my attention. It seems like I can handle everything all month until my period comes. Then I go nuts and start screaming at everybody."

"You two are lucky," said Gloria. "You can relax into it now. We'll be your moon lodge. You can lay around all day in the sun and water, and the rest of us will take care of everything. How about it?" she asked, looking at the rest of us. This sounded fine with everyone.

"My grandmother used to tell me that this is the most powerful time in a woman's month," said Doris, a brightly patterned sarong wrapped around the lower half of her body and nothing on top. "I never could understand what she was talking about because it always has felt like the opposite to me. But as I've gotten older, I'm beginning to get it. Our period is all about transformation. But change doesn't always feel that great when it's actually happening."

"Especially when it's not supported by the people around you . . . or even ourselves for that matter," said Susan.

"I imagine myself like a snake shedding a skin every month," Lisa said. "Or sometimes I see myself walking through a gateway into something unknown. But if I have no time or space to pay attention and be with myself, it sort of gets away from me without any real awareness."

"Yeah," replied Merle, "and right now I feel like it's time to go slither down, melt into one of those boulders, and take a nap."

One of the more important things women discover when they meet together is the primacy of their biological realities. Despite heroic efforts of will, our bodies are inextricably cyclical by nature, at least for the first half of our lives. Because of our menstruation cycles, we change hormonally, waxing and waning both physically and emotionally throughout the month.

Some of us spoke among ourselves about what an effort it is to conform to the standards of heroic culture—that women seeking power feel they have to deny this uniquely female experience. This denial contributes to some of the physical and emotional discomfort so many of us experience during our menstrual cycles. Tamara Glenn of the Menstrual Health Foundation says that PMS is a result of a society that doesn't know how to integrate the female fertility cycle into the fabric of the culture.

It has continued to be a mystery to me that despite some progressive thinking about female psychology, there is still very little written about the psychological effects of the onset of menses. What is well documented, however, is that self-esteem in adolescent girls takes a serious dive at that time. There continues to be an enormous taboo for us women—even unabashedly feminist women—against acknowledging the differences that we experience because we menstruate.

There is a very deep-rooted cultural assumption that these differences render a woman dysfunctional and inferior.

At the onset of menstruation, most of us learn that there is something taboo, dirty, and disagreeable about the experience. We are taught that it should be hidden, sanitized, and denied in the presence of men. And we learn that society discourages us from expressing our feelings when we menstruate.

We learn early on that being moody, "coming unglued," and other expressions of emotion are considered inappropriate in a culture that places a high premium on controlling feelings. In our society, ego loss—loss of conscious will over emotion—is often considered undesirable unless it is part of a woman's sexual experience with a man. Many of us are taught to look upon the emotions surrounding menstruation as a disease. All too many of us are robbed of the potential value of the menstrual experience as a focal point to feel securely rooted within feminine-gender culture.

For some time it has troubled me that throughout western history menstruation has been described in disparaging terms. Saint Jerome said, "Nothing is so unclean as a woman in her periods." In the *Rule for Anchoresses*, Christian women are queried, "Art thou not formed of foul slime, Art thou not always full of uncleanness?" Pliny said, "A menstruous woman's touch can blast the fruits of the field, sour wine, cloud mirrors, rust iron and blunt the edges of knives."

Some native American men did not allow menstruating women in their sweat lodges, lest the scent of their blood linger and scare away prey or attract predators. Even today Orthodox Jews will not shake hands with a woman in case she might be menstruating. Contemporary women are still derided for having "the curse" or being "on the rag."

Because of such disparagement, we have lost the deep soul journey connected with this biological experience. The soulful side of menstruation is a potential gold mine for women. It is a process that, when understood and integrated into our psyches, can become a significant tool in our healing and empowerment. The menstruation cycle provides a window into the deep emotional power of the unconscious.

I feel that through menstruation, we are often brought in touch with our deepest feelings. Monthly, we have the opportunity to surrender to the depths of emotion, allowing feelings to surface that are uncontrollable. It is a unique time, when the ego loses its powerful grip on our personality. It is this relaxing of the ego's grip that makes menstruation so frightening for women as well as for men. Our culture worships the god of reason. It pathologizes deep feelings. Consequently, the soul-making possibilities of the menstrual experience are lost, leaving many women feeling diminished.

As we relaxed at the campsite, I reflected that in other times and cultures the female fertility cycle was considered the prime source of a woman's power. It was evidence of her awesome and mysterious capacity to create life. Many indigenous societies understood the deep meaning of this phenomenon. Rites of passage were built into cultural practices that, at the onset of menses, welcomed adolescent girls into the larger circle of womanhood. The practices varied widely, from the Mescalero Apache and the Navajo, to the African Swahili, to the Australian Tiwi, to East Indian and Cambodian tribes, to countless others. What seems common throughout the world, however, is that the rites allowed all the girls of the tribe to experience initiation into the collective body of adult women.

In indigenous cultures, at puberty a girl would be taken aside from the larger community and instructed by the older women. From them she would learn all she needed to acquire the full rights and responsibilities of a mature woman. Through initiation she would also learn about the sacred meaning of her menstrual-fertility cycle. In our culture, however, there is no comparable experience for young women. They are not welcomed by older women who themselves have an intact sense of self-esteem and value in being female.

We need to embrace and accept our female nature that manifests uniquely through each feminine body. This acceptance is something that can never be given to us by men. It is unlikely that men will ever be able to recognize and affirm our needs without our first understanding and expressing these needs to ourselves.

When we are in touch with the feminine soul, we can move into the world with strength, depth, and femininity. We can reweave the broken strands of female culture. Initiated women are a source of inspiration and wisdom for younger women who are struggling to find self-worth in a difficult and changing world. Susan and Merle caught a glimpse of this strength and healing when they had the opportunity to take time out from their usual responsibilities, with the full support of other women.

As we continued discussing this issue, Gloria wistfully commented, "In some ways, as I go through my change of life, this awareness is coming too late for me. Although menopause is a blessing in certain ways, I also feel sad about it because I'm just beginning to really understand the deeply spiritual nature of menstruation. Well, maybe now at least I can start teaching younger women about it. What I'm also getting out of all of this is that like menstruation, I've been conditioned to regard menopause in a negative way.

"Menopause means my blood is now being held within my own body. It's not being mobilized for motherhood. Instead of my focus being the nurturing of others, it's now turning toward the nurturing of wisdom within, toward deepening my feminine soul. I think we should change the name from menopause, which focuses on a cycle ending, to 'wisdoming' or another word that exemplifies the positive metamorphosis this change represents for women. What we usually hear about is hot flashes, our raging hormones, and our 'empty nest' syndromes. It seems that every stage of women's transformation can either be regarded as a horror or a blessing. It just depends on how you approach it."

✿ FIERCE BEAUTY, FEMININE FIRE

The sun rose higher in the azure sky as the second day of our gathering continued. The day turned hot. We draped ourselves over the large white boulders bordering the creek and let the sun soak into our bodies.

"This feels incredible," said Lisa. "I can feel the stress of my life melting away."

As we relaxed into the seclusion of this private spot, most of us felt secure enough to take off our clothes. The scene was reminiscent of a group of nature spirits bathing in a sacred pool. I was moved by the sight of these lovely women, in all their shapes and sizes. "Look at us," I said. "We're beautiful."

"Oh come on, Liz." Gloria reacted. "Don't get carried away here. I don't feel very beautiful. I'm fat, wrinkled, pale, and flabby. It's pretty hard for me to let anyone see my body anymore. I feel embarrassed."

"Yeah," said Marie. "I can totally relate to that."

"It's tragic how we've internalized this negative view of ourselves." I sighed. "It's been a long time since I've been in a group in which any woman has said that she genuinely feels good about her body."

"We've really lost a sense of our innate beauty and special-ness, as women," agreed Lisa. "When I teach my women's studies classes, I bring in myths about goddesses from other cultures and times. There are wonderful ancient images of the feminine soul that seem to elude most modern women. One of my favorites is Inanna, the ancient Sumerian goddess.

"Inanna was known as the Queen of Heaven and Earth. One of her sacred hymns says, 'When she leaned against the apple tree, her vulva was wondrous to behold. Rejoicing at her wondrous vulva, the young woman applauded herself.' Can you imagine feeling that good about your body and your sexuality?"

"It's hard," admitted Merle.

"Not likely," chimed in Marie.

"Women have gotten so lost in the pursuit of superficial beauty," Lisa continued. "And then in reaction, there are so many women who've gone to the opposite extreme and have completely denied their feminine sensuality. In one of my classes, one guy continually insulted some of the women by calling them 'Birkenstock mommas.' But you know, there were an awful lot of women in the class with short hair, no makeup, baggy sweats, sensible shoes, and a perpetual frown."

"So what are you saying?" challenged Gloria, lounging in her Birkenstocks. "That women have to be frilly and fruity or they're not feminine anymore? What a load of crap!"

"There must be another alternative," said Doris, "one in which our sense of beauty is aligned with being fierce and powerful in our own right. Not just as objects for the pleasure of men, but beautiful for our own delight and self-satisfaction."

"What we seem to be groping for here," I said, "is an image of femininity that is beautiful and powerful at the same time, sort of a fierce beauty."

"Yes," said Doris. "Exactly! Fierce beauty. That really captures the image I have of myself as a woman."

We lay sprawled on the boulders, drinking up the warmth of the day and periodically cavorting in the creek. We spread lavish amounts of sunblock on ourselves to protect our skin and lay like pagan worshipers in adoration of Great Sol. We chatted together amiably as the afternoon wore on. It was a very satisfying and nurturing way to spend the day.

"All this sun is really good for me," said Merle. "I feel like I lose my vital energy from being indoors most of the time."

"I know," said Doris. "At my agency we have these awful fluorescent lights. I hate the way I feel when I spend too much time under them. It doesn't seem natural or healthy."

"I notice as this day goes on that I am feeling much more comfortable with my body," said Gloria. "When we first came down here this morning, I felt incredibly self-conscious. Now with all this talk of Inanna and fierce beauty, combined with the sun and the water, I am beginning to feel very sensual and soft."

"Yes," Marie chimed in. "I feel more relaxed than I have in a long time. My work has been eating me alive. But why do you think we feel more feminine from being in nature and lying in the sun? I always thought that the sun was a symbol of male energy."

"It usually is," said Lisa. "Which is something that has bothered me for a long time. I don't know why exactly. I guess it makes me feel excluded. I don't understand why we divide up the symbolic world into one gender or the other. It doesn't even make much sense to me. From what I understand about biology and physics, there are male and female elements in everything."

"You're right," Susan said. "Now that I think about it, in all the stories I've ever read, the earth is always the Great Mother and the sky is the Great Father. So what's wrong with that? I like identifying with the Great Mother."

"Well," argued Lisa, "I've always felt more at home on mountaintops than in valleys. Since I was a little kid I've been fascinated with the sky and the sun. I used to pretend I was a bird and that I knew what it was like to fly on the wind. But I've always been told that this part of nature was male. So where does that leave me as a woman? I don't relate to being like an earth mother with bountiful breasts, feeding all her children. I love my son, Gabe, but my career has always been very important to me. I want to soar and shine like the sun, not be merely relegated to the dark and mysterious earth."

❦ THE GODDESSES OF THE SUN

"Well, Lisa," I said. "There's no reason why you can't. There are actually lots of cultures around the world who imagine the sun as being female, a solar goddess who is partnered with a male earth god."

"Come on, Liz," said Lisa. "I've been in a dozen women's groups and I've never heard a thing about a solar goddess. Every woman knows the earth is our mother. I think you're just making this all up."

"No, I'm not. There are lots of examples of sun goddesses. In Norse creation myths there is a man named Mundlifari who has two children, a daughter, the sun, and a son, the moon. The feminine sun in these myths has many names: Orb, Everbright, All Glowing, Fairwheel. There is also a Swedish sun goddess named Lucina who appears at the winter solstice with a crown of lighted candles, symbolizing the return of the light.

"Among the North American Indian tribal groups, the sun is considered female by the Eskimo, Yuchi, and Cherokee. The Celts have a sun goddess called Sulis who was later called Sulis Minerva by the Romans. In Bath, England, there are ancient healing hot springs whose heat is said to come from her. In Australia the majority of tribes identify the sun as female and the moon as male."

"I like this idea," said Susan. "It fits right in with the discussion we had earlier about fierce beauty. I imagine a woman with fierce beauty to be one with some of this solar energy.

She's someone who determines her own life instead of always just reacting to the people around her."

"I like it, too," said Merle. "I have always felt pretty passive in my life. I seem always to be reacting to Alan's needs and the needs of my children. I hardly even know most of the time what I want. I don't think a solar goddess has any trouble knowing what she wants."

"That's exactly my point," I continued. "The Egyptian solar goddess Sekhmet, for example, is one tough lady. She's a lion-headed goddess who's extremely fierce and violent, but paradoxically is also associated with the healing arts. She is called the Lady of Life. She's often depicted holding an anhk, the Egyptian symbol of eternal life. In *Women's Mysteries*, by Esther Harding, there's a wonderful image of Sekhmet standing guard over women as they go through the phases of their moon cycle. I like to think of her standing guard over me when I'm at my most vulnerable."

There are countless images of solar goddesses in all parts of the world. The Japanese sun goddess, Amaterasu, is perhaps the most well known. The imperial line of Japanese emperors claims her as their founder. One of Amaterasu's most famous myths revolves around the seasonal cycling of the sun. Amaterasu argues with her brother, known as Impetuous Male, because he is always disrupting her court. She becomes so angry that she withdraws into a cave in the earth.

The Kami (the other gods and goddesses), recognizing the potentially dire nature of this situation, create a large mirror in the shape of the sun, called a Sky Mirror. Then they throw a big party. There is much noisy merriment and bawdy humor. Finally, Amaterasu peeps out of the cave to see what's going on. She sees her reflection in the mirror and is tricked into thinking that they have found a Kami more beautiful than herself. So, she emerges from the cave to confront the usurper and thus the sun is restored to the world.

Those who love her fool Amaterasu into declaring herself "the most beautiful." It is the need to claim her beauty in the world that causes her to leave her dark, depressed refuge in the cave. Based upon the myth of Amaterasu, Japanese feminists, lamenting the decline of vigor and vitality in women, adopted the slogan that opened this chapter: "In the Primordial Age Woman Was Once the Sun."

Aphrodite is another goddess of the sun. Jungian scholar Karl Kerenyi notes that her magic is "warm and genuine, like the rays of the sun. It is the warmth and truth of passion that shine through Aphrodite's nature, as sun-like gold shines through her whole appearance." This energy is the alchemical heat and passion that bring about transformation from one state of being to another. Solar movement, solar warmth, solar fire infuse a woman's being and enable her to bring herself forth into the world while retaining her femininity, her sensuality, and her grace.

Through understanding solar femininity, we also create the potential for both lunar and earthly masculinity to emerge for men as well. It is possible to extend our worldview and see both genders expressed in all elemental and natural forces. This style of imagination breeds partnership. The alternative is to continue to divide the universe, allocating one domain to the female gender and the other to the male. This now-outmoded style of imagination breeds war between the genders.

Because myths generate culture, we must ground our visions on new mythological foundations. In reimagining gender roles, we must stretch beyond the familiar and habitual. We limit ourselves when we think about elements of the natural world being assigned to one gender or the other. The mythological world is a vast caldron of symbol and image. Out of it we can weave the fabric of a new sacred partnership in which women and men can freely support and embrace both their solar and lunar strengths.

As we sat around the fire that evening and looked at who we were, we realized how much value our shared experience had brought to us, short as it had been. Some of the women expressed that they had never before felt what it was like to be in a group of women without men. We realized how special it was. I reminded them that sometimes we, like Amaterasu, cannot see who we are, as women, without the mirrors of other women. It doesn't mean that men do not have an essential place in our lives. Rather, it means that there is a field of feminine energy created in a group that helps us to feel and identify who we are on a deeper level.

We had shared a good deal of intimacy and trust during our time together. This bonding and sense of strength as women were important as we moved into our next task: to begin to explore our feelings and issues with men and to discover how we contributed to the war between the sexes.

As the moon came up, I wondered if the men had made it up to Summit Lake. I hoped Aaron was okay. I was having a great time with the women, but I missed him and was looking forward to rejoining the men the next day. But morning would bring an unexpected obstacle to our plans.

CHAPTER FOUR

IN THE
MEN'S CAMP

From time to time there passes, as it were,
a wave a frenzy through the ranks of men
too long constrained within the limitations of their culture.
Antiquity experienced it in the Dionysian.

— CARL JUNG

I T WAS LATE MORNING by the time we finished our morning meeting, said all our good-byes, and packed our gear. I sat alone with Liz at the far edge of the camp. There we had a final breakfast of nuts, granola with powdered milk, and our last few pieces of fresh fruit. We shared our impressions about how the council was going and made a plan to check in with each other about halfway up the trail, at midmorning on the following day. After that, both groups would reconnect around noon at Grace Lake, a glacial cirque that was a roughly equidistant two-mile hike from our respective camps at Blue Water Creek and Summit Lake.

As I picked up my gear and headed up the trail, I had mixed feelings. On the one hand, I was looking forward to getting to know the men better and to having the opportunity to talk about our issues away from the women. On the other, I felt some trepidation.

Separating the groups after the first conflict council seemed risky. When Liz and I work at growth centers and for corporations, we divide the groups, in separate rooms, only for a few hours at a time. Now we were going miles apart and for a longer time. A lot of energy had been stirred up the night before and I didn't want the enmity to fester. I was eager to move toward the peacemaking intent of our gathering. Also, I found myself already missing Liz. I had been on the road lecturing so much lately that we had not spent much time together. And here we were in this astonishingly beautiful place. I wanted to go swimming, laze around, and hike the moonlit ridges with her.

I found myself regretting our commitment to dealing with gender conflict and same-sex group work. Suddenly I wanted to be in a gathering where everybody just tried to be nice to each other. But our experiences to date had already taught us that hosting conflicts is an essential first step to genuine peacemaking. Furthermore, the experiences we gain from the solidarity and comfort of a same-sex group inevitably provide a foundation for potentially more valuable councils between the sexes. So, with all this in mind, I headed out with the men toward Summit Lake.

As we crossed the ridgeline, I looked back toward the women's camp. I was too far up to make out individual figures, but it looked as if they were breaking camp. Where was Liz going? I wondered. Moving camp wasn't part of the plan. Oh well, I guessed I'd find out the next day when we'd have our agreed-upon rendezvous below Blackheart Ridge.

❧ MALE PRIVILEGE OR PRIVATION

Early afternoon brought us to an old forest ranger's cabin, where we stopped for a break. We were now high above Blue Water Creek. It was tumbling and cascading through the narrow canyon below us. The porch of the cabin afforded us a fine view of a small waterfall and white-water rapids below. The spray from the water hitting the rocks created a fine mist. It caught the sunlight in such a way as to make sparkling rainbows dance and shimmer in the air above the canyon's edge.

I noticed a small weathered brass plaque set into the concrete of the native-stone porch. It stated that the cabin had been built in 1935 by men in the WPA. As I thought about the men who had camped and worked in this place two generations ago, I felt touched with sadness.

The Great Depression was a hard time for this country. The nation responded to the out-of-work masses by instituting welfare, mostly to benefit women, and public-works programs, mainly for men. Now our society is once again experiencing economic disruption. The welfare rolls of women and children have swelled. This alone is a social disaster. And most unemployed men not only lack direct public assistance, but, unlike their grandfathers and fathers in the thirties, often have no work programs at all. The growing numbers of men, who comprise about eighty-five percent of the homeless living on our streets, bear mute testimony to this problem.

I couldn't help but reflect that today there are no new Grand Coulee dams to build, no meager funds for the construction of wilderness cabins and trails like these, and few public-works programs to repair our decaying infrastructure.

There is currently a dearth of honorable endeavors dedicated to restoring men's self-esteem and generating a continuing sense of worth. Instead, we now pour public funds into building more prisons to house men who, often in desperation, strike out against a society that seems to have abandoned them. Grim thoughts for such a benign sylvan setting, somehow evoked by the fantasy of men from another era sitting in the same spot, working with pride, eating, swearing, spitting, resting, and gazing at the same rainbows, dreaming of a better life together.

As we continued resting in the shade of the cabin, I thought about the council the night before and about how poorly most men's issues are understood by women and by society at large. I showed the men the plaque I had discovered and shared some of my thoughts with them.

Andy said, "Yeah, I can relate. You know, I've been underemployed for several years. I barely make a basic survival wage at the group home. I want to learn new skills, go back to school or something. I see a lot of special classes and reentry programs for women. But there don't seem to be any special training programs or support systems that are specifically oriented toward men."

"One of the things that feels unjust to me," said Alan, "is that women now get a lot of special considerations at work. And I agree that they have a lot of legitimate complaints about unfair wages. But anytime there is something physically strenuous or dangerous that must be done, it's always a man that's designated to do it. As a contractor, I'm painfully aware of the fact that when it comes to getting seriously injured or killed on the job, men are getting hurt and dying twenty to one over women."

Larry then spoke, saying, "I've noticed that most of the people on the streets of my city are men. There are numerous women's shelters, but we don't even have a single men's center in my city."

"Maybe you should start one," interjected Jerry.

"Yeah, well, that's not such a bad idea," Larry replied, "even though it would be tough since, as I understand it, most public funding available for women's centers is not equally available for men. But the point I was trying to make is that if there were more women on the street, society would be doing something about it. It's just like war. The only reason we tolerate it is because it's men's bodies on the line, not women's. When it comes to our health, safety, and well-being, it seems that society doesn't care about men as much as it does about women."

As we continued working our way up the trail to Summit Lake, I thought more about the sentiments the men had shared at the cabin. In our conversations along the trail that afternoon, we continued to share our concerns about the double standards most men face. As we hiked above the treeline, onto the granite backbone bursting through the thin alpine soil of Blackheart Ridge, I pondered Gloria's belief that men are so much more privileged than women.

Clearly, I thought, we create much of our own suffering. We are, as Gloria noted, the primary perpetrators of physical violence. It's a tragic legacy all men must bear. It is rarely noted, however, that we men, in almost every category, are also the primary victims of violence. We account for seventy percent of all assault victims and eighty percent of homicide victims. Over the last few decades, the important and needed focus on women's wounds seems to have unintentionally also created a drought of compassion for males in its wake. While hiking in silence through the thinning pines, I had more time than usual to think about these issues.

As I looked at the men winding their way up scattered boulders amid the glacial moraine, I was struck by how beautiful they looked, sweating in the sun, their colorful garb and gear standing out against the mottled grays of the native stone. Sadly, there seems to be little initiative toward protecting that beauty. I thought about how there are massive public campaigns to educate women about breast cancer, but little information for men about prostate cancer, a deadly disease that affects about one in eleven men but receives only about one-tenth the funding of breast cancer. About ninety percent of persons dying of AIDS in America are male. If this were true for women, I wondered, would there not be more public funding for research and victim support?

Yes, I thought, it's true, as Gloria, Marie, Jerry, and others pointed out in our council, that some men enjoy access to significant political and economic power as a result of their gender privilege. But they account for only the upper one to two percent of the population that controls more than one-third of the nation's wealth. The other ninety-eight percent are sorely in need of our compassion, understanding, social activism, and support. I was hopeful that these men would experience some overdue understanding before the journey ended.

SUMMIT LAKE CAMP

Although the trail to Summit Lake was not very long, it was steep and rocky. The climb was hot and we proceeded slowly. Consequently, it was midafternoon by the time we arrived. After a rest, most of the guys wanted to go fishing or exploring around the lake.

Toward dusk I found that Jerry and I were the only ones in camp. Grasshoppers were flickering through the alpine meadows, and crickets had already started their evening concertos. Night was coming, and even midsummer's eve at this elevation can be quite cold. So, Jerry began collecting a night's worth of firewood while I set up a hearth, built a fire, and started boiling water to get some soup and coffee started.

As the men trickled into camp they seemed grateful for the hot water and fire, but no one said anything. Dave, Alan, and Joel were triumphant. They had caught eight trout among them. They laid out the glistening fish on a log next to the fire for all to admire. We lavished a fair amount of praise on them for their prowess as fishermen.

The fish were already cleaned and ready to fry. I was happy that I had had the foresight to bring some garlic, herbs, and a small container of oil with me instead of leaving all that stuff with Liz. Although I was delighted to have the fish for dinner, I resented it that everybody had split without giving any thought for the camp. This experience gave me some insight into one of the issues many women are angry about. I felt a little like a neglected wife who had to make sure there was a nice home for the men to come home to after a day of hunting. I realized how often the domestic, traditionally feminine role is underrated while the traditionally male, hunter-provider role gets all the glory.

The issue wasn't so much about the amount of time put into the job, but rather how much the work was honored. No one had praised Jerry and me for our contribution as fire-builders and coffee-boilers. Part of my current experiment as a man is to no longer automatically sit on my feelings, but rather to express them, even at the risk of violating the heroic-male taboo that equates feelings with weakness. I told the men that I felt taken for granted. Jerry seconded my opinion.

Although Jerry had begun to get on my nerves with his habitually subservient attitudes toward women, I suddenly felt sympathy and solidarity with him. I had enjoyed sharing the few hours of being domestic with him. I experienced how undervalued the domestic role is for men. Men often wind up rejecting such occupations as fathering, home care, child care, or participation in early education because they are conditioned to believe that these are not "manly" occupations. In any case, our complaints were duly acknowledged by the others. We let it go and got on with making dinner.

After dinner we sat around the fire picking our teeth with trout bones. Dave reflected, "It was very relaxing to be without the women today. I felt really smooth and easy with you all. I especially enjoyed the silence and listening to the sounds of this place as we fished together, side by side. It felt like the first time I really heard the birds, the sound of the water, the wind in the trees. Women are always talking, always wanting to relate. I felt very connected to all of you today, but we didn't have to talk about anything. We just used gestures and nods to communicate our desire to move from one place to another or to display our enjoyment of the moment. I think this is a way that men are fundamentally different than women. We communicate a great deal in silence." Several men nodded in agreement.

After a pause Larry said, "Another way men are different, and one of the things that I appreciate about men, is how easily they can let go of things. They don't seem to hold grudges to the same degree women do. Like when Aaron complained about having been made 'camp wife' by default. It was said, heard, and finished. And we then all went back to having a good time. If that had been a woman we would have had to endure a lecture about how inconsiderate men are and then she would probably have been upset all evening."

"Why do you think that is?" Joel asked.

"I think it's because women never feel heard by men," replied Andy.

"If that's true, one of the reasons women may feel that way," I offered, "is because of what Dave was just talking about: our male mode of communication. When I told you all about how I felt this evening, I could tell by the way you looked at me, by your body posture, and by your expressions that you received my complaint and nothing more needed to be said. But many women seem to need more verbal input. So when we don't give them a lot of feedback, they don't think we heard them and then they say it again. Then we call it nagging. But it's not, really. It's just the more verbal, female mode of communication."

Joel then said, "I talk at work all day and then I'm supposed to come home and have intimate conversations with my wife. But I don't even have time for intimacy with myself, much less her. I try to be there for her, and yet somehow it's never enough. I wish she could understand that sometimes I just need to be quiet for my own restoration, but that doesn't mean I don't care about her."

For a while we uncharacteristically continued talking about not talking. Then we discussed some of the binds inherent in the social stereotypes that define who we're supposed to be as men. We spoke about what it was like to be men in this culture, how it felt to be raised never to show feelings, to always have to be cool, "to be a man."

Dave reflected on this topic, saying, "I've always believed that I could only be loved for what I produce, never just for who I am."

Alan stated, "I feel like I have to be everything to all people, a good father, good lover, successful in business, and my wife's best friend. I don't feel that there's ever any room for me to fail at anything without it somehow reflecting on my worth as a man."

Andy shared, "Men can never show fear and I've always had to be strong. Since I was a little kid it's been clear to me that no one was ever going to come along and take care of me just because I was beautiful, nurturing, or fun to be with. I was not only going to have to work to support myself, but if I didn't want to be alone in this life, I'd have to figure out how to support a family as well."

Jerry, surprisingly, admitted, "I've always felt it was sexist that men are the only ones who have to register for the draft. I grew up knowing that in a time of war, I'd be expected to die or go to prison if I resisted. Women have a lot of legitimate fears about the possibility of violence entering their lives. But they don't have this threat of potential future military induction hanging over their heads. Even though there's currently no draft, men are still subject to fines and five years' imprisonment if they fail to register. If we're truly going to create a non-sexist society, I'd like to see women confronting this issue in the same way that I and many other men have been active in supporting women's initiatives."

As we continued talking about our lives and the lives of our fathers, our sons, and other men we knew, it became clearer that most men still feel they have to live up to a pain-negating, heroic image of masculinity. This role, however, often has little to do with how we really feel as men. In most cases the old ideal of manhood does more to imprison our souls than to liberate our spirits. Many of us feel caged by our stereotypically prescribed roles and responsibilities.

The more recent "sensitive" image of masculinity, however, does not seem to offer a solution to our dilemma. This vision denies men's passion and fierceness and, as such, does not feel like a realistic possibility for most men. So, where do we turn for a new myth of masculinity? When we can't break out of the old one playfully and creatively, we often may choose destructive behaviors like drinking, drugs, sexual obsessions, and putting our bodies at risk in a misguided attempt to cope with our emotional numbness. The need for a new way becomes evident whenever men sit together and instead of shucking and jiving one another somehow find the courage to tell each other the truth about their personal lives.

STICKS AND STONES

We continued talking deep into the night. For a while we sat silently around the fire, listening to the hiss and crackle of the burning, sap-filled pine. Incense from the resin filled the night air. Bats flickered ominously at the farthest edge of the fire's glow. The night's hush was occasionally punctuated by distant owl calls. Jerry answered back: hoo, hoo, hoo. Joel chimed in, hooting too. Others then joined the chorus, making various sounds and tones. Andy clacked two sticks in rhythmic accompaniment. Larry pounded on a log, and Dave clicked two stones together. We were making some very odd yet, in some strange way, completely familiar music. Most of us as little boys had done some such thing at one time or another.

Finally, everyone got into the rhythm. Sticks and stones . . . it must be true, that's exactly what boys are made of. After a while Jerry started shuffling and dancing around the fire. Joel and I joined him as the others clapped and urged us on to wilder dancing. We leaped around, over, and even right through the fire. After a while, sweating, laughing, and exhausted, we stopped. I looked at the stars, now seeming somehow brighter, and realized I hadn't felt this alive in many months.

Larry then spoke. "That was really fun. I feel great. I don't think I've done anything like this since I was at camp when I was ten years old. You know, it seems ironic to me that drumming, dancing, and the open display of feelings amongst men are the activities that are the most ridiculed by the media in their strange and twisted reports about the men's movement.

"If the media must ridicule men," he went on, "why not lampoon the absurdity of men battering each other uncon-

scious in boxing, breaking their bones in football, or splatter-
ing their bodies in warfare. Dancing, singing, making music,
laughing, and just being silly feel pretty good once you give
yourself permission to break out of the 'Be cool and take it like
a man' cage most of us have been stuck in."

Joel fished a slim volume of Rilke's poetry out of his pack.
He said, "I've got a poem here that expresses some of the feelings that I have about feeling caged as a man."

> **"Der Panther"**
> *His weary glance, from passing by the bars,*
> *Has grown into a dazed and vacant stare;*
> *It seems to him there are a thousand bars*
> *And out beyond those bars the empty air.*
>
> *The pad of his strong feet, that ceaseless sound*
> *Of supple tread behind the iron bands,*
> *Is like a dance of strength circling around,*
> *While in the circle, stunned, a great will stands.*
>
> *But there at times the pupils of his eyes*
> *Dilate, the strong limbs stand alert, apart,*
> *Tense with the flood of visions that arise*
> *Only to sink and die within his heart.*

We all fell silent once again.

I walked away from the fire and paused for a while gazing
at the moonlight shimmering on Summit Lake. I looked at the
range of mountains to the west and for a moment felt like a
giant owl that could leap into the chasms beyond, soaring into
the cool and starry night. Savoring this momentary feeling of
intensified freedom, I thought about how many men in the

United States are not merely prisoners of social stereotypes that deny them access to their deeper feelings, but also are being physically imprisoned at a rate exceeded by no other nation on earth. About 1.5 million American men now have no freedom at all.

I felt frustrated as I thought back to the many men I had counseled over the years who were demoralized by their experiences with the criminal justice system. Most of them never had a chance to experience the beauty that was now before me. I thought about the councils ahead and how I wanted the women to understand that not all men are advantaged. One of the reasons that ninety-five percent of prisoners are male is that although men are arrested for drugs six to one over women, they are incarcerated ten to one. Even though the vast majority of crime is related to substance abuse, there are few recovery programs for these men, many of whom are non-violent. On the other hand, women are much more likely to be referred to intervention programs, social welfare organizations, social services, and mental health practitioners for the same disorders for which men are routinely incarcerated.

In prison men usually serve longer sentences than do women for similar crimes and are raped in numbers matching those of free women. However, we have few programs, if any, to deal with the post-traumatic stress disorders of men who have been victimized in the penal system. This, too, must change if we are to create a just society for both sexes. But this night at Summit Lake camp we were all free men, shaking off our grief and frustrations for a short time. We felt freer than usual by simply doing what men had done for thousands of years before us—sitting around the fire, swapping tales, drumming, dancing, and howling at the moon.

THE MAN IN THE MOON AND THE EARTH FATHER

The moon began to crest over the eastern ridgeline as we sat, silent for a while around the fire. Andy put some water on for hot chocolate. Alan said, "God, it's been years since I just sat around and looked at the night sky. It's so clear out tonight. Look, you can really see the man in the moon."

Jerry then said, "You know, that's a real patriarchal way to look at nature. Every other culture in the world sees the moon as a goddess. But since our culture puts down women, we get told as kids that the moon, just like our Big Daddy god in the sky, is a man."

"So, Jerry," I challenged. "You seem to see everything in nature as feminine; do you have any positive images of masculinity that you believe in?"

After thinking for a moment, he replied, "No, I guess I don't. You know Robert Bly chides so-called soft men. And I feel that you've sometimes got kind of an attitude, too, Aaron. But even though I'm not gay, I've always identified more with the feminine. There are no male models that support me in the way that I experience myself as a man. I've always been more sensitive and emotional than most men. Women understand me. I relate to my soul, the moon, and the earth as reflecting the beauty of the Goddess, and I think other men would be more balanced and whole if they embraced their inner femininity, too."

"That may be true," I replied. "But what's confusing to me is the fact that in many cultures the moon has been viewed as an image of masculinity."

"I think that's just some men's movement jive," Jerry replied. "I've never heard about a moon father before."

"What about Jerry Brown?" cracked Alan.

Everyone laughed.

"Exactly the point," I continued. "Men often get ridiculed for being spiritual, thoughtful, inward, passionate, idealistic, or emotional. But that doesn't mean they are more feminine. They are simply masculine in a different way. Jerry, you seem to have what could be called a lunar style of masculinity. But your feminist friends have framed your character for you in a way that makes you feel less aligned with men. It's kind of sad, because you're really a beautiful man. You've been told that your sensitivity must come from your feminine side. But if you don't have an image of masculinity that feels sacred to you, how can you feel sacred yourself?

"Through my readings in mythology I've encountered the Egyptian gods Thoth and Osiris, the Eskimo Brother Moon, the East Indian Chandra and Soma, the Sumerian Nanna, and countless other sacred images of masculinity throughout time that have reflected this lunar quality of masculinity to men of those cultures. So from that point of view, Jerry, I can't relate to you as a feminine man. It seems that you are deeply masculine in a manner that diverges from the hard, heroic, solar masculinity that most of us have been conditioned to emulate."

"Well, when you put it that way," Jerry replied, "it makes me feel more aligned with all you men and my male body as well. I've never heard myself described that way before and there's a part of me that feels pretty good about hearing it. You know, I never look at strong women as unfeminine, so why should I think of myself as unmasculine? I guess I've got some sorting out to do about all this."

Many of us who are in quest of masculine soul are attempting to reconnect with our bodies and our emotions, and to seek our place in the natural order of things. In the absence of male initiation, over the last few decades many men like Jerry have sought reconnection to soul through the feminine. However, femininity is not the primary cure for masculine wounds. Indeed, the trend to personifying the soul and nature as a feminine entity effectively perpetuates the divorce of the male psyche from its own, inner-masculine, life-affirming nature.

"Where did we get the idea that nature was our mother only?" I wondered aloud to the others. I recalled that many cultures imagined personifications of nature as masculine. In ancient Sumeria, the Earth Father was called Dumuzi. In other parts of the world, he was also known as Adonis, the Green Man, Iacchus, Freyr, Karora, and Ymir, or, as in medieval Germany, simply the Wilde Man. The potency and wild magnificence of the ocean was imagined by the Greeks and Romans as Poseidon, Neptune, or Oceanos.

In Egyptian mythology he was Osiris, son of Earth Father Geb and Sky Mother Nut. The overflowing of the Nile River deposited fresh alluvium that fertilized the crops each spring. The annual regreening of the world was depicted in ancient paintings as resulting from the overflowing of Osiris's ejaculate fluid. Kokopelli, the hunchbacked native American trickster, planted seeds, like Johnny Appleseed, wherever he went. He was always dancing and making music.

I looked around the circle as flickering half-light and shadows played upon the men's faces. They suddenly appeared to me as if they could have come here from any time or place in history. I shared my perception with them and the thought that moving through the wilderness together in small groups was the most ancient occupation of men. We are at home in nature and clearly as much a part of it as are women. Something sleeping in the depths of the male psyche seemed to awaken in us as we allowed ourselves to appreciate nature free from the numbing noise of urban life. Sitting around the fire that night, it seemed that we were resonating with the countless generations of men who had come before us to dream, hunt, play, and simply be at peace in the great green natural world.

A NEW MYTH OF MASCULINITY

The moon began to cross the ridge tops to the west of Summit Lake, and we let the fire die in anticipation of calling it a night. However, though we were all very tired, there seemed to be no end to the conversation. The floodgates of feeling had begun to open and as a consequence most of the men had a lot to say. The topic shifted from talking about myths of Father Nature to fathering itself.

As the myth of masculinity is undergoing transformation, the image of fatherhood is also changing. Instead of the postindustrial father who is isolated from his children, many men are downshifting from work away from the home in order to spend more time directly parenting their children.

Women are finding that the Earth Mother alone is an oppressive ideal that limits their imagination. In a similar manner, men are finding the spiritual ideal of the Sky Father insufficient for reimagining masculinity as nurturing and life supporting. The psychological and spiritual development of men becomes unbalanced when only solar archetypes form an ideal of sacred masculinity.

The heroic model of masculinity, by itself, is dominating and oppressive. The solar gods are abstract or even transcendental. They are often inaccessible to our imagination—the very images of remote or disembodied fathers. These images, moreover, have served for centuries as the primary ideals for masculinity in western culture. Such ideals do not feed men in quest of soul any more than a diet dominated by earth mother images feeds women. Our gender myths are changing. But for most men, the shift toward the hearth, the earth, the community, and the family is not an easy one.

"What's happening to fathers in our culture is sad," said Alan. "Women blame every problem in the world on men. But more and more homes are without fathers. It doesn't seem to be the presence of fathers that is screwing everything up, but rather their absence. At least that was true for me growing up without my father. He was killed in the Korean War when I was only eight. I really miss him. I wish he was here tonight. I was remembering today how he used to take me fishing when

I was just a little guy and how happy I felt around him. We had so little time together. How was I supposed to learn how to be a man and how to become a father myself when there was none around for me to imitate?

"I guess I'm doing okay with my kids, just making it up as I go along. But I wish I had more memories to draw on and could ask myself how would my old man have dealt with this or that issue. After being here tonight I think that maybe a regular men's group, like one some of you guys already have, could help me learn more about how to be a good father."

Joel then said, "It troubled me last night when Lisa complained about me not doing more parenting. I handle all the home maintenance and repairs, keep the cars maintained, do all the bookkeeping and the yard work as well. These things aren't hobbies. I also work more overtime than Lisa. Where am I supposed to find the time to equally coparent?

"The bottom line is that I really miss my son. I love spending time with him. I just can't seem to figure out a way to hold up my responsibilities and be a full-time father at the same time. I also find it difficult to know how to be a good father at times. Lisa always seems to have it so together. Whenever I do try to get more involved, I experience her taking over, as the resident expert. But maybe fathers nurture in a different way. I tend to involve him in activities that are directed toward becoming competent in the world. She seems to focus more on his emotional life. I don't think either way is better or worse. Kids need both. But my style of parenting seems to be lesser rated. Lisa gets validated as a parent by nature itself, but I somehow have to earn it."

"I can't even see my first two kids anymore," said Dave, "cause their mother moved back East. I've got a business on the West Coast and she knew I couldn't leave. She didn't have to move. Her new boyfriend is in some play in New York and she wanted to be near him. I wanted custody and the kids would have been happy to stay with me. But the court gave her custody because most people these days still believe that mothers can do a better job with the kids than fathers. And there's nothing I can do about it.

"I can now only see the kids on vacations, twice a year. I really miss them. They're growing so fast. I'm missing all the little day-to-day stuff that a solid relationship is built on. And yet I still make the support payments even though she has a more lavish lifestyle than I do. There's no way for me to enforce that she spends the money on the kids. I pay because I want the kids to have what they need. But the way it's all set up makes me more and more resentful as time goes on."

"Yeah, I know what you mean," said Andy. "I got a girl-friend pregnant a few years ago. She decided to have an abortion even after I told her that I would assume full custody and financial responsibility for the child once it was born. She just said, 'Don't be ridiculous, a man can't raise a child without a woman. And I don't want to be that woman. So I'm going ahead with the abortion.' I was devastated and still feel sad about it as I speak tonight.

"I just don't get it. There's all this controversy about women's choice, but men don't have any choice at all. It's kind of ridiculous to call our society a patriarchy since men have almost no parental power. If she chooses to have a baby you don't want or simply are unable to care for, then you pay or go to jail. But if you want a child and she doesn't, then you lose your opportunity to be a father. It seems that when it comes to parenting rights, fathers are becoming second-class citizens."

"Fatherhood is certainly a less-valued male institution than it was in the past," I agreed. "In my own life, my experience as a stepfather has taught me a lot about how men are unseen and undervalued for their fathering. I'm very committed to my stepdaughter, Noelani. And Liz both admires and takes pleasure in my parenting. But in the world at large, I feel the only thing I am ever recognized for is my performance in my profession.

"I turned down a valuable appearance on CNN last year because it conflicted with our family plans for Thanksgiving. It was hard for my publicist at the time to understand how I could make that kind of choice. And there are many other occasions when I feel it's necessary to put my family commitment ahead of my career. I don't mind that. In fact, I believe that my family is more valuable than anything else in my world. It feeds me more than any possible success in the world at large. But it's rare anyone says, 'Hey, Aaron, you're really a great father.'

"People tell me they love my writing or my teaching or were touched by a workshop I led, which is great. Really, I'm very fulfilled by my professional success and am not knocking it. But why is it that if men fail as fathers they are raked across the coals, yet most committed and engaged fathers are simply taken for granted? Impoverished fathers are put in jail and called 'Deadbeat Dads.' On the other hand, men who attempt to downshift from work or even take advantage of parental-leave programs in order to become more involved parents tend to be seen by employers as uncommitted to their careers and thus at risk for losing promotions.

"As a society, we see fathering as a somehow lesser role than mothering. Last Mother's Day, for example, the phone company broke its record for the number of calls made in a single day. On Father's Day, however, there wasn't a significant change in volume from any other day, except that there were many more collect calls than usual. It's a sad commentary on the state of fatherhood in America."

For several decades now, I have listened to an unending stream of rhetoric from the women's movement against patriarchy. But just what is a patriarch? According to the dictionary, a patriarch is the leader of a family or a venerable old man. A father is a male who has begotten or adopted a child, any male who originates or establishes something, any elder man, a leader of a council, the senior member of a profession. To father means to create, support, nurture, and protect. Robert Bly has observed that what we have in our country is not really a patriarchy—a society ruled by the father—but rather a society in which the father is mostly absent, more like what Jungian psychologist Robert Moore calls a "puerarchy"—a society ruled by puers, that is, immature men.

At almost every public talk I give, at least one single mother comes up afterward and asks what she can do to help her adolescent son become a man. It's always a painful question because I, too, wonder how we can learn to be men without our fathers. A mother's love, no matter how committed or mature, is still not enough to move a boy into mature masculinity. I believe she must draw some ethical and committed lover, husband, uncle, brother, father, teacher, clergy, or friend into her and her son's lives.

I feel that men must restore honor and celebration to the vocation of fatherhood. The dying myth of masculinity was primarily concerned with material success and the acquisition of power at any cost. The new myth defines success according to the capacity to father our children, nurture the earth, achieve balanced partnerships with women, and codirect our institutions in a manner that empowers everyone around us while increasing our own well-being.

It's only in the last decade of developing deeper friendships with men, and through fathering each other in circles like this one at Summit Lake, that I've begun to have an unabashedly positive regard toward my own masculinity and that of other men. And from my work across the nation, I know this is also true for tens of thousands of other men. To those whose fathers did not prepare them for mature masculinity, a second chance has been given to grow up in the security of councils with other honest, open, and caring men. All is not lost.

"In many ancient cultures," I shared with the group, "it was the 'second birth' of a young boy that made him ready for both the sacred and mundane responsibilities of an adult man. In the myths of Dionysius, the god's resurrection comes after his dismemberment, which is a reminder that through letting go of our old ways of being men is born the possibility for a new life to emerge. There exists the possibility, however, that lacking the fierce protection of the father, we become utterly annihilated by our vulnerability. That's why most of us never risk revealing our authenticity to one another.

"In the old myth of masculinity, we used each other's weaknesses competitively to gain advantages. In the new myth, however, we are exploring our vulnerabilities cooperatively, offering mutual support and healing. We are creating contexts, like this wilderness gathering, through which we can safely experience falling apart and then being supported, rather than shamed, for expressing our authentic feelings and trying to put our lives back together in a better way."

We talked a while longer and then began to bid one another good night. Though we had left the women behind only that morning, it felt more like a week had gone by. It was a good group of men. We were diverse in many ways, yet all of us felt a common bond from both the wounds and the hopes we shared. We had all been deeply affected by the stereotypical ideas about manhood we grew up with. And we were all, in our own ways, trying to find a better way of being in the world without relinquishing our self-respect, dignity, and identity as men.

It was hard to believe that we would be meeting the women again the next afternoon. After the men were so intimate for a day, the gender work was now beginning to feel like an alien idea, though it was part of the plan. I reminded them that I would be hiking down in the morning to meet Liz and that I would rendezvous with them in the afternoon before meeting with the women at Grace Lake, about an hour's hike away. I gave Andy the topo map, and he agreed to lead the pack the next day. The last glimmer of moonlight shimmered for a moment above the western ridgeline and was gone. Moments later, in the deep and silent dark of the mountain night, I fell asleep.

CHAPTER FIVE

DROWNING
IN OUR FEARS

Men and women, women and men, it will never work.
— ERICA JONG

"WHAT?" AARON CRIED. "You're kidding, Liz. What do you mean the women don't want to meet with the men? That's not the deal. We have an agreement to have these meetings. That's why we all came out here, isn't it?"

He was obviously feeling a little worn out. After hiking up to and down from Summit Lake yesterday, he had developed a large blister on his right toe, which he was examining when I arrived after the short hike up from our camp at Blue Water Creek.

"Well, Aaron," I explained, "one of the women called for a meeting this morning before I left to come here. She said she didn't want to spend any more time with the men. We went round and round about it, but couldn't get a consensus. Eventually two of the others agreed that they were enjoying being with the women more than when the men had been there.

They sided with the first woman, saying they also felt it was too soon for us to come back together. That's why I'm so late. I just kept meeting with them, hoping we could work it out. But this one woman in particular was adamant. She doesn't feel safe and won't go on until she does. So, they're all waiting for me to come back to camp so we can talk about it some more."

"The guys are probably already on their way to Grace Lake at this point," Aaron laughed wryly. "You know, the funny thing is, we were having a great time together, too. But it never occurred to me to put off the council. What's going on?"

"It's mostly Gloria's trip," I replied, realizing I had been reflexively upholding my gender solidarity in trying to keep the women anonymous. However, Aaron was my partner and he needed to know the whole story if he was going to help me find solutions to our problem. "I think she's very afraid of men. But the way it comes out is as a sort of hatred. And when she goes on and on about how screwed up men are, it infects the others. The next thing you know, half the group has got you guys cast as the bogey men and suddenly we're doing a women's group instead of a gender council."

Aaron took a deep breath, laughed again, and said, "Oh well, it's not so surprising that this could happen. So, where do we go from here?"

We sat on a fallen cedar tree and for a while silently watched a woodpecker hammering away at the far end of the log. This was a familiar way in which we sometimes approach problems. Instead of a lot of discussion or argument, we sometimes give up for a while and hang out together until some clarity starts to bubble up. I sighed, just relaxing into the beauty and comfort of the moment as I lay down with my head in Aaron's lap and thought about how we women got to this place with men.

THE NEW SEXISM

I've been attending and leading various women's groups for almost two decades, and hearing anger against men as a class is nothing new. But this morning I was disappointed and frustrated. We had come here to meet with the men, not to start another separatist women's group. Yet, it's so easy for rage to come up in a group of women. I thought about our meeting this morning. After the anger council two days earlier, Gloria had seemed outraged about hearing the men express their issues. Then this morning, as we were about to rejoin them for a second session, she began to vent the feelings she had been sitting on since the first meeting.

"I'm just not willing to hear any more wounded male shit from the men. I simply refuse to meet with them until they first apologize to us for all the damage they've done to women for the last two thousand years. Where do they get off having anything to complain about?" Gloria demanded. "They're the ones that made the world a mess. And now they have the nerve to have issues with us? Women have been the victims of the patriarchy, not men! And it's clearly women that are going to save the world now. This is a great group of women and I treasure this time we have to nurture one another. I don't want to sully our time together by rushing right back to the men. Okay?"

I understood how Gloria felt. Even so, I had finally come to the point where I was no longer sympathetic with her position. The habit of blaming men for all our problems can help create a sense of common identity in women's groups. Anger is a powerful source of energy and motivation for many women who are trying to create new, more authentic cultural roles. Yet there is a serious downside to the habitual expression of anti-male sentiments. This sort of female bonding has, in many cases, transformed women's 1950s false sense of inferiority into an equally false sense of 1990s superiority. Neither position has much to do with partnership and creating a more just society for both genders.

"Hey, Liz, it's getting late," Aaron said, jolting me out of my reverie. "I'd better get on up to Grace Lake and let the guys know what's going on."

"What are you going to tell them?"

"I'm not sure yet. I guess I'll tell them the truth. Without naming names I'll tell them that some of the women don't want to get back together yet. But we can't leave it at that. We need to develop some sort of alternative plan so the guys are not hanging in the wind waiting for the women to come around."

"Yeah. Here's what I think we should do." I took my copy of the topo map out of my pack and said, "How about if you gather the guys, about here, at the north end of the lake? And I'll suggest to the women that we move to the south end. That way we can easily go back and forth to communicate or negotiate, but the camps can still remain separate."

"Sounds right to me," Aaron said, leaping off the log. "What would be helpful at this point, Liz, is if the women would let us know just what their issues are or what they're afraid of, if anything. If they don't want to tell us directly, maybe they could communicate with us through you. What we can do as men to facilitate the next step and make the council a safer space is to offer simply to listen to them, without response, if they wish."

"Okay. I'll propose that, too. And one way or the other, I'll meet you at Grace Lake sometime this afternoon." Aaron hitched up his day pack, winced a little as he took the first step on his sore toe, and then scooted off toward Grace Lake.

Aaron told me that he wasn't completely surprised when I told him the women didn't want to come to the second council. After all, what we were trying to do was daring and threatening. According to Aaron, in men's gatherings when he proposes the idea of creating gender reconciliation councils, he sometimes hears comments to the effect of, "Well, that's a great idea, Aaron. Maybe we'll be ready for that meeting in about five years, after we develop a solid sense of our own masculine ground." Others say things like, "Women are always asking us to share our feelings with them, but I'd bet you my Buck knife that five minutes after we told them the truths we share in our meetings, they'd be trying to shove the cork back in our mouths as fast and as hard as they could."

As I strolled back toward the women's camp, I had a lot to think about. The women clustered around me expectantly when I arrived at the creek, where they had been having their morning swim.

"Well, Liz, what did you and Aaron discuss?" asked Merle.

"We've agreed on a compromise that I want to suggest to you," I responded.

"Oh, Liz, come on," said Lisa, wincing, as Gloria started groaning.

"Wait a minute, hear me out," I continued. "What women usually do when we are afraid or angry is to separate from men. In fact, what I often hear from women is that they feel powerful when they are apart from men, but when they're with men, they lose their voice and their will. Our challenge here is to stay connected with this wonderful female power we've been experiencing together and at the same time be in dialogue with the men. Have you ever noticed what happens when you feel afraid or threatened in your relationship? What do you usually do with that fear?"

Susan answered. "Whenever I reach the point in a relationship where I start to feel vulnerable or needy with a man, then I usually back off like a bandit."

"When I feel threatened by something that Joel does, I usually get mad at him right away," said Lisa. "It's sort of a first strike approach to gender conflict. When we were in counseling together, however, the counselor would have me express the fear behind the anger. When I could do that, it was amazing how receptive he became. He would sit still and listen to me, instead of heading for his study and slamming the door behind him."

"So, Gloria," I said. "This morning we heard a lot of anger from you about men. What I'm wondering about is if you also have some fear under that anger that isn't being expressed?"

"Yeah, I'm afraid of what you are doing now, Liz. You go off with Aaron and then come back and want to sell out the women's group by psychoanalyzing us all about our fear, instead of showing your unity with us by acknowledging that the men are jerks and we are clearly having a lot more fun now that they are gone."

"But, Gloria, we came out here to meet with them, right? So, just because it feels better with the women is not a valid reason, in this context, to not reconnect with the men. This has nothing to do with selling out! It has everything to do with seizing an opportunity to deal with these very issues in a more productive way than we usually do. It's clear that some us are afraid we can't be with the men and at the same time hold on to the special feeling we have found together."

"Yeah," said Doris. "I sure don't feel that I can hang out with the men in my sarong with my boobs hanging out."

Marie then said wistfully, "The issue for me is that I've been feeling so relaxed and comfortable with all of you, I just don't want to give it up."

"So, what should we do?" I asked, persisting. No one responded, and I said, "I propose that instead of being stuck here with these feelings, we go to Grace Lake, make our own separate camp, and communicate to the men exactly what we fear about the effect their presence has upon us. The reality is that sooner or later we will have to coexist with men. We might as well find out if there's a way we can do it better here, while we have the chance.

"In the interest of making a safe space for us, Aaron is going to ask the men to come and silently listen to what we have to say. Then they'll leave to consider our issues among themselves. We don't even have to discuss anything with them if we don't want to. Is there anyone who doesn't want to agree to do this?"

No one protested, and then Gloria said, "Well, then, what I want to do is tell the men this: I'm still pissed off about having to listen to all that crap they said in the anger council. I hope the poor little wounded boys can handle it."

℘ FEAR AND LOATHING AT GRACE LAKE— THE WOMEN'S STORY

By the time we had set up our new campsite at the south end of the lake and had cooked our evening meal, it was after dark. We then gathered at the spot Aaron and I had decided would be a good council ground. I heard a few grumbles as we all sat around the fire Aaron and I had built before everyone arrived. Most of us looked a little edgy as we arranged ourselves in a semicircle facing the men's camp. Then the men filed in and sat in a semicircle opposite us.

Aaron and I reminded everyone in the group to take responsibility for holding good boundaries around what they were willing to do. They were cautioned to care for themselves and one another in this process and to risk only what they cared to risk, nothing more. This wasn't est, and nobody was going to get points for not going to the bathroom or for not participating in any process that felt wrong.

Aaron and I then spent some time talking about what we hoped to accomplish. We wanted the men to listen with "soft" ears. That is, our intent at this point in the process was to further develop the ability to hear and receive the other gender without the need to criticize, respond, analyze, or fix anything.

We asked everybody to take a brief moment to become a little more aware of themselves: to be aware of their bodies, the space they occupied, and their connection to the earth and the sky and the great round of life all around us. We then began our council. I spoke to the men, saying, "I guess that Aaron told you we had some difficulty coming back today. Many fears came up that we would like to share with you." I turned toward the women and asked, "Who wants to begin?"

After a few minutes of awkward silence, Doris spoke up. "When I was in the women's camp, I walked around bare-breasted with only my scarf wrapped around my hips. I felt free and easy with my body. And I felt proud. Now I notice that I want to keep it covered up and instead of feeling like a beautiful nature spirit, I feel fifty-something, dowdy and chubby. I guess I'm afraid of your hard, critical eye and how unattractive it can make me feel," she said, looking at the men.

Lisa was next. "I've felt so carefree most of the last two days. For some reason, when I was with the women I stopped working so hard at being the perfect responsible wife, mother, and teacher. I kind of let it go and it felt as if I was appreciated by the women just for who I was in the moment. Some new part of me is showing up, kind of a wild woman," she said with a laugh. "I'm afraid of losing her. She's a lot of fun and I guess I don't know how to be that silly and free around men. I'm afraid of your scorn."

"I second that," Marie jumped in, looking at her husband, Larry. "I'm also afraid of men's anger. Men are scary when they get really angry. I guess the bottom line is that even though we've all agreed that there would be no violence allowed in our council, and it seems unlikely that anything would happen in this context, I'm still afraid of men's rage. I just can't feel totally relaxed when we are all together."

"I feel vulnerable right now, too, and somewhat emotionally ragged," Merle said, looking close to tears. "When we were apart from the men, I felt like it was okay to be this way. But here I'm afraid that I'll be judged for being weak. I don't feel nearly as safe and accepted for being who I really am in all my changing moods."

Susan, who was sitting next to Merle, reached over and put her arm around her. "I have felt very powerful as a woman in these last few days." She stood up while keeping a hand on Merle's shoulder. The fire shown brightly on her tousled mane of red hair. She looked radiant, protective, and fierce. "I feel really big right now. I don't want to lose this feeling. I'm afraid," she said, looking at the men, "because you have the power to make me feel small again."

Then I spoke up. "I'm often afraid of doing or saying the wrong thing when I'm with men. I feel like I have to be careful around you, especially when I am exerting some kind of leadership. I think that if I don't communicate just right, you'll think I'm a bitch. So sometimes I find myself tiptoeing around. But with the women I just let it rip, saying and doing whatever I want. Somehow the rules of engagement are all so much clearer when we're women alone."

Gloria was the last to speak. She looked miserable. "I'm so angry and so hurt, it feels like a bottomless pit. I'm afraid of that anger. I want to hurt you with it," she said, looking across the fire at the men. "And I can't believe I'm saying this to you, but it's my truth. Sometimes I become so enraged at men that I feel like a hurricane just waiting to happen. I think that anger toward men has become the center of my identity. It's been driving me for years. But feeling angry all the time doesn't feel very good.

"I've been abused by men. I was molested by my drunken father. I was also beaten by my first boyfriend. I want to just relax and feel alive around men again, but I don't know what to do with all these feelings. I've had them so long, I'm afraid I won't know who I am if I let them go. I also feel my anger keeps me safe, that as long as I keep my guard up, you guys will never be able to hurt me. So I'm afraid of being changed by you, it feels safer to keep you at bay, as my eternal enemy.

"It feels pretty scary to do this," she said, taking a deep breath. "But it feels pretty good, too," she said, sighing. Gloria suddenly looked more relaxed than I had seen her since the trip began.

 # THE MEN'S STORY

We were all silent for a few moments, letting this all sink in. The men appeared more subdued than I had seen them thus far. I think they felt a little overwhelmed by the honesty they had just encountered. I looked across the fire at Liz and then made direct eye contact with the rest of the women for the first time that evening. After a time I said, "I appreciate the courage it took for you to share what you did with us, to make yourselves so vulnerable and to trust us in this way. I realize that it's a lot easier for you to share your anger with us than your fear. In either case, it's not easy for any of us to tell the truth to one another, so I honor you for that.

"As I agreed with Liz, we're going to leave now and discuss what we've heard. But first I want your permission to repeat back to you what we heard you say, just as we did in our last council, so that you're sure that we got the messages you sent. Does anyone object to that?"

No one objected. And then the rest of the men and I paraphrased, and in some cases reiterated almost word for word, what the women had said. Whenever we didn't get one of the points right, which happened several times, a woman repeated what she had actually said, then we repeated it back to her. I watched the faces of the women soften as we continued. Then I asked them, "Is there anyone who's unsatisfied, who still doesn't feel heard?" No one replied, and so we were done with this phase of the council. But then as we stood up to go back to our camp, Susan said, "Hey, wait a minute here. We just spilled our guts. And I'm glad you're going to go talk and then come back to share what you think about all this. But I want to know what's going on with you guys. Don't you have any fears of women?"

"Of course we do," I replied. "I believe that we have as many fears of women as you do of us. Tonight, as a condition of making the council feel safe enough for you to return, we came to just listen. But my hope was that in time you would also be willing to listen to our fears." I slowly looked around at the women. "Would you like to hear them now?"

They looked at one another and nodded in agreement.

Then I asked the men, "Is there anyone here that doesn't feel like sharing their fears with the women?"

Dave said, "Yeah. I don't really want to. In fact, I'm not sure that I have any fears of women."

"Then do you object to the rest of us doing that while you're here in council with us?" I replied.

"No, go ahead, knock yourselves out."

Andy stood up and faced the women. "I'm afraid you'll ridicule me if I expose any weakness to you. But in the men's group I felt compassion and understanding when I told them I was tired of trying to be a hero all the time."

"I fear that I can't just be myself in front of you and joke around the way I do with the guys," said Alan. "I guess some of our humor is kinda raunchy, but I like it. And I especially enjoyed the horsing around and dancing we did around the fire last night. Even though nothing we did or said would offend women—at least I don't think so—I still can't imagine carrying on like that with the women around."

I saw Liz casting a curious eye toward me, and I noticed quizzical looks on the faces of some of the other women. Nevertheless, I believed we were entitled to our male mysteries, and so at our meeting that morning I hadn't told Liz anything about our midnight moon dancing.

Joel continued. "I feel that I have to be very careful about what I say and how I say it so that I don't violate any of the new codes of political correctness. It's exhausting at times to filter all my comments through a gauge of what's likely to offend or not offend women. Around men I know what's offensive or not and if I do inadvertently step on a guy's toes, I know he's going to let me know right away. But around women, I'm never sure. I'm also afraid that if I do offend a woman, I might only hear about it secondhand—days, weeks, or even years later. So it makes me feel cautious. It's harder to relax around women."

Larry looked at the entire group of women and then said hesitatingly, "Basically, I'm afraid of your anger. I feel that women's anger often comes at me sideways or jumps me from behind and then totally throws me off balance. Men seem to come more straight on and, although I fear that, too, I understand it better than women's anger. When Marie gets mad at me, I suddenly feel like I'm about five years old. It leaves me feeling ashamed and paralyzed. When men get angry at me, I still feel like an adult, I know how to defend myself. I have no inhibitions about mobilizing all my power to meet it."

I said, "What I fear the most is being criticized by women. I feel that I can make mistakes around other men and they will understand that everyone has their limitations. But I'm afraid that women will hold me up to a standard of performance that's unreasonable and be unforgiving when I fail."

"What I fear most about women," Jerry said, looking toward Gloria, "is that they're going to abandon me. I feel that I need Gloria a lot more than she needs me. So I'm always going out of my way to make sure that I please her, that I don't do anything to make her angry. I usually put her needs ahead of my own. If she left me, she'd have her women's groups for support, but all I have is her. It leaves me feeling pretty unbalanced in the relationship."

Then Dave stood up, facing toward us, and said, "Okay. I've changed my mind. I do have a fear I want to express. I'm afraid of how attracted I feel toward you, Susan," he said, slowly turning his head away from the men until he looked directly at her. "I fear women's sexual power over me. I don't even know you and yet you have this sway over my thoughts and feelings in a way that none of these guys ever could, no matter how much male bonding we do.

"Now I fear that all you women will think I'm some kind of harassing pig or sex fiend. But the truth is I'm affected by Susan's beauty and strength and I just don't see what's so wrong with that. How do you say you're attracted to someone these days without offending them? I really want to learn that from you women while we are out here, 'cause lately all the rules have changed and I just don't get it anymore."

When the men had finished, the women mirrored back what they had heard. Then Liz told us, "I want you to know that we have genuinely listened to you. We hear your frustration and your grief. We don't know how to fix it. We don't even know what part is ours to fix, if any. The knots in which we have tied both ourselves and you are very large and complex. But I honor you for your openness and your honesty. Hopefully, we are coming to understand you better as a result of listening to your fears."

❧ WE ARE COMMON IN OUR GRIEF

After Dave spoke, Liz and I asked all the members of the group if they would like to continue being in council. Everyone agreed that this was a fruitful meeting and affirmed that they wanted to go on. We then opened the circle to feedback. We asked people to try to make "I" statements, to talk about how the information they had just received made them feel rather than to critique the comments of others. And we acknowledged that all of us had already come a long way by being able to sit together and listen to one another.

It was clearly impossible to unwind all our issues in one evening, but everyone seemed deeply engaged and fascinated in wanting to hear more about the wounds each gender was struggling with. As the evening progressed, it became clear that underneath all the anger and the fear we had shared with one another during the last several days lay a deep well of grief.

"I'm having trouble taking in what the men said," observed Lisa as she sipped a cup of hot tea. "I keep taking it personally and feeling somewhat ashamed."

"Me too," said Merle. "I'm having the same problem. Although I can't help but hear the truth in much of what the men are saying, it's painful to look at all this stuff."

Because women have a history of being shamed by the old sexism, they are understandably sensitive about any hint of blame or negative characterization of their behavior. They are used to being told that every problem in parenting and relationships is their fault. Consequently, women in quest of empowerment and in need of high self-esteem are often reticent to look at their "shadow," that is, the parts of us we would rather disown. And yet, Aaron and I felt it was imperative that both sexes do just that as a step toward breeding deeper understanding and trust.

Dave told us about how hard it had been to share his feelings with us honestly, saying, "Now that I've said what I did, I feel very exposed." Other men agreed that talking this way was uncomfortable for them. Several confessed that they did not know how to cope with women's tears and that they, too, noticed a tendency toward feeling ashamed after listening to the women.

The shame cycle in women and men is clearly one of the reasons both genders have had so much resistance to hearing about the other's past wounds. However, in the present context, instead of being swallowed by feelings of shame and winding up enraged, we were able to talk out our feelings and witness the habitual patterns we fall into. As we continued to talk, many of us realized that we felt considerable hopelessness about our capacity ever to heal our wounds.

Marie got up and threw another piece of wood on the fire. Warming her hands over the coals, she said, "It makes me feel sad to hear about how afraid everyone is to just be themselves around one another."

"For all my anger at men as a group," said Gloria, "I really love Jerry. It makes me sad to hear how insecure my independence and connection to other women makes him feel. I wish he could get as much comfort from other men as I do from other women."

Jerry admitted that he felt spiritually and emotionally inferior to women. He felt lost and unable to connect with being sacred or special in any way that equaled the beauty he saw in women. Andy acknowledged that he was completely confused as to what women wanted from him. Joel talked about how difficult it was to balance his inward, artistic nature with meeting the needs of his family for his attention and his time.

"When we talked together back at the men's camp," Alan told us, "we realized that we felt caged. Men were once free like the antelope on the prairie. I've heard that many native people only worked about three or four hours a day. Now we wear ties or heavy boots and work all the time. But we've lost sight of just what it is we're working so hard for. We've lost our wildness and our freedom. It feels like a terrible price to have paid for love, security, and acceptance. We're not completely sure about how to change. I feel like we need your help and don't know how to ask. I'm afraid that if I do ask, you'll say, 'We've got enough problems of our own without trying to help you out of your mess as well.'"

We continued talking less formally while holding an open conversation between the women and the men. The issues were vast and complex. Many of the women's issues centered around their fears about the ways in which men make them feel threatened or small. Many of the men's issues focused on their fear of women's power to transform or overwhelm them in a variety of ways.

One of the things men fear is that they can feel driven into violent competition with one another to win women's affections. This is one of the reasons why we need to meet apart from women at times. Men who are seeking peace and brotherhood often find it more easily in a same-sex group.

When we men discuss the need to separate from the mother, as an integral part of our individuation, women often consider that need a condemnation of women. Consequently, the men's movement has generated a great deal of animosity from leaders of the women's movement. Our society, however, desperately needs men to find a way to instill the virtues of brotherhood in one another while developing vital and egalitarian partnerships with women. The women asserted that they felt an identical hunger for developing a deeper sister-

hood that could help bring about a more nurturing community with men. But they also felt that men, who felt threatened
by women's collective power, would ridicule their periodic
need for separation.

As we talked late into the evening, the moon came up,
casting dappled shadows on the lake and trees around us. This
group of adventurers clustered around a small fire surrounded
by vast forest seemed an apt symbol of the gender wilderness
we found ourselves in. It was becoming clear that although the
problems of the men and the women were often different, the
feelings of anger, frustration, and sadness were similar. Several
people said that they realized men and women alike felt
equally victimized or misunderstood. We concluded that both
groups equally tended to blame some of those feelings on the
other sex.

Liz and I made some observations about the group process
thus far. Instead of increasing the sense of alienation between
the sexes, by bringing conflicts into the open and speaking our
truth we appeared to have increased a sense of shared humanity.
I reflected that we still clearly had much work to do before we
could be in equal partnership. Liz suggested that our needs to
dominate and control, or to be controlled by, the other gender
came from a loss of a sense of our deepest beauty and power as
women and as men. The challenge for the coming days was to
learn how to access that beauty and power in the presence of
one another. Real partnership between the sexes must have
beauty, pleasure, and mutual empowerment at its foundation.

One of our favorite authors, Jungian analyst Marion
Woodman, writes in her book *The Ravaged Bridegroom* about

how the unconscious feminine and the unconscious masculine get in the way of women and men claiming a new vision of partnership. She says,

> The old petrifying mother is like a giant lizard lounging in the depths of the unconscious. She wants nothing to change. Her consort, the rigid authoritarian father, passes the laws that maintain her inertia. Together they rule with an iron fist in a velvet glove. Mother becomes Mother Church, Mother Welfare State, Mother University, the beloved Alma Mater, defended by Father, who becomes Father Hierarchy, Father Law, Father Status Quo.

Clearly, many of our old ideas about gender do not work anymore. And, as we were discovering, even some of the more recent visions—the strident woman warrior and the overly sensitive male—are already worn out and obsolete. In our group we were attempting to move into new territory. In order to do that, we needed to get rid of some of the baggage that was weighing us down. We put our anger, our fears, and our grief on the table as first steps in that direction. We had to do much more, and again the question came up: Where do we go from here?

It was not enough merely to inform one another about our problems. As Gloria had so clearly stated to Liz that morning, she needed to hear the men state their accountability for the ways in which they have wounded women. And we suspected that the men had a similar need. Thus far, both sides had avoided taking much responsibility for their parts in the war. Therefore, as our council drew to a close for the night and the women and men prepared to go back to their respective camps, Liz and I asked each group to ponder the same question we had asked at the last meeting, before returning for further dialogue: What do you contribute to the war between women and men and, furthermore, what weapons are you willing to lay down in order to make peace?

The group broke up, and for a while all the couples and most of the others paired off for private conversations. One by one they found their way back to their separate camps.

The midway point of our gender council had been reached and no one had become injured, died, gone insane, attacked anyone, or split the scene. It had been a little hairy at times, but, to some extent, that had been expected. As Liz and I said good night, a brilliant shooting star streaked across the midnight sky, doubled by its reflection in the lake. Fire, Water, Earth, and Sky all in one potent moment. It seemed like an auspicious sign that light and wholeness were returning to our work together, and we were filled with hope for the coming days.

CHAPTER SIX

FACING THE
MASCULINE AND
FEMININE SHADOW

*Doing shadow work means peering into the dark corners of our
minds in which secret shames lie hidden and violent voices are
silenced . . . [it can] result in an authentic self-acceptance and
a real compassion for others.*

— CONNIE ZWEIG

I WOKE UP EARLY the next morning, just as the sun was
emerging over the ridge. It was quiet and peaceful. All I
could hear were the sounds of a few jays squawking and the
occasional plop of fish jumping in the lake. There was already
a plume of smoke rising from the men's camp. I imagined,
with some envy, that they were cooking trout for breakfast.

In the past I always relished eating the fish Aaron caught.
Now I wondered, Why does he have all the fishing gear? And
how come I've never bothered to learn how to fish? I guess it's
because I don't like to get my hands all slimy with fish guts
and so I let Aaron do it all. However, now with him on the
other side of the lake I was resenting my lack of hunting
power.

Last time we camped I ran through the meadow and gathered live grasshoppers with Aaron. He said, "If you want to eat

fish, you've got to help catch bait." Yech! But I got over my bug aversion. Now perhaps, I could also bait my hook, catch, and ugh, even clean my fish. I was tempted to walk over to the men's camp and demand a fishing pole and tackle from them, but just about then Doris sat up sleepily and gave me a big grin.

"What a day!" she exclaimed, looking at the mists swirling on the lake.

"Yeah, and what a night!" I answered, referring to last night's council.

We laughed together. One by one the women got up and gathered around the fire. After four days in the wilderness, we were a motley crew. Yet, despite lack of makeup, styled hair, and clean clothes, we looked more relaxed and vital than when we had begun our trip. When I am in the woods with Aaron, I sometimes wear a little bit of makeup, even though Aaron always quits shaving. Because I was in the women's camp, however, I didn't bother and neither did anyone else. The other women actually looked more beautiful to me now than they had looked the first day. Each woman had courageously shared intimate parts of herself over the preceding days. It made me feel a special closeness with them that transcended the brief time we had spent together. I felt as if we had been sisters for years.

While Lisa stirred a large pot of hot cereal, we started hashing out our feelings about the previous meeting with the men. One of the observations that surfaced, after some discussion, was that although we obviously fear men's violence, we also resent their denying their real vulnerability. The hero thing really turns us off.

Now, all of a sudden we were confronted by a group of men who were admitting that underneath all the bluster they weren't so tough after all. They were angry, hurt, afraid, lost, and troubled. Hey, they were human! They had feelings, just like us! At times, however, because of our conditioning to regard "real" men only as stoic warriors who never complained, we felt a resistance to hearing men "whine."

Would so-called sensitive men be able to protect us in a time of danger? Perhaps not. That was a troubling thought. As we talked about the council, however, we realized that we felt less angry with the men because they had stopped bullshitting and had started telling us the truth. And maybe, if we really wanted men to change, it was time for us to begin counting on ourselves for protection rather than expecting men to keep on being the tough guys.

THE VICTIM AND THE PRINCESS

"When I heard the men speak, with such honesty and sincerity, I was able to hear them in a whole different light," said Gloria. "It somehow helps me feel less angry to know that they also suffer. Honestly, before last night I've never heard a group of men admit it. I guess that in the past I've really believed that men had all the advantages. Now I'm beginning to see another side to the story."

"I'm glad to hear Joel share his fears with other people," said Lisa. "It's no secret to me when the guy is in pain. The whole family is aware if it, even when he won't admit it. He'll come home after a stressful day and get mad at me or at Gabe. But when I ask him how he feels, he usually just says he's fine."

"Aaron says that FINE is a secret male code," I offered. "He calls it an acronym for Fucked-up, Insecure, Nervous, and Exhausted." We all laughed.

"That's great," said Marie. "It sounds to me like a more accurate appraisal of the way most men really feel."

"It's sad that it's so hard for men to talk about their pain," said Doris. "Talking to other women about my problems keeps me going through the hard times. I couldn't do without it. Who do men reveal themselves to as they really are? How do they survive without brothers that they can confide in?"

"They don't survive," said Lisa. "That's the problem. That's probably why men drop dead eight years earlier than us. They can't ever show their real feelings. They get so bottled up that they explode with heart attacks."

Women have always shared with each other both the challenges and the pleasures of being mothers, lovers, wives, and workers. This process is an integral part of our female culture. We have found a lot of self-empowerment both by getting mad about the inequalities we face and by revealing our wounds to one another.

I probably share the belief with many women that most men, on the other hand, act as if they don't feel much pain. So of course it is easy for us to assume that life must be much better for them. They have been keeping up the old John Wayne pretense that they can take a bullet in the chest and still keep riding hard, killing bad guys, and saving little ladies in distress.

It makes us feel weak and stupid when we appear to be the only ones struggling. Now we began to realize that men, because of their conditioning to act like heroes, have been lying to us all along. But they are not alone. We have been lying, too.

Several women have shared with me their awareness that when women feign helplessness, it pisses men off just as much as men's pumped-up posturing angers us. It's no secret to us that men lie about their real vulnerability and that among themselves they are quick to reveal, and even exaggerate, their wealth, power, and sexual prowess in the hope of being accepted and admired by their peers. At the same time, women are in the habit of denying their real power to one another as well as to men, but they are quick to share and even exaggerate their disadvantages and vulnerabilities in the hope of gaining sympathy and sisterhood.

I grew up watching old movies like *Gone with the Wind* and Errol Flynn swashbucklers. I listened to powerful women like Aretha Franklin sing sadly codependent songs like "Rescue Me" on the radio. Wherever I turned, the same Cinderella messages, like "My Boyfriend's Back" (he's gonna save my reputation) came at me. None of the gender fables I heard said, "Someday, Liz, you will be a powerful and successful woman in your own right."

Most women of my generation were raised to believe that someday the right man would come along and make our lives meaningful. The Knight, we hoped, would rescue us from the dragon of our own emptiness, loneliness, and unrealized dreams. Although many of us now consider ourselves beyond this expectation, when I talk intimately with powerful women around the country, I'm surprised how deeply ingrained this belief remains in our collective psyche.

We know that waiting for the perfect lover, perfect father, and perfect provider-protector to rescue us is a no-win situation. Nevertheless, this expectation persists and contributes significantly to the anger and resentment we feel toward men—because no man can actually live up to the ideal. At least not for long. Disappointment is inevitable if we hold men to this standard.

One of the major archetypal gender themes of our epoch has been that of the Hero rescuing the Maiden from the Dragon. This theme is the central model for our old gender culture. I don't think anyone misses the fact that in this myth the rescuer is almost always male. The victim in peril is female. In most stories in modern romantic literature, the dragon stands for the male victimizer whom a hero must defeat on behalf of a helpless woman. This theme sells tens of millions of books to women every year. One of the historical goals of the women's movement, however, has been the reimagining of this myth, a goal we are still struggling to achieve.

Identifying ourselves as victims of the patriarchy has clearly been an important step in our recovery and empowerment. It is part of waking from our slumber, from the "feminine mystique," as Betty Friedan called it more than thirty years ago. There is a downside, however, to all our railing at men. In our anger at men for having some kinds of power that we lack, we frequently imagine that we are powerless. I think that our devaluation of men, as discussed in the previous chapter, is often done as an attempt to make ourselves feel bigger by making them feel smaller rather than simply to focus on becoming more powerful ourselves. When we believe that men have all the power and cause all the problems, we believe things will change only when men change. At the core of this mind-set is the same dynamic that creates codependency in relationships.

As I voiced some of these ideas to the group, I saw several heads nodding in agreement. "Right," said Merle. "Like when I think that if only Alan would change, our relationship would get better."

"I think," said Susan, "that if all power is seen as being outside us, then we feel no responsibility to change ourselves."

"Yes, that's the problem," I said. "Our protected and 'special' status of woman-as-victim puts the source of healing outside us. The victim carries all the wounding and helplessness; the victimizer carries all the power and responsibility. This is familiar ground for many of us because it has always been part of our traditional upbringing to view the world in this way. Even many of us 'new women' of the nineties, who have had our consciousness raised, habitually fall into the same patterns. In many cases it seems like we have formed our sense of community through a shared sense of victimization rather than through developing a deeper knowledge and joy about our feminine power and magic.

"Blaming men for not doing it right clearly casts us in the role of helpless and passive princesses," I continued. "I like the way Camille Paglia puts it."

It is women's personal responsibility to be aware of the dangers of the world. But these young feminists today are deluded. These girls say "Well, I should be able to get drunk at a fraternity party and go upstairs to a guy's room without anything happening." And I say "Oh, really? And when you drive your car to New York City, do you leave your keys on the hood?"

"So, the Princess-Victim has no responsibility," said Lisa. "That must be part of the great allure of that role. Through embracing it, we seem magically to become absolved of all our sins—'It's all his fault,' we sincerely believe."

"Exactly," I replied. "Any attempt to identify the ways women take part in their abuse or disempowerment is now called blaming the victim. But the victim has no power! This sort of thinking has left us in some very abusive relationships. It has also, historically, left us out of the rough-and-tumble core of politics and business. Princesses genuinely believe that they should never have to suffer and that in a just society, others should protect them from the hardships of the world.

"The recent changes in the gender mix of politicians and business owners is testament, however, to the power of women who state what they want and go after it instead of just blaming men for not relinquishing power to them. We still have a long way to go. Therefore, I think that it's in our best interests, as we start trying to improve our relationships with men, to look carefully at our habitual identification with victimization and to stay aware of the consequences that this identification can bring us."

As I looked at this group of strong women, it occurred to me that women's arenas of power are often different from men's. There's no doubt that men in our culture have had more political and economic power than women have had. On the other hand, we women have incredible power to create and sustain the relationships that make up the fabric of our culture. We have tremendous social, emotional, and intuitive powers plus enormous sexual power, which we have used throughout time to manipulate the world and achieve our desired goals. As many capable women have demonstrated, these areas of power do not limit us or deny us access to men's traditional domains, but simply establish us as intrinsically potent beings in our own right.

Female identification with being helpless both fuels and colludes with the old male conditioning to be heroes—tough, capable, fearless, and "on top of it." It's a bad dream that men and women dreamed together. Now we are attempting to wake up. It is not an easy task. And it is especially difficult for one side of an equation to change, in a vacuum, without the other. That is why the gender diplomacy work we were doing together felt so important.

THE HERO

I went fishing with some of the men at dawn. The freshness of the morning uplifted my spirits. Everything was perfect in our silent world until Dave suddenly cried, "Shit!" He had made a cast that somehow wound up with the hook stuck deep in his thumb instead of in a trout. The only thing to do was push the hook through so the barb came out the other side. I cut it off with the wire cutters on my leathermaker's tool and then backed the shaft of the hook out of the wound. It left two holes in his thumb.

A lot of blood spurted out and it was clearly very painful when I pushed the hook through. But Dave never winced or cried out. When I asked him if it hurt, he replied, "Nah! It's just a little prick." I thought about the countless times I had heard a man or a boy deny his pain. "Big boys don't cry" is what just about every man is instructed along the way.

I was reminded that just as many women find solidarity and membership by identifying themselves as victims, many of us men find brotherhood and community with other men by joining the cult of the Hero. All our cultural directives — from early education and parenting, through adolescent sports, to military induction and initiation into the work-place — inform us that to be well regarded by others we must learn to model ourselves after a heroic ideal of masculinity.

When I go to the movies, I see the archetype of the near-invincible male hero represented in roles played by actors like Arnold Schwarzenegger, Steven Seagal, Sylvester Stallone, Jean-Claude Van Damme, Mel Gibson, Clint Eastwood, and Bruce Willis. In the past, the heroic roles were played by John Wayne, Kirk Douglas, Errol Flynn, and Charles Bronson. These few men, and others like them, account for hundreds of millions of dollars in box-office receipts every year and cannot help but influence how we feel about ourselves as men and how others perceive us.

It seems that regardless of whether the Hero is Rambo, Rocky, the Terminator, or a super hard-ass kung-fu cop, the theme in most of these films is remarkably similar. Like the mythological character Hercules, the hero defeats a seemingly superior opponent against impossible odds. Often he is up against an extraordinary number of vicious, powerful, heavily armed men. Yet, he has absolutely no fear in the face of superior forces and he is never confused about the best course of action to initiate.

The Hero inevitably suffers a great deal of physical abuse. He endures hardships that seem far beyond the endurance of any mortal man. Yet he, like Dave, expresses no complaint in response to his wounds or to his apparently hopeless situation or his exhaustion. In most cases, along the way, he rescues a woman in distress. Most often he uses superhuman strength and fighting ability to defeat all the bad guys.

In some cases I've begun to notice a variation on this theme. We now have a new, modern, "soft" hero who is less heavily armored. He is represented by characters such as Daniel Day-Lewis's Last Mohican, Harrison Ford's Indiana Jones, and Richard Dean Anderson's MacGyver. Instead of brute strength and ultraviolence, these more politically correct heroes in almost every case use uncanny stamina, superior reflexes, and brilliant ingenuity to rescue the woman.

When I discuss these thoughts with other men, someone inevitably asks, "What's wrong with men being heroes?"

The answer is, essentially nothing. Every one of us must connect with our own personal heroics in order to write a book, raise a child, start a business, confront injustice, face an illness, or engage in any of the hundreds of human endeavors that require us to overcome our fears of transformation, failure, injury, or death. For many of us, however, the problem is that, like Dave, who was still oozing blood as he baited a fresh hook, we feel we must always be heroes.

Even a completely rehabilitated chauvinist, as depicted by Bill Murray in the movie *Groundhog Day*, must also face his own death several times, perform a variety of charitable acts, save a little boy's life, learn to play classical piano, and learn everything about the personal likes and dislikes of the woman he is pursuing. He must perform at a level of accomplishment way beyond the capacity of most mortals in order to be loved by a woman who only has to look cute to win this heroic attention from him. For many of us men, cinema imitates life to the extent that it articulates the unreal, heroic ideals we feel we are expected to live up to.

One way we can look at the Hero and the Princess—and the Victimizer and the Victim—is as aspects of a wholeness separated into its parts. In Jungian psychology we call this dynamic a split archetype. Each of us has a courageous hero and a sensitive child within our psyches. Each of us has a ruthless streak and a portion of ourselves that feels wounded by others' ruthlessness. Problems arise when any of these psychological elements dominates our character. We become "possessed" by the split-off part, which, in acting out its polarized role, is also constantly seeking its missing counterpart.

We all know that the Hero seeks dragons to slay and maidens to rescue while the Princess languishes and pines for her prince to come. After reading decades of women's books, most women are probably now painfully clear about the perils of Princesshood. However, after only a few years of reflective thought about masculinity thus far, the deadly trap of the Hero does not seem to be as obvious to most men.

The Hero embodies the idea that the ultimate goodness of a man is expressed in his willingness to die for others. This belief led countless generations of men who marched off heedlessly to wars and slaughter. My generation was called cowardly for suggesting to the world that the time for peace had come—not through more fighting to end war, but by ceasing fighting altogether. The Knight needs armor to fight when there is clearly no other recourse. But as I discussed in my previous book *Knights Without Armor*, when the Knight forgets how to remove the armor, he becomes trapped within his strength and is unable to tend the wounds hidden beneath his hard exterior.

Another shadow of the Hero I think we can all easily see in these films is his incapacity to forge meaningful connections with others. The Hero, like so many males these days, is often excessively narcissistic—solitary and self-involved. Whether the character is Clint Eastwood's Man with No Name or Dirty Harry, Charles Bronson's vigilante killer Paul Kersey, or Steven Seagal's kung-fu cop, all these icons of heroic masculinity believe that they, and they alone, can solve the problem of the day. They have contempt for conventional rules. They often solve their problems—one of which often is rescuing the maiden—by direct, compelling ultraviolence.

Of course, we need heroes in times of distress. And it is commendable that women and men, in times of great danger, do reach beyond the ordinary limits of their bodies and emotions. As Liz articulated earlier, the problem for women occurs when they habitually act like victims. And, similarly, the problem for men lies when they are habitually heroic.

Heroes can't ask for help when they need it. This presents a serious problem for those of us who are caught in the heroic archetype. We often suffer greatly and, as many men have told me when discussing their fathers, die early deaths. We have been trained to believe that we don't need anyone but ourselves. This is the dark side of the heroic archetype. Just as overidentification with the Victim-Princess cuts women off from their power, overidentification with the Hero cuts us off from our feelings and our capacity to provide sustained care for ourselves and others. I suspect that domination of women is intimately linked with the abuse we inflict on ourselves. This self-abuse often takes the form of excessive alcohol and drug use, workaholism, and other obsessions that enable us to continue to deny pain, fear, and the human need for connection.

❧ THE DARK GODDESSES

"I was surprised to hear about how afraid the men are of women, Liz," said Susan, leaning against a tree as she caught her breath. We had decided to take a hike up a trail to a smaller lake. On the topo map it had looked nearby, but we had yet to find it and had stopped for a break on an outcropping of rock that offered a panoramic view of the Grace Lake valley.

"Me too," agreed Marie. "I was floored. I've always thought of women as the 'gentler sex,' but to hear the men talk, you'd think we were going to murder them while they slept."

"More likely bewitch them and steal their power," laughed Doris as she used her bandanna to wipe the sweat off her face.

I reminded them that men's fear of women is nothing new. World mythology is replete with images of the destructive aspect of the feminine. In India, for example, there is Kali, a goddess of death with a necklace of skulls, wielding knives and scissors, fanged, drooling, and wrathful, who sits astride the corpse of her husband, Shiva, in necrophilic conjugality. Her images are absolutely terrifying.

"I've always thought of the feminine as being compassionate and merciful," challenged Lisa. "The Goddess, as I understand her, is the embodiment of the 'good' mother."

"That's certainly one aspect of the Goddess," I replied. "But there are also many nasty and violent goddesses. In this country people have primarily worshiped the Virgin Mary, who's very pure and good—an image that many women have felt they must live up to. And the more recent resurgence of interest in women's spirituality has also emphasized the all-nurturing symbol of the Earth Goddess. But that's only a piece of the story."

Our culture is very divided in its thinking about good and evil. Unlike some cultures in other parts of the world that hold the view that their gods embody equal portions of good and evil, we tend to locate all light or all darkness in one or the other deity. This thinking also fuels the tendency of both genders to locate all goodness in one sex and all evil in the other. I think that the degree to which any group denies its own shadow is inevitably equal to the need it has to project the blame for all its sorrows on others. If we fail to attend to our shadow, we breed denial about our own capacity for abuse. And we know that denial about the potential for abuse of power is dangerous in any group.

At this stage in our council, we were trying to move forward by looking at some of the shadow issues we drag along.

One is clearly our addiction to being victims. Another is our denial of both our real power as women and our capacity for violence that, in many cases, matches that of men.

I began unpacking the idea of the feminine shadow, saying, "I think it's apparent to us all that men, because of their greater strength, do significantly more damage in domestic assaults. But many of us don't know that most studies indicate women instigate just as much domestic violence as men. We actually strike the first blow in a majority of domestic disputes and commit more than one-third of all domestic homicides. It is culturally sanctioned for us to slap men when we're angry; we see it in films every day. We also perpetrate the majority of physical abuse, battery, and neglect of children. The incidence of child battery is over twice that of sexual abuse, a category dominated by males. Current studies indicate that we females also commit about one-third of the sexual abuse of boys and a significant minority of girls as well, another fact that is usually unreported when we berate men for their abusiveness.

"The essential nature of women, as well as men, is a complex mixture of qualities. I feel that it does us a disservice to deny our capacity for violence because then we also inevitably deny our power as well. We create huge fallacies when we idealize the feminine principle as being only benign, because the Dark Goddess is also an integral part of the feminine principle."

I continued presenting this idea to the group, noting that in Greek mythology, for example, "there are harpies and shrews, the Gorgon Medusa who turns men to stone, and Scylla of the whirlpool; dismembering maenads, furies, and sirens—all seducing men to their deaths. The crone Hecate, who on one hand has a rich store of ancient wisdom, is simultaneously dry, cold, and withering. Demeter—a goddess of generativity, the Harvest Goddess—also has a wrathful form in which she threatens to destroy all human life unless her daughter is released from the Underworld. Artemis is a beautiful nature goddess who loves wild animals, but she also wields arrows and transformative spells, and destroys men for simply sighting her in the woods.

"Golden Aphrodite also has her dark side. She is a wrathful destructress and a jealous, manipulative dominator of her son, Eros. She reflects the same dark face of matriarchy as do Psyche's vain and jealous sisters, who, in the story of Psyche and Amor, oppose her marriage with Eros, calling him a monster when in actuality he is divine and beautiful.

"Snapping Vagina is a mythological character of the Navajos. She is malevolent, violent, raging, and destructive. She is eternally hungry, embodying a vast emptiness, and kills by engulfing her victim. Also in Navajo myth, which, by the way, springs from a matriarchal society, there is a power-driven, plotting sorceress named Changing Bear Maiden, who kills her brothers after turning into a monstrous bear. She wears sharp deer hooves that cut and hurt men, and then she possesses them. In her book *Changing Woman and Her Sisters*, therapist Sheila Moon says that this aspect of the Goddess has 'a marked and negative ambivalence towards that which is living.'

"There exist hundreds of other personifications of the Terrible Mother from almost every culture, throughout the millennia," I continued. "I don't think that these images—like the ravaging mother protecting her young in the film *Alien*— are mere apple-eating Eves invented, as many feminist writers would have us believe, by a patriarchal culture. I believe that they express an essential element present in human conscious- ness and nature itself—the wild, primitive aspect of feminine sexuality and the all-devouring aspect of the earth itself.

"When we embrace the role of the innocent victim, all our power, willfulness, and rage gets stuffed in the closet, into the shadow. When we relegate the Dark Goddess's heat to the closet, it starts to smolder. Before you know it, what might have been a small flare turns into the eruption of Mount Vesuvius."

I suggested to the women, as we got up to continue on our hike, that we open the door of the closet and see what might be lurking there. I reminded them that, before our next coun- cil, we still had to explore what gets in the way of creating gen- uine partnerships with men.

"What kinds of things do we do that are abusive to men?" I asked. "What are our feminine styles of dominating and deceiving? Are there ways we attempt to cope with our victim- ization by evoking the Dark Mother? How does our sup- pressed power come out? Do we cut them to shreds verbally like the Navajo goddess with her sharp hooves? Do we domi- nate and possess men by swallowing them like Snapping Vagina?"

We walked in silence for a bit, doing some heavy think- ing. The trail rounded a bend, and there was the long- awaited lake. Within minutes we stripped off our clothes and jumped in. Later, as we dried off in the sun, Doris picked up the topic.

✸ WITCHES, BITCHES, AND WHORES

"Okay, I'll begin. I have a nineteen-year-old son. His father ran off with another woman years ago, when Danny was small. I was terribly hurt, and as Danny grew up I continually bad-mouthed his father. I feel bad about it now, because it ruined their relationship. My ex-husband tried to keep in touch over the years. He clearly wanted to be part of Danny's life. But I wouldn't let him. It's been very hard on Danny not to have a father, and I could have made it possible if I hadn't been so angry. His father really isn't such a bad guy, he just didn't love me anymore. I never forgave him for that."

Marie then spoke about her ex-husband. "I was married, before Larry, to a man who put me through law school. He got me started in my career and then our marriage fell apart. I used all my new legal skills and my feminist 'take no prisoners' approach to men and money to take him to the cleaners financially. He ended up paying me alimony for years before I remarried, even though I was making more money than him.

"If I had been treated like a man in the divorce, I'd be paying him or putting him through school until he could make as much as me. Now I have a great career, but he's stuck with a contracting business that's going bankrupt. And he's getting too old to be a carpenter again, the only other trade he knows. When I was listening to the guys talking the other night, I started thinking about Daniel and how I really should make some kind of amends to him."

"Well, I find this difficult to tell you all," Lisa began, looking at the ground. "Even though in my women's studies classes I'm a champion of women's and children's rights, something I've never disclosed is that I've abused my own kid. There was a period in the early years of our marriage when we were very stressed out. We were struggling financially. Joel was working two jobs, one of them at night. I was also working at a lousy job during the day. I'd come home at night exhausted, and Gabe was often fussy. Sometimes I would just start screaming at him. A few times I lost it altogether and just started smacking my son around. It was as if I was possessed by one of those furies you mentioned, Liz."

"It's easy for me to imagine how that could have happened," said Merle. "I've been very close to hitting my kids at times. But my shadow is that I had an affair behind Alan's back. It was pretty sleazy and didn't last long, but it still almost destroyed my marriage. When he found out about it, instead of taking responsibility for getting sort of swept away by this hunk at the health club, I blamed Alan for not being a good lover. I really made him feel like shit."

"I've done some pretty outrageous sexual things, too," said Susan. "I seduced my boss last year and ended up with a promotion that beat out several other, equally qualified men. That's probably the real reason there's so much hostility towards me at the office. I think they've guessed. I've also sexually used men purely for my own gratification without any intention of forming a relationship with them. I've been pretty ruthless when it comes to my sexuality. By the time I was thirteen years old, I learned that I had a lot of power over men. I like using it, but clearly have a double standard about men who behave the same way."

Gloria was next. "I guess what I need to get out of the closet is the raving bitch that I am with Jerry sometimes. I'm good with words. I can tear him to shreds. The poor guy doesn't even know what hit him. When I'm angry, I shame him without mercy. He doesn't even defend himself anymore, which seems to make me even angrier. I'm ashamed to say that there's a part of me that feels strong knowing I have this power over him."

After a few minutes without anyone else speaking, I said, "I seduced a sixteen-year-old boy when I was about thirty. I was married to my ex-husband then, and he had this cute young guy working for him on his crew. I became totally possessed and just couldn't keep my hands off this kid. He thought it was great to have sex with an older woman. But if it had been reversed, if I had been an older man with a younger girl, it would have been considered statutory rape or child molestation. Men go to jail for that!

"I don't know if it screwed him up or not, but since I've been with Aaron and heard about how many men in his groups have psychological problems and sexual dysfunctions related to early seductions by older women, I've begun to wonder about this. Was I an educator-initiator, as I've always imagined, or just a selfish user? I'll never know. But it's clearly in our shadow as women that we carry such double standards about sexual encounters with minors."

One of the most startling revelations that emerged from our conversation that day about the modern myth of the ideal feminine and the evil masculine, was the tremendous denial we have about our capacity to abuse our feminine power. In his book *The New Male*, psychologist Herb Goldberg sums it up by saying, "For every chauvinist who uses women, there is a woman who uses wiles, coyness, helplessness and other 'feminine' manipulations to gain her end and goad him into proving himself the big man, the succeedor, the dominant, fearless, powerful protector." I believe that if we are ever to have peace with men, we must begin by openly acknowledging our part in creating the conflicts between us.

THE MALE MONSTER

The morning's fishing had been fruitful, despite Dave's accident with the fishhook. This time I went with Joel and Dave while others stayed behind tending camp. That felt good. As I returned to camp I was thinking about the topic for the next council. What do we do as men that gets in the way of partnership with women? What is our part in the war between the sexes? When I talked to the men about it, I noticed there was a lot of resistance to this step in the process. It was easy to talk about our anger, somewhat more difficult to talk about our fears and our grief, but it felt significantly harder to consider taking responsibility for things being the way they are.

Over the years, as I have worked with thousands of men, a primary issue that keeps presenting itself is our struggle to recover from a deep, personal, and collective sense of shame. This feeling is not easily articulated by most men. More often than not it is denied until we have done some trust-building and have created a safe environment in which we feel we can authentically reveal ourselves without being castigated for how we really feel.

Shame often makes its presence known by the destructive behaviors we engage in when we try to escape from the debilitating depressions associated with it. These behaviors, as we discussed earlier, often take the form of excessive drinking, drug abuse, workaholism, addiction to high-risk excitement, sexual obsessions, and even violence against others who are perceived to be the inculcators of that shame. We returned to camp and as we ate our breakfast trout together, we began discussing last night's council, which, in turn, led us to the topic of shame.

Andy mentioned, "More and more these days, teenage boys are shooting one another on the streets for 'dissing each other.' I recently read that in 1992, over eight hundred young men were killed in the Los Angeles area alone. That's more than in the war zones of Beirut, Palestine, or Dublin! Did you know the slang word 'dis' comes from 'dis-respect'? The street code says, 'If you try to shame me or my friends or family, I just might kill you.' I think this is one of the most extreme examples of our incapacity to bear shame."

I replied, "Yes, and for many of them, their feeling of shame has probably grown over a lifetime of emotional impoverishment and lack of economic and educational opportunity. Even though their violence often appears to be way out of proportion to the acts that provoked it, it only appears senseless, when we overlook the sorts of social injustices men face, like the ones we talked about the other night. Science seems to indicate that we men are biologically programmed to be more aggressive than women, but I don't believe that means we're destined to be more violent. There've been many cultures in which men were not significantly violent. I don't think that violence comes out of a vacuum, like a virus from outer space, do you guys?"

"No, of course not," answered Joel. "We have to consider the broader social context that shapes our character and either directs our aggression into creative acts or fuels our rage and pushes us toward destruction."

"From my conversations with men over the years," I continued, "I've begun to think of low self-esteem as a life-threatening disease. When it gets bad enough, we commit suicide, as young men are now doing five to one over young women. Or in many cases, when someone aggravates that low self-esteem, we strike out. Most of the feminist writing I've seen depicts violence toward women as part of a conscious male conspiracy to keep them from having power. What seems more true, however, is that some of us become abusive of women because we are afraid of their power to shame us. In the work I've done with battering men, I hear over and over again about how powerless they feel in their lives, but only a very disturbed few view their behavior as powerful in some way.

"I think all of us have experienced shame as demoralizing. Guilt makes us feel that *what we did* is wrong. We can survive it and learn from it. That's good. Shame, however, makes us feel that *who we are* is wrong. That's bad and many of us will go to violent extremes to avoid that deadly feeling. Consequently, we are often reticent to consciously reveal our dark side. We can feel that to do so will only put another nail into our coffin."

As I thought more about our resistance to this step in the process, I realized that a good portion of my work had centered on helping men recover from shame. In my role as a leader of men's groups, I've tended to resist the prevalent "monsterization" of masculinity in our society and have focused instead on supporting what I believe is the inherent goodness in all men. Now, however, my companions and I generally agreed that the time had come for us to look fearlessly at the ways in which men are also monsters. If there is ever to be peace between the sexes, we must begin to acknowledge our real responsibility for destructive past behaviors and make amends wherever possible.

Women do have good cause to fear us. Not only because we are capable of destroying nature and dominating, raping, beating, torturing, and killing women, but because—all sociological analysis aside—something deep within our male psyche that is cold, dark, and utterly unfeeling allows us to behave in this manner. Mythology is full of these images of the dark masculine—the Monster.

In the same manner that ancient mythology gives us a glimpse into the collective psyche of a particular culture and epoch, I feel that cinema and television are the primary arenas in which the archetypal forces moving through our collective consciousness today are displayed. We began to discuss ways that contemporary media is fascinated with the male monster. The conversation quickly turned toward horror films. As we talked about the themes in these films, it became clear that most are not concerned with the Dark Mother that men so fear, but rather with the hidden, dark, monstrous male who sexually exploits, stalks, terrorizes, wounds, rapes, or kills women. More than two hundred films have been made on the theme of the vampire alone, as well as dozens of books, the vast majority of which are bought by women. It's been my observation that even though there are female vampires, they are usually servants of the primary male monster or mortal women whom he has subverted to his will. Vampirism is imagined as a masculine force that preys upon the life's blood of women, particularly young and attractive women. The werewolf is also usually male, as are most other creeps, beasts, things, and its.

Another related genre in films and literature is the human monster—the psychopathic killer. From *Scarface* to *The Silence of the Lambs* and in more than ninety percent of thrillers we could recollect as we went around the circle, the human monster is male. Freddy Krueger of the *Nightmare on Elm Street* series and Jason of the *Friday the Thirteenth* series take this genre to macabre new heights, adding an otherworldly dimension to their psychopathic powers.

What do these stories tell us about the male psyche? What was fueling the fear the women at Grace Lake were so openly sharing with us? Scapegoating and projecting our own shadow on the other gender are clearly one aspect of the enmity between the sexes. But another aspect is the genuine destructive powers of the other sex. Just as the dark feminine has the power to smother, dominate, poison, seduce, and sexually manipulate men, the dark masculine has equally strong powers to batter, dismember, and utterly destroy the lives of women.

As we talked about common themes we have noticed in the hundreds of horror movies we had seen over the years, the following list emerged:

1. The monster is male.
2. He is ruthless (*Cape Fear*), obsessively focused on his prey, relentless, and devoid of compassion.
3. He preys on women (*Psycho*), usually very young, sexually alluring women (when he kills men it is generally incidental, because they somehow got in his way).
4. He is either utterly devoid of feeling or takes a certain sadistic glee in his slaughter (Freddy Krueger).
5. He is usually immune to tactics that would kill ordinary men and often repeatedly rises from the dead (*Terminator 2*).
6. He is cold-blooded, dead-eyed, and often has hypnotic powers over his prey (Dracula). In short, he has many reptilian qualities. As Jerry pointed out, some of the epitaphs for a man who exploits women are "snake," "worm," and "slime."

One way to look at the Monster is as a creature that lives hidden in the shadow of the Hero. As we talked about it in this way we became aware that the Monster shares many of the characteristics of the Hero.

"The Monster is strong, purposeful, fearless, and practically invincible in battle," noted Larry.

"He's also a relentless and dauntless hunter," added Dave.

"If we could somehow probe more deeply into the ancient structure of the male psyche," I suggested, "we would probably find at its foundation the archetype of the Hunter. For thousands of years, the primary occupation of men was hunting. It's what we were biologically built for."

"I agree, Aaron," said Dave, who, with the authority of his bandaged thumb, suddenly emerged as our resident expert on hunting. "Men's greater stamina, muscular strength, skill at stealth and stalking, capacity for one-pointed focus, and stoic response to pain and discomfort are all required skills for successful hunting."

"These are also the attributes a man needs to be a skilled warrior," added Andy.

"So when these abilities are used in the service of others, especially where they protect and support women, then we call the man a hero," offered Joel. "When these same skills and powers are used to stalk and prey on women, however, then the man becomes a monster."

I observed, "Much of our modern language regarding the sexual pursuit of women uses the idiom of the hunt. One of the most monstrous serial rapist-murderers in recent history was dubbed by the media as the 'Night Stalker.' Men go out 'cruising' (stalking) to get 'a piece of ass' (game, meat) and say they 'scored' (hit the target). Unless he misses, a man hunts an animal only once. As soon as he has scored, the animal is dead and no longer exciting. After satiation and rest, he hunts another animal."

Even after thousands of years of civilization there appears to be something still buried in the male psyche that is interested only in the hunt and is completely uninterested in developing an ongoing relationship or intimacy with his prey, except as some sort of lure with which to capture it. This is the mode of sexual predators such as the young men who gained notoriety for their participation in the 'Spur Posse,' a sex-point scoring gang in California whose members collected one point for each young woman they had sex with. Some of the teenage boys boasted publicly that they had collected more than sixty "points." This sort of behavior infuriates women. Women feel betrayed when men use the promise of intimacy as a lure for sex, and it breeds the deepest of resentments against men.

The Monster seems connected with the older brain in men, a structure neurophysiology calls the "reptilian brain." There is an aspect of male sexuality that is purely reptilian, predatory, and narcissistic. This is what women fear. So, the Hero, who is in the business of rescuing women from their fears, slays the reptilian bad guy, the "cold-blooded" killer. But there is a problem, for both women and men, with this old story.

On the one hand, many of us men are now trying to escape the bonds and burdens of living up to the Hero archetype. It is oppressive for us to feel that we always have to be strong, can never show fear, and can never ask for help. But on the other hand, there is an aspect of the Hero, what one might call the sacred Warrior or the Hunter, that is sorely needed today. There is real evil in the world. Our cinema monsters hardly do justice to the true monsters of our century: Hitler, Stalin, Ceaucescu, Pol Pot, not to mention Serbian "ethnic cleansing" through the systematic rape of tens of thousands of women.

The horrors of this world, the starvation of entire populations, the destruction of entire species and whole ecosystems, the degradation of the ozone shield above our heads, are all human-made. We need real, heroic warriors, male and female, to confront these monsters. A first step toward becoming a sacred warrior, however, must be to confront the monsters within. If we have not done so, how can we ever act in a trustworthy manner in the world? That seemed to be the task that faced us now before we met with the women again.

I attempted to sum up our conversation by saying, "The Monster seems to be representative of when man's best capacities to defend, nurture, and create life are turned toward destroying life."

"Just the way Darth Vader (Dark Father) was a noble Jedi Knight before he was seduced by the dark side," added Jerry.

"Exactly," I replied. "The Monster and the Hero are another split archetype. All the exploitive power is on one side and all the nurturing power lies on the other. The Monster, Hero, and Victim are all part of the same complex. We all know that in most stories, it is the male Hero who defeats the male Monster in the service of the female Victim-Princess. Instead of the concept of defeat, however, what we may need more is reconnection with our split-off parts. Because, as our horror tales tell us, the Monster is never really defeated. He just vanishes for a while, only to rise again in the sequel. So, now we are being presented with an opportunity to wrestle with our darker sides.

"Are women right to fear us?" I asked. "Are we so evolved as to be free from the sorts of behaviors women fear? Or have we, in resistance to our shame, been in denial about the ways in which we are monsters alongside whatever noble capacities we possess to nurture and defend?" I then asked, for the first time in a gathering of men, "Who amongst us has raped or battered women or simply had fantasies of hurting, dominating, or sexually exploiting women?"

BASTARDS, BATTERERS, AND FIENDS

Dave was the first to speak. "When I was in the seventh grade we used to have folk dancing after school once a week. There was this one girl, Nancy, who would usually wear a pleated skirt. When we twirled around, her dress would come up and I could see her pink panties underneath. Those panties, and the shape of her buttocks standing out against them, had the most disturbing effect on me. For months afterward I would masturbate with the fantasy of touching her naked bottom. I don't know why she affected me that way, but I used to sit in class behind her and frequently think about those pink panties coming down around her knees.

"I don't remember ever having a sexual fantasy before then. Certainly I never saw any dirty pictures and no one ever told me about sex. I just started out my sexual life obsessively. I don't know why. Now it's Susan's ass that's on my mind. A part of me is much more into women's asses than their personalities, and I know that is degrading to women. I feel like if I ever shared this story with women, they'd regard me as some sort of deviant. But I really don't know how to not think about it. It's like not thinking about an elephant after someone mentions one."

"The head of my department is a woman," said Joel. "She's very demanding, critical, and humorless. Some of the students refer to her as the 'High Priestess of Political Correctness.' I've begun to have fantasies of raping her. It's weird, I guess. I really love Lisa and I don't usually have many sexual thoughts about other women. But with this woman, my fantasies are about getting even somehow for all the humiliation I and other men have suffered around her.

"Another way I deal with her is by trying to make her feel stupid and incapable even though she's a brilliant scholar. I'm always vigilant for the slightest inconsistency in her ideas. I feel that if I was more of a warrior, as you say, Aaron, I'd confront her more directly about her behavior without attempting to shame her in public meetings or dominate her in my fantasies. But the way I deal with it is by thinking about tying her up in her office and bending her over her desk and . . . well, you get the picture."

"I battered Merle once," said Alan. "It's a family secret I've never told anyone about. It was early in our marriage. I had just lost a major contract, was scared about my business failing, and was drinking too much. She started giving me a hard time about something or other, I don't even remember what. But I slapped her pretty hard. And then when she started screaming at me, I slapped her a few more times.

"She ran out of the house with a split lip and drove off to her mother's house. She didn't come back for over a week, after many phone calls and assurances from me that it would never happen again. And it hasn't, even though there have been other times when I felt like it. It scares me. My mom used to scream at me all the time. I often wished I could have hit her and made her stop. Maybe a shrink would say I was getting back at mom. I don't know, but in any case I don't ever want that to happen again. I still feel bad about it, especially when we visit her mother, who's never returned to the level of friendliness she had toward me in the past."

I confessed that when I was fourteen I slapped around my girlfriend for going out with another guy. In the working-class street culture I grew up in, that was expected. But then the next day her big brother showed up and punched me in the nose a few times. He told me that if I ever hit her again, he would kill me. I never hit another woman after that. As I told the story, it made me think that as part of men's accountability to women about their own violence, it was also necessary to confront and prevent the violence of other men. We can do this through education, mentorship, and, when appropriate, as in the case of my girlfriend's brother, a serious display of strength.

Andy told us about a time when he was a freshman in college. After a night of partying with a date, he invited her back to his room. They started making out, and when the girl asked him to stop, he didn't. He said, "By the time she said no, she was half undressed and I was completely aroused. And so I just kept persisting until she finally gave up and had sex with me. Now I understand it was date rape. Even though I think of myself as a gentle man, who is generally respectful of women, it's also true that I have the capacity to rape."

Larry told us that he had had a sexual affair with a close friend of Marie's. "Even though I didn't beat or rape anyone, I feel that this is a violent thing to have done. I betrayed my marriage vows. And by doing it with a friend of Marie's, I feel like it was a double betrayal. The affair lasted about six months, during which time I had very little sexual interest in Marie. That just added to her hurt."

Jerry was the last to speak. He was silent for a while as we looked toward him expectantly. "Soooo, Jerry," said Dave eventually. "What about you?"

"Well, I just don't have any violent thoughts about women and I don't have any weird sexual needs either," he said, somewhat defensively. "I'm glad to hear the rest of you finally admitting that you have problems with women. But I love women. I haven't ever wanted to hurt them."

"Bullshit," said Andy. "I just don't believe you. Come on, Jerry, 'fess up, what's your deep dark secret? If you leave here without saying it, I think you'll never be free. You'll always be feeling guilty around Gloria. Look, I've seen the two of you together and I know something is going on in that relationship that you're ashamed about. I can see it in your body language. You're the one that's always challenging the rest of us to come clean about our attitudes towards women. I don't think you're being straight with us now."

Jerry just sat there, glowering at Andy and avoiding eye contact with the rest of us. After a while he took a deep breath, looked up at us, and said, "Okay. You're right. I'm copping out here, doing the very thing I have accused most of you of over the last four days. I'm going to tell you something that I've never told anyone.

"I have a sister who's two years younger than me. One summer, when I was about sixteen, we hung out a lot together. We had a lot of fun taking hikes and going to the beach. She was pretty mature, physically and emotionally. She was already having sex with boys and into other stuff, and I began to notice that she was starting to look terrific in a bathing suit. Anyway, one night she and I were home alone for the evening. I got stoned and she was in our parents' spa. She invited me to join her. I did, and after a while I put my arm around her. We were just sitting there. It felt very innocent. We had always been close. Anyway, I had my eyes closed and she leaned over and kissed me, very sweetly and tenderly.

"Instead of pushing her away, I sort of kissed her back. She was so pretty and it just felt so good. I kissed her some more and then I fondled her breasts. I felt full of love for her and got very turned on. I kissed her breasts and one thing led to another, until we had sex. I knew we shouldn't, but I just couldn't find any restraint. During the next few months, we had sex a number of times until she got a steady boyfriend and demanded that we stop.

"We never told anyone about it and we've never talked about it. But she's in therapy now, almost thirty years later, and I recently got a letter from her requesting that I help pay her bill. I'm painfully aware of the fact that she must be dealing with her feelings about the incest. I guess that's one of the reasons I've been so involved in all this women's work with Gloria and even facilitated groups for abuse victims and offenders. I've been living a lie all these years. It's a relief to finally admit the truth to someone."

Andy put his arm around Jerry and comforted him. Here we were, good fathers, committed husbands, environmentalists, psychotherapists, educators. We were men who, for the most part, were consciously concerned with the betterment of humankind. And yet it was undeniably clear that within every one of us lay the seeds for violence and the abuse of women. To ensure that those seeds did not find fertile soil in our souls and those of other men was one of the tasks that lay ahead of us.

Both our groups had taken a look at some of the secrets locked away in the dark and dusty rooms of our psyches. The next step in our council was to find a way to reveal the paradoxical truths of our existence to one another. We had to find a way to help one another come to terms with the fact that we were all capable of violence toward the other gender while desiring to learn how to love and nurture the other more deeply.

CHAPTER SEVEN

LAYING DOWN
OUR SWORDS
AND SPEARS

Never apologize son, it's a sign of weakness.
— JOHN WAYNE

WHEN I GOT BACK to the women's camp at Grace Lake, it was midafternoon. I could see Aaron hanging out at the council ground, where we all met the previous night, midway between both camps. He was skipping stones across the lake and waved me over to him when he saw me coming down the trail. I told Lisa I was going over to meet him, walked over, and plunked myself down on a large, smooth, warm granite rock.

Aaron came up from the water's edge, greeted me warmly, and then said, "The conversation in the men's lodge has been moving to new depths, Liz."

"Yeah, us too," I replied. "The women have been taking a long, hard look at their personal shadow and something that's usually a taboo subject in women's groups—the dark side of femininity."

"The men have also begun to talk about the personal and collective pain they've caused women," Aaron noted. "But it's not enough for us to merely confront these taboo issues in our same-sex groups. We need to become accountable to one another. That's what needs to happen in order to bring a deeper healing between us, don't you think?"

"That's exactly what Gloria was asking for two days ago," I reminded him. "But clearly people can't become accountable for their own abusive behaviors in an atmosphere that's charged with blame and shame. This group has come a long way now towards building an atmosphere of empathy and trust in which some genuine healing can take place."

"Yeah, we weren't ready to tell the truth about our own contributions to the gender war two days ago," Aaron replied. "And I'm not completely sure that we are now. Some of what the guys revealed is pretty private. And some of it, if it were shared with the women they're in relationships with, might create more interpersonal conflict than we can realistically deal with in the couple of days we have left together."

"So we won't push anyone," I offered. "We'll keep some boundaries around how far we go with this next step. Let's just open the council and suggest that there's an opportunity for anyone who wants to, to offer something to the other sex about the way in which we, or our sex as a whole, have contributed to the pain, anger, and distrust between women and men."

"Okay, Liz, but before we go back into the hard work of facing our shadow, I feel we need to strengthen the empathy and trust we've been building by making an affirmation about the positive attributes of each sex. I suggest we build an altar of some kind, at the council ground, that symbolically holds the strength and virtue of each group, so that as we continue to struggle with the dark side we don't lose sight of the beauty and healthy power each sex holds. What do you think?"

This sounded like a good idea to me. We decided to ask all the women and men to bring an object to the next council that they felt symbolically represented their deep masculinity or femininity. Thus agreed, we went back to our camps, gathered everyone together, and met again about an hour later.

HOLY WOMAN, HOLY MAN

We assembled at the council ground and sat at the base of a giant cedar on the flat, rocky ground made comfortable by a covering of soft forest duff. Liz brought out a brightly colored Moroccan cloth from her seemingly bottomless pack of decorative materials. After designating one side of the cloth as feminine and the other side as masculine, we invited everyone to place his or her object on the cloth and say a little something about why it was meaningful.

In most of the homes and churches I've visited around the world, there is usually a masculine image on the altar—Jesus, Buddha, Krishna, Shiva—or a feminine one—Mary, Tara, Kuan Yin, or an earth goddess. Rarely, except in some Hindu, Taoist, and Tibetan temple art, have I seen the sacred masculine and feminine principles equally represented. How can we ever have partnerships between women and men when mythological, religious, and philosophical icons tend to exclude either gender from that which is holy? We can't. That's one of the big problems we face in our culture. The religious ideals that infuse our social philosophies have no images of men and women in a balanced, sacred alliance with one another.

We wanted to create a little island of gender-balanced iconography to symbolize the wholeness we were seeking before we went any further in our quest for healing. A Taoist symbol for wholeness is the yin-yang sign. It shows the masculine and feminine principles as separate areas within a circle that also have a little piece of the other in them. They touch each other along a wide boundary and even flow into each other's territory while still retaining their own distinct arenas. In this manner they create a balanced whole without losing individual identity.

Gloria stepped to the altar first. She placed a garland of wildflowers on it and said, "I picked these flowers in the meadow on the other side of the lake this afternoon. They represent a lost type of femininity for me that I've been getting in touch with on this trip, a kind of fresh, open part of myself. I made this garland and later, much to my surprise, found myself sort of dancing around the meadow. I haven't danced for over twenty years. I didn't feel foolish at all. Quite the contrary. For the first time since I was a girl, I just felt completely spontaneous and free. I want to honor that."

Larry then laid down a picture of his children. "When people ask me what I do, I usually tell them that I'm a computer program designer. But when I think about it, what really means the most to me is my kids. It's my kids that really give my life meaning. I don't know why I never answer that question by saying, 'I'm a full-time father.' Many women are comfortable primarily identifying themselves as a mother, but I've been shy, as a man, to primarily identify myself as a parent.

But today I'm putting this picture down to identify fatherhood as my most sacred symbol of masculinity."

Lisa went to the altar, and she too laid a photograph on the blanket. "I also want to put my child on the altar as a symbol of my femininity. I've struggled for so many years with balancing career and motherhood. My female colleagues support me for my aspirations around work. But I always get the feeling that my commitment to motherhood is seen by them as a less worthy occupation. The bottom line is, that as much as I enjoy my work, I've learned more about being a woman from my son and been more enriched by him than anyone or anything else. I feel a lot of appreciation for him right now. And even though I was delighted at first to get this week off without him, I am starting to miss Gabe quite a bit."

Jerry offered his red cotton bandanna. "In the animal world the males are the most colorful. But in America, except for the punks and some artists, we are the most drab. Bleh! I like to wear bright colors and mix up my apparel with a lot of variety. At times I've been ridiculed for expressing my male beauty. It seems that women have a lot more permission to be playful with their appearance. But I think that a little flash is good for the masculine soul, too. I'd put a peacock feather down if I could find one, but in its absence, I think this bandanna can hold my message that men can be beautiful, too."

Merle sauntered to the altar with a grin on her face. "This is probably not your typical feminine symbol. But when Liz asked us to think of something, this is what came up for me." She laid a small, black Maglite flashlight on the cloth. "For me," she continued, "this symbolizes finding the feminine light in the darkness, the female spark of creativity that illumi-nates the way for me."

I put my leathermaker's tool on the altar. "During the dozen or so years it took me to work my way through college and graduate school, I made my living fixing up old houses, boats, and building movie sets. It was through my side-by-side working relationships with men that I learned to respect them for their artistry and capability in the material world.

"Now my life is filled more with psychological and spiri-tual relationships. In certain ways my current friendships are deeper and more satisfying than those I had on the job sites. But I often miss the simple pleasures of lifting walls in syn-chrony, the elegant ballet of heavy equipment, materials in motion and men balancing, sweating, testing the limits of their bodies and the world, and all the while looking out for one another's safety and success. So, for me this tool symbol-izes the beauty and utility men make with the raw stuff of nature and the beauty of men working in concert with one another."

"I found this rock in the creek," said Susan, as she placed an oval green rock on the altar. "It reminds me of a vulva. To me it symbolizes the deep healing power of my feminine sexu-ality, the power to create life, and the pleasures of the body. I also just like the way it feels in my hand when I hold it, kind of soft and smooth and warm." She said this with a lascivious chuckle as she sat back down in the circle.

Alan laid a rounded smooth, straight stick of driftwood on the cloth. The phallic implications seemed obvious, and sev-eral people laughed. But Alan surprised us, saying, "I feel that my steadiness as a provider is the way in which I express my manhood. So for me this straight and solid stick represents the strength and consistency I bring to my work and my support of my family, even though I gather that to some of you more dirty- minded folks —" he looked around with a grin — "it holds other implications."

Doris got up next and went to the altar. "I love the way this altar looks. It's beautiful and I'm glad that we are talking about our beauty together, at last. I'm going to add one of my favorite possessions." She took the brightly colored scarf from her waist where it had been decoratively wrapped. It was hand-painted with green and lavender waves and spirallike images. "These colors and swirls remind me of women's beauty and the silk is sensual and soft, yet strong and resilient, like me."

Joel laid down the slim volume of Rilke poems he had read from back at Summit Lake. "Many of the great poets who have touched my life have been men. Women write good poetry, too, but for some reason it's mostly male poets who've really touched my soul and spoken directly to my inner life as a man. One of my secrets is that I also write poetry. I've been reluctant to read it to others or attempt to publish it, but writing it is one of the more deeply satisfying things I do. I'm placing this book on the altar in the hopes that it will help me to embrace the poetic side of my life without shame and inspire me to risk sharing more of that part of myself with the world."

"I had a really hard time with this for some reason," said Marie as she stood up hesitantly. "It made me sad because I couldn't get in touch with a symbol of my femininity. But as I was lying on the ground contemplating this, I realized that the earth feels feminine to me. I feel most grounded in my female body on those rare days that I have time on the weekends to work in the garden. I love to stick my hands into the dirt." She sighed wistfully. "So I brought some dirt in this little bowl as a symbol of my fertile female ground."

Dave laid down his hunting knife. "I'm placing this here because, like Alan, I feel that my ability to hunt, to provide, is one of my greatest strengths as a man. But this is also a weapon that can be used to protect or wound. So I feel that my desire to use my power in the service of the community, and my willingness to protect others from harm, is also a deep quality of masculinity that I feel good about."

Liz was next. "I found this bone on the trail this morning. I think it's a rabbit pelvis. I love the shape of it. It reminds me of a woman's pelvis and how women contain and nurture life in the bowl of their hips. Bones also symbolize for me the indestructible essential parts of our being, the parts that never get lost regardless of what we might undergo in our lives. Many women have triumphed in life sheerly through their awesome capacity to endure adversity. So I admire the strong bones of the feminine soul that hold the flesh and organs of the community together."

Andy was the last one to place a symbol on the altar. He had a curious look in his eye as he got up and began fishing something out of his backpack. He withdrew a small bundle wrapped in a leather pouch. It looked a little strange, and at first it was hard to figure out what it was until he began unrolling it. It was the snake from our first camp, or at least its skin.

"I buried its body back at the camp," he said. "But I didn't want its life to have been simply wasted. I skinned it without knowing exactly why or what I wanted to do with the skin. But now it's clear."

He laid the long skin between the two sides of the cloth. It had the visual effect of creating a bridge between both groups of objects, which was exactly what he intended.

He then said, "I offer this up as a symbol of the natural and wild life force that moves through all of us and draws us toward each other. Although we clearly have a lot of differences, I think our life force, like our blood, is the same. I pray that we can cross over the chasm that separates us by walking across this bridge and that we can find some deep pleasure and healing in one another's company before our time together ends."

Almost everyone acknowledged this prayer in some fashion, saying, "Amen, brother" and "Ho!" or as Liz and I have begun to borrow from one of our favorite television characters, Jean-Luc Picard of "Star Trek," "Make It So!"

Similarities and differences between women and men were evident from the altar's offerings as well as at dozens of similar tableaus at our workshops. Photographs of children seem to occur fairly evenly between women and men. Women, however—even very contemporary career and executive women—inevitably tend to place a lot more bowls, baskets, and other vessels; jewelry and other decorative objects; crystals; goddess figurines; heirlooms from their mothers and grandmothers; symbols concerning their relationships with nature; and vulva-shaped objects.

Men generally display metallic tools, knives (once, a man brought a pistol), keys, talismans, credit cards, heirlooms from their fathers and grandfathers, handmade artifacts such as carvings, and phallic-shaped objects. We've had men bring in bicycles and once, in a large hall, a man went to the parking lot and brought in his Triumph motorcycle. Jerry was unusual in displaying a decorative piece of clothing as a masculine symbol, and Merle, as she mentioned at the time, was unusual by choosing a tool.

Women certainly have just as much capability as men when it comes to using tools, just as men share equal ability to nurture life. However, when you ask a man or a woman to produce a gender symbol, with a few exceptions the objects usually fall into somewhat stereotypical, traditional categories. Many women tend to identify their femininity with a symbol of receptivity, nurturing, beauty, relationships with others, plant materials, and the female sex organs. Men tend to identify their masculinity with an object symbolizing capability in the world, physical strength, material success, relationships with male ancestors and animals, and the male sex organ.

As I gazed at all the objects on the altar, it occurred to me that the more we investigate the authentic expression of masculinity and femininity, the more it seems that, regardless of all the modern political attempts to convince us that we are the same, we remain different in many ways. It's not easy to say why. Neither our journey nor this book will unveil the entire mystery. Certainly, as we have discussed, some of this difference comes from social stereotypes and some of it is biologically determined. What's more important is that, as in life, those differences made our altar more interesting than had we all chosen similar symbols to represent our gender. And that is the point, isn't it? Our differences make the tapestry of our lives more varied and rich.

❦ MAKING AMENDS

Andy's prayer for peace and healing sounded good to me. After five days of meetings, I was more than ready to lay down our differences, rich and interesting as they were, and have some fun. I was sure that at this point, Aaron was feeling the same way. But it was also clear that we could never have a true peace between us without taking the next step: accountability.

We began by cautioning our people to reveal only those issues they felt could be adequately received in our gathering. We suggested they hold off discussing deeply personal relationship issues that had the potential to consume all our time together and to wait for when they had the ongoing support of a counselor or a couples' support group.

The point of our next meeting was not to claim accountability for every rotten thing we had done in our lives. Rather, the point was to demonstrate to one another that both sexes had an equal hand in creating the enmity between them and were both equally empowered to bring about peace. We were attempting to create a model for reclaiming projections and reducing conflicts. We wanted to move beyond the adolescent blame game so many of us have been stuck in, into a more adult encounter in which we took full responsibility for our actions and attitudes toward others.

I reminded the group how we have all heard that "Love is never having to say you're sorry" and how that is one of the many guidelines for the "Let's just flow together; you do your thing, I'll do my thing and if by chance we meet, groovy" romantic philosophy of the last few decades. I shared my belief that real love, however, and the foundation for peace and equality between the sexes grow out of a willingness to admit when we are wrong coupled with a commitment to changing problem behaviors when it is possible to do so without diminishing our wholeness as individuals. When changes are implemented bilaterally and amends are made in the name of peace, they have the capacity to expand our individual sense of worth rather than reducing it.

I raised the proposition that most of the damage women and men do to one another is not done out of malice. Rather, most of the harm comes from ignorance about the cultural expectations of the other gender, frustrations about our own lives, thrashing about in our own unhealed pains from the past, and a habitual avoidance of healthy conflict that can eventually lead to unhealthy, even explosive behavior. When we understand that we are not cursed either by nature or by acculturation to war endlessly with one another, there's hope for creating genuine partnerships.

Women and men's relationships often vacillate between being either totally shame based and apologetic or scapegoating and blaming each other as the repository of all our pain. When each gender regards the other's humanity, morality, and sense of justice as fundamentally inferior to its own, then war is the only recourse. How then is peace achieved? Who makes the first move?

I cautioned the group that each gender may fear that listening to the other's issues could overwhelm its sense of self. Men have felt afraid to expose their wounds in the presence of women's vehemence and negativity toward their gender. And women have feared that to show some compassion for men will make them appear weak and place them at risk for slipping back into the old feminine mystique that encouraged women to focus on men's needs at the expense of their own.

"In the same manner," I continued, "we may be afraid that if we take responsibility for our contributions to the problem, even in an act of candor with a desire for reconciliation, then later that information may be used to blame, shame, and wound us. So we fight. We blame each other. We refuse to admit when we are wrong in order to protect ourselves from the immobilizing pain of shame. However, we need to take some risks if we are going to find peace." This was the challenge we faced when we returned to the council ground.

Health, for both gender groups, I reflected, is ultimately derived from the acknowledgment of, and communion with, all our parts, "positive" and "negative." When there is empathy and trust, with both sides acknowledging responsibility, some mutual healing can be activated through a process of accountability. It has to be done in a safe space where the participants agree not to use the information in a retaliatory fashion, but rather to receive it as a gift of honesty and acceptance of failure from both sides. The aim is toward improving future relations rather than to express shame in a self-flagellating, mea culpa way.

We discussed these ideas with the group. Then we invited those who wished to do so to become accountable for how they have significantly wounded the other sex. The council was declared open, and straws were drawn to see which group would go first. The men won—a dubious gain.

THE MEN'S PEACE OFFERINGS

Liz handed the talking stone to me and I held it out to the men, asking, "Would anyone like to take this opportunity to make amends to women by taking responsibility for their abusive past behaviors or by committing to some sort of change in the way they relate to women?" To my surprise most reached for the stone. I figured a few men would be willing to take this step, but, as it turned out, all the men, and subsequently all the women as well, went through the process.

Dave spoke first, saying, "I want to openly acknowledge that, for most of my life, I have treated women as sex objects. I've been much more fascinated by their body parts than their personalities. And I want to admit that even though I often blame women for not being more honest and up front about their sexuality, in fact it's been my attitudes that have been the primary obstacle to me having a satisfying and stable relationship with a woman. As a representative of all men, I apologize to all women who have suffered from this sort of male behavior."

Alan then said, "I want to acknowledge that I once hit Merle and furthermore, even though it hasn't happened again, I still feel violent towards her sometimes. I've also, at times, used my physical power to intimidate other women. And this sort of behavior is pretty much what I've been trained to believe I should do as a man. You know, be in control all the time. But I'm making a commitment here to seek out a support group for men who are prone toward violence, so that I can work more deeply on this issue and ensure that I never strike a woman again."

Larry stood up and began to speak. "This isn't a secret from Marie, but I want to tell the group that I had an affair a few years ago. I didn't even like Karen that much. She was kind of ditsy. I certainly was not looking for a new relationship to replace Marie. We have a good marriage and a great sex life, too. But there was something about Karen's youth, beauty, and availability that I just couldn't resist. And just about every other man I know also secretly compares their lover, in some way, to the fantasy image that we're all fed and then hooked on from every magazine cover, film, and television show. So, on behalf of all men who make their lovers miserable by holding them up to an unreal standard of beauty and thereby wind up missing the deep beauty that lies within every woman, I apologize."

Andy then said, "A way in which I've abused women is by not respecting it when one woman said no at some point during a consensual sexual encounter. It was in a gray area, for me, between seduction and dominance. But now I understand that even if, in any given situation, we think women don't mean it when they say it, men need to start respecting what women say instead of what we think they really want. So, on behalf of all men, I want to apologize to all women who have ever been sexually dominated, against their wills, by men."

Joel decided to introduce a different subject than the one he talked about in the men's camp. "During most of my marriage I've assumed that my wife should do all the child care. I've got lots of rationalizations about why I think it's okay, but the truth is, I know it's unfair and that this attitude causes Lisa a lot of pain. So I apologize on behalf of all men who take advantage of women's commitment to keep the home running smooth and take it for granted that they are always standing on the front lines of child care."

The rest of the men went on to share most of the information discussed at the last men's lodge meeting and more. We were mostly dealing with personal issues in these encounters. But it seemed to many of us, when we talked about it later, that we were also in some way talking out these issues for society as a whole. Our admissions reflected the reality that men are responsible for the majority of violent acts. We acknowledged that, even though men comprise the majority of victims of their own violence, one of the great inequalities between women and men is that men also commit more acts of physical violence against women than women do against men.

We admitted that we were often afraid of the psychological, emotional, and sexual power of women. Because of this, we sought ways to control women. As we discussed this issue, we realized that paradoxically we wanted women to be weak and dependent, and then considered them inferior when women acquiesced to our dominance. Although all of us consciously supported women becoming more empowered, most of us admitted we found women's changes intimidating. A painful truth emerged: a part of men still wants women to stay "small" so they can continue to feel "big." We recognized, however, that this is a dysfunctional strategy that makes our own empowerment conditional on women's lack of power.

Several of us acknowledged that our feelings of superiority over women have led us into abusive and dominating behaviors. Because we have been systematically trained to disregard women as equals, we felt at times that we were more entitled to privileges than they were. We were indoctrinated to believe that we did the most important work in the world and made the more serious sacrifices. From the male perspective, the lives of women seemed easier, softer, and more protected. This way of seeing the world has led many men to feel that women owed them. The conversation did not justify these attitudes, but was, rather, a confession, a forthright admission that men possess certain deeply conditioned perspectives that are getting in the way of gender peace.

As the women continued to listen in rapt silence, we reflected that attitudes of male superiority had caused some men to think, or simply take for granted, that they deserved to make more money than women because they worked "harder" and longer hours. Some of us felt we shouldn't have to do our fair share of housework because what we did outside the home was more dangerous, demanding, and debilitating. We felt it was demeaning to do "women's" (read: unpaid) work.

Some of us believed at times in our lives that women owed us sex if we paid a lot of attention to them or spent money on them. We acknowledged that this attitude was a factor fueling the increase of date and spousal rape in our society. We were coming to realize that women often had different standards about sex and intimacy. We needed to learn how to listen more attentively to the ways in which women set limits without trying to overwhelm or control them all the time.

As we discussed these issues, it became evident that the traditional philosophy we had all been raised with was still deeply ingrained in our psyches. Even in this group of men, who were willing and desirous of change, there were strong residues of traditional psychological conditioning. Even though it might take generations, we wanted to begin laying down the whole institution of male superiority. It was clear, however, that this was not going to be a simple task. We thought it should be a subject for the next meeting, a sort of disarmament conference with both sides discussing how they could bilaterally start standing down their missiles.

The only reason we were able even to admit these things now, however, was because we knew the women would be doing it, too. Unilateral admissions inevitably result in increased shame. That is one of the major problems with most psychological and social services that attempt to treat men who have problems with violence. The unidirectional blame many men experience in groups led by those who still believe in the myth of universal male privilege creates a climate in which men find it difficult to achieve any lasting change in their behavior, even though aversive training may effect some noticeable, short-term changes.

Even though we were not sure about how to do it, we emphatically stated our desire to lay down the sword of superiority, and we made a commitment to keep searching for a just peace between our genders. As a first step, all the men agreed to make a commitment to do all they could to reduce violence toward women by educating other men and boys and to continue to confront their own attitudes of entitlement and superiority. On behalf of all men who have dominated, abused, controlled, and damaged the lives of women, we expressed our sorrow and our intention to stand with women as equal partners, allies, and committed brothers.

THE WOMEN'S PEACE OFFERINGS

Aaron passed the stone back to me. The women sat in silence for a while, absorbing all that had been said as the late-afternoon sun began to infuse the lake and surrounding mountains with hues of lavender and rose. A flock of ducks landed in a flurry at the far edge of the lake, and far above us a large hawk was circling in the rising currents of air. I watched intently as it suddenly swooped below the ridgeline. Then, as it started to climb nearer and I could see it more clearly, I realized with a thrill that it was not a hawk but an eagle. We all took a moment to watch its flight in awe. It inspired me to remember that we all have the capacity to rise above our conflicts and soar with beauty and grace. We still had a lot of excess baggage weighing us down, however, and it was time to see if we could jettison a little more.

Then, turning our attention back to the council, Lisa said, "Well, I'll get the ball rolling for the women. This is not an easy thing to do. I want to tell all of you that I lost control of myself and hit my son on several occasions. It was at a time in my life when things were really hard, but that's no excuse. I'm realizing that some of the anger I have at men for their violence is being fueled by my own guilt and fear about my own capacity for misplaced aggression. So, I want to apologize to men for supporting the belief, as a teacher of women, that men are the only perpetrators of violence in this culture and for not having been willing to cop to my own violence before now."

"I want to acknowledge that I was responsible for denying my son access to his father and caused a deep rupture between the two of them," said Doris. "I know other women who have done similar things that resulted in separating fathers from knowing and enjoying their children. I was hurt and angry and felt justified at the time, but it was no excuse. I want to apologize to men for the pain that I created and that other women create when we fail to include the father in our families."

"Well, I've had enormous resistance to doing this process, as you all know," Gloria declared. "But I'm beginning to understand why we are doing it. I want to admit to the men, and to Jerry in particular," she said, glancing his way, "that I've tried to dominate and overpower you. I've used my verbal arrows to make you feel like shit in order to get my way. And, like Doris, I know a lot of women do this and don't admit that it's a form of aggression. So, on behalf of all women who abuse and manipulate men verbally, psychologically, emotionally, and even psychically, and then in the same breath make men feel like they are the assholes of the world, I'm sorry. I really am. I'm beginning to see that this war between women and men really is a two-sided affair. It's just been completely opposite to my feminist political beliefs to look at it this way up until now."

I looked over at Jerry. He looked stunned at this admission. In fact, all the men seemed deeply moved by Gloria's statement. It had really struck a nerve, especially given the amount of hostility that she had conveyed toward the men earlier.

Marie spoke next. "I've taken advantage of men financially, actually one man in particular, my ex-husband. I've had an attitude towards men that they had it better than me, and therefore they somehow deserved to be used. I used my assumed victim status as a woman to justify using legal means to rip off money from an innocent man. Lots of women use men for material gain, let's face it. Some men use us for our bodies and some women don't care anything about a man except what he can produce or pay for. I'm not proud of this at this point in my life, but it feels good to acknowledge it openly here to the men and to commit that I will strive for fairness in my financial dealings with men in the future."

The women continued to share with the men some of the issues they had discussed when they were in the women's camp. Many points were expressed. We acknowledged that we had quite a few privileges of our own that women rarely, if ever, admit. We told the men that it was clearly unjust that only men are forced to put their lives on the line for their country in time of war. We also admitted that in most other dangerous circumstances, ranging from hostage takeovers to sinking ships, it was automatically assumed that our lives would be more protected than the lives of men.

We observed that even though women have demanded equality as political and business leaders, doctors, lawyers, and other high-paying white-collar professionals, we had not sought much entree into other high-paying, but physically dangerous blue-collar professions such as logging, heavy construction, machine operations, road building, or mining. We wanted to share men's "goodies," but not their pain. We speculated that perhaps one of the reasons women's life spans are now so much longer than men's (more than seven years) is because, like men's privilege to make more money and gain political power, we possess a greater privilege to care for ourselves and be protected by others. We had taken it for granted that our lives were more valuable and should be more protected than men's.

As we talked and listened to one another, we realized that all of us had been feeling morally superior to men for quite some time. One of the more secret, yet mutually agreed-upon, assumptions in contemporary women's culture is that many women believe they are essentially better people than men. This is not just a politically idealistic belief, but a statement of an actual collective worldview that has emerged over the last few decades.

Somehow over the years, in the course of breaking free of the past and redefining ourselves, we came to hold the belief that men are in many ways inferior to us. Some of us even believe that men are less spiritually evolved than women. Others feel that something is essentially wrong with men and essentially right with women.

Women are not alone in this view. In his book *The Natural Superiority of Women*, anthropologist Ashley Montagu proposes that women foster life, men destroy it; he states, "It is the function of women to teach men to be human." He also comments that "women have always been superior to men but until recently they have had the good taste to keep quiet about it."

As we brought this attitude into the light, in front of the men, I felt a little embarrassed. How had this happened? We were exhibiting the same sexist thinking that we had long held to be the exclusive domain of the "patriarchy." Upon further reflection during the course of our accountability council, several women also revealed the deeper and more difficult truth that they believed this "new" feeling of superiority was compensation for their ingrained sense of vulnerability and inferiority.

Psychologist Alfred Adler believed that "every neurosis can be understood as an attempt to free oneself from a feeling of inferiority in order to gain a feeling of superiority." We had all felt, or still did feel, inferior on some levels, and it was easier to cover this with an attitude of superiority than to address the core of the problem honestly. We agreed collectively that it was time to lay the whole thing down. It kept women and men separated, and there was really no proof as yet that women could do a better job of running the world than men could. What was clear was that we had the right to have an opportunity to prove we could do just as well if we wanted to.

We come out of a women's culture that has compensated for our experience of inequality in the world by creating a belief in the intrinsic moral superiority of women. Because the power dynamics of our society have often been unfair to women, we have sought many times to redress the situation through passive-aggressive behaviors that undermine male self-esteem rather than to focus more attention on building up our own.

We shared with the men our recognition of the way in which we had "set down our own basket" by abdicating responsibility for ourselves in many ways. We realized that many problems we blame men for are created just as much through our inaction or helplessness. As the men had done, we wanted to lay down our poisoned arrows of superiority and make a commitment to the men and to ourselves to learn more constructive and life-supporting ways to find power in the world.

It was clear to us that in order to shift toward a new way for men and women to relate, we were going to need the help and alliance of men. We agreed with them that this should be the topic of our next meeting. We expressed regret on behalf of all women who had used their sexual powers to manipulate men; abused or neglected their children; verbally shamed, physically battered, or emotionally dominated their spouses; disregarded men's humanity as a group; allowed men to do an unfair share of income-producing work or let them face danger and death alone; and habitually blamed men for the problems of the world instead of taking responsibility for how we, too, contribute to those problems.

We told the men that our intention was to change these patterns in the hope that we could revision ourselves and our relationships. We felt that just an awareness of the problem was an enormous step forward. It was also our intent to take the work that we had done here, both separately and together, into the world to share with other groups of women and men.

We offered this information with a mind toward promoting healing between the sexes. This, and more, was given to the men as a peace offering, a forthright admission of women's responsibility in co-creating the war between the sexes. On behalf of all women who have dominated, abused, controlled, and damaged the lives of men and boys, we expressed our sorrow and our intention to stand with men as equal partners, committed allies, and sisters.

IN THE PLACE
OF GATHERING STORMS

We took a short break. When Dave returned from the tree line north of camp, he looked concerned and said, "Hey, there's some serious clouds boiling up over the ridge." From where we were sitting, though, we could see only clear skies to the south, east, and west. "Well, it doesn't seem to be anything to worry about," said Jerry, who was stretched out on the ground soaking up the last slanting rays of the sun as it starting dipping below the western ridgeline.

"I don't know," said Dave. "Maybe some of you should come look and see what you think."

"I'll go," cried Susan, leaping to her feet and quickly out-pacing Dave up the short climb to the northern ridge that rose above the lake bed. In about fifteen minutes they returned and Susan said, "We've got trouble, kids. There's definitely a storm headed this way. There's big black thunderclouds across the sky to the north and the wind is blowing them straight at us."

"Well, I guess we'd best get ready for rain then. Class dismissed," joked Liz.

We briefly discussed who had what for rain protection. I had the extra-large tarp and twine in my pack, and Dave also had an extra tarp. Because Joel and Lisa, Gloria and Jerry, and Alan and Merle had packed as couples, they now had their tents and tarps in different camps. Neither camp had a suffi-cient amount of gear to build a large shelter. If we were going to confront the storm and still keep meeting with one another, the best idea would be to get our stuff from our separate camps and come together at the council ground.

By the time we packed and returned from the opposite ends of the lake, we didn't need a scout to tell us what was going on. Rain was already falling at the ridgeline and we could hear distant peals of thunder. The first thing we did was attempt to rig a big lean-to over the fire pit and the council ground using my big tarp plus Dave's and a few smaller ones contributed by others. The wind was coming up. It kept whipping the large tarp out of our hands as we tried to set it in place. We weren't making much progress. Alan suddenly took charge of building the shelter, shouting over the wind to pull lines here, plant stakes and heavy stones there, and rig tie-lines where needed.

"Hey, who made you boss?" asked Marie defiantly. "What happened to all the talk about equality?"

Alan just looked pained, as did everyone else. This was not the moment for a gender council. The rain had suddenly reached us. We were getting wet and it was starting to get cold, too.

"Do you have a better idea about how to do this, Marie?" asked Liz.

"No," she replied. "I don't even know how to erect a tent, much less a big shelter like this. I just think that it's a little weird that all of a sudden now that we have a problem, some man is the one taking over."

It was clear to me, and to everyone else, that Alan knew exactly what he was doing and no one else questioned his authority. We were grateful to have someone take charge, and women and men alike submitted to his direction and kept on working while Marie stood there, looking pissed-off. After a few minutes she got off her trip and pitched in with us.

Andy and Dave shinnied up trees to rig lines. Several women and men hauled rocks from the shoreline to weight the sides of the lean-to and pounded stakes for ground lines. A few of the couples set up their individual tents near the main shelter. In the midst of all the activity, I noticed Liz hauling up a large pot of water from the lake. Several other people, under her direction apparently, were gathering still-dry firewood and putting it under a tarp.

Suddenly, I heard a horse whinnying on the trail above the camp. Wow, just in time, I thought. Here comes the cavalry—cowboys with shovels, more tarps, and rope (we were quickly running out of twine). But the cavalry had not arrived, only one riderless horse. I went up the trail with Andy and Lisa to meet it at the edge of the clearing where the trail came into the lake side. The horse appeared frightened and exhausted. It was very skittish and had a lot of brush tangled in its reins. We tried to approach it, but it just kept snorting, rearing up slightly, and backing away with a wild look in its eye.

Lisa said, "Guys, no offense, but why don't you just hold back and let me try?"

I thought, okay, why not? I don't know beans about horses. I stepped back about thirty feet. Lisa advanced slowly, talking gently and making clicking noises. The horse calmed down. She continued advancing, making reassuring sounds until she was able to walk right up to it and grasp the dangling reins, just below the horse's mouth.

Lisa patiently stroked its side and neck as the rain plastered her hair to her head and water streamed down her face.

She then proceeded to lead the horse toward our camp, motioning with her head for me to keep walking ahead of them. By the time we got back, the horse was completely calm. She tied it under a large fir tree next to our new camp. I was very impressed with how she had tamed this huge, frightened beast in the midst of a storm.

It was after dark by the time we had the camp secured. Many of us were wet and cold. The storm started to drop fierce bursts of hail. Thunder and lightning were crashing to the north and moving closer to us. A strong gust of wind lifted Jerry and Gloria's tent and hurled it into the lake, where it sank before anyone could do a thing about it. Fortunately, our main shelter was holding strong.

We had prepared for the possibility of rain, but a freak summer storm of this intensity was unexpected. It was valuable, however, that our accountability council had ended with an experience that demanded we all be able to work together for our mutual survival and well-being. Despite the hassles and even possible dangers of being exposed to the mercy of the elements, I was glad we were having this opportunity.

It seemed that some of the men, by virtue of their experience in construction and their physical strength, were a little more able at shelter building, even though Marie felt that our task should be equally shared. And Lisa, though the most slightly built person on the trip, was clearly the most capable, by virtue of a lifetime of horseback riding as it turned out, of dealing with the horse. We are often the most capable at that with which we are the most familiar. My first inclination, however, was that I should have dealt with it because I was a man and men are supposed to be the ones that face danger when it arises.

I thought about how the whole political move toward equality through sameness ignores the practical reality that in any given situation a woman or a man may be the most suited for leadership by virtue of experience and ability, rather than because of any stereotypical gender expectations we might have of them. There are times when a woman or a man must exhibit leadership on the basis of personal characteristics, rather than gender authority.

The experience we just had in the group clearly demonstrated to me how our society needs to enhance its capacity to support people on the basis of their authentic authority. All too often we get immobilized by a more superficial analysis of equality that obscures the truth. For example, the truth may be that in a divorce, the father could be the most able parent and should be awarded custody even though gender prejudices might tell us wrongly that women are intrinsically better parents. Men also make capable nurses, primary teachers, and school counselors, and can excel at other traditionally female-dominated fields if they want to. Even so, they continue to encounter prejudices that make it difficult for them to enter these fields.

I thought about how, as Lisa had just demonstrated, a judgeship or a military leadership position may best be filled by a woman if she is the most qualified person available for the job, even though our gender prejudices might tell us, again wrongly, that women are less rational and just than men are. Women also make capable carpenters, truck drivers, senators, and CEOs, and can excel in other traditionally male-dominated fields if they wish to.

With ninety percent of our primary educators still female and the majority of congressional leaders still predominantly male, sexism is obviously still keeping qualified women and men out of fields where their differences are needed to bring balance. As I mulled over our group's experience, it seemed to me that at this point in the national dialogue on gender entitlements, the most useful attitude might be to accept the paradox that males or females may both have special insights and abilities that stem from their biology and traditional roles, and that they also have equal abilities to cross over and exhibit excellence in arenas traditionally held by the other gender.

As our discussions together revealed, old gender prejudices limited women's and men's freedom to enter each other's traditional domains. Then we tried to eliminate any awareness of differences. That has failed. Now new gender prejudices limit our capacity to take advantage of, and enjoyment from, real differences, whatever they are. We need to keep moving beyond rigid orthodoxies that hurt us and find ways to embrace paradoxes that can liberate us.

✿ WHAT WOMEN AND MEN LOVE ABOUT ONE ANOTHER

During the chaos of securing gear and building shelter, Merle and Doris had the presence of mind to keep the fire going and get several pots of hot water boiling. As the shelter builders came in to dry off around the fire, they had plenty of coffee, tea, and soup to warm their bones. Then we all polished off a big pot of stew. We sat back, getting warm and dry, with our bellies full, as the storm raged around us. I was glad to see Aaron smiling again and felt more at peace than I could recently remember.

After days of dwelling on our differences and disagreements, in a few short hours we demonstrated our capacity to cooperate in the service of our common good. For the most part, egos and power struggles were at a minimum. We all pulled together and did what we could to survive. In the midst of the storm, it seemed natural to let more of the guys handle the building of the shelter and for me and a few other women to focus on the fire, wood, food, and water, even though some members of both groups worked on both tasks.

I was sure we could build a shelter without men and the men could cook without us. But that wasn't the point and we didn't need to prove it. We had to get it all done quickly and it didn't matter to me who did what, just that the task got done. After all, weren't we equal?

The women carrying firewood and hauling water were no more oppressed than the men who were carrying large stones or climbing trees in the rain and lightning. We were equally wet and equally cold. We all did everything we could to secure the camp. But to some degree, we did different things. Our roles, in this case, were asymmetrical but equal. Instead of becoming immobilized in squabbles about which job had more status or who was boss for any given project or how to make our roles symmetrical, we became allies. This spirit of cooperation between the sexes is too often missing today.

As I compared our group's experience to the world at large, I realized that the problem of sexism in society cannot be solved by attempting to create perfect symmetry; by everybody doing the same thing and then somehow magically becoming equal. As our group demonstrated, the problem is more when one sex's contribution is seen as of lesser or greater importance than the other's. Now, if the shelter builders got twice as much food as the fire tenders, then that would have been sexist. Or if women were not allowed to build or men were not allowed to tend hearths, that would be a problem. But the way it all happened, traditional or politically incorrect as it was, it felt perfectly natural even in this context. It was just an exercise in common sense and the best use of our skills.

In the face of survival, our preoccupation with gender discussions suddenly seemed a little ludicrous. I was just happy to be dry. A celebration seemed in order. I dug into the bottom of my pack and brought out my secret stash of chocolate bars and raided Aaron's pack for the package of Jiffy Pop popcorn I knew he always brings along for a special moment.

"Who else is holding out on goodies?" I asked, holding out my hat.

My hat was passed around the circle while I started popping the corn over the fire. It came back with some slightly melted Gummi Bears, hard candies, chocolate-covered raisins and peanuts, dried pineapple, and, to my surprise, a pile of jellybeans. Dave produced a plastic, still mostly full pint flask with apricot brandy in it. Incredible what people will carry in a pack for ten miles, and lucky for the group. We passed the brandy around with the chocolate-fruit-nut-popcorn ambrosial hat of plenty. After almost a week in the wilderness, it tasted like a royal banquet.

When the flask came to Doris, she said, "I want to propose a toast to Alan. I really love men's strength and capability in emergencies, and I want to thank you for taking charge and getting us out of the storm."

We all cheered him.

"You guys really made me feel safe and supported," agreed Lisa.

"I want to say that I appreciate all the men on this trip for the honesty and vulnerability that you've shared. It's kind of blown my mind and gone a long way to restoring my faith and trust in men," said Gloria.

"What else do we like about the men?" I queried, egging the women on.

"I think men are a lot of fun to hang out with; they have a zany sense of humor," said Susan.

"Well, I love the way Larry is with our kids. He's a wonderful father and husband," exclaimed Marie. She was curled up with him under her shawl and seemed happy and relieved to be reunited with her husband after the days of separation.

Other women joined in, saying things like, "Men are sexy." "Men know how to fix things." "Men are courageous."

During the round of toasts, some of the women shared brief stories about the benefits they had received from men in their lives. While the wind whistling around us lessened and the storm began to abate, they talked about deepening compassion and understanding about the valuable qualities of their fathers, husbands, teachers, friends, lovers, and sons.

These are some positive qualities the women said they deeply appreciate about men:

Men love adventure
Men are great lovers
Men are strong
Men are reliable
Men understand cars
Men have stamina
Men give comfort and reassurance
Men risk their lives to protect others
Men are good at making money
Men are logical
Men are wild
Men are independent
Men have a good sense of humor
Men are confident
Men are big
Men are good hunters
Men take out the garbage
Men can build
Men keep their cool in an emergency

Men are creative
Men are leaders
Men can be silent
Men are capable
Men are great dancers
Men are wise
Men are good cooks
Men are good planners
Men are loving fathers
Men are focused and goal-directed
Men are compassionate
Men are adaptable
Men hold us in their arms
Men are loyal
Men are problem solvers
Men are generous
Men are stable and grounded
Men smell good
Men have hard muscles
Men sacrifice for their families
Men are thoughtful
Men are tender

After hearing these statements and some of the stories that engendered them, most of the men responded by saying how refreshing it was to hear women making positive comments about men and masculinity. It is tremendously healing for men to receive unqualified praise from women. Unfortunately, in our culture, this kind of support and applause by women for men about the positive side of masculinity is a rare event.

When the women had finished telling their stories, Dave proposed a toast to Merle and Doris: "If it wasn't for you two sheltering the fire with your bodies until we got the tarp up and then preparing food and heating water during this whole scene, we might be out of the rain, but we'd still be cold and hungry. I appreciate your thoughtfulness in getting a meal together in the midst of all this wildness, and the others who secured dry firewood with Liz while there still was some to be had. Something that I really love about women is their attention, even to the point of sacrificing their own well-being, to the details of caring for the comfort and health of others."

Aaron offered a toast to Lisa: "I admire your personal courage. That horse was threatening and frightening. It could have bolted through our camp and made a mess of everything, hurt itself or someone else. I was grateful when you took charge because I didn't really have a clue about what to do. I was also impressed by your caring and humanity in trying to calm the animal, rather than just try to scare it back down the trail, which is what I was about to do."

"Yeah, here's to women's strength and fortitude in the face of adversity," said Joel.

"What else do we love about women?" Aaron asked.

"I love women's laughter," Andy stated. "Women are playful, they lighten things up."

"I admire women's grace and sensuality," said Jerry.

"Women are responsible," offered Joel. "They demand that society pay better attention to its problems."

The men continued talking about many things they love and appreciate about women. They shared stories regarding the various blessings they have received from the women in their lives, their mothers, teachers, lovers, wives, sisters, and daughters. The list of qualities they honored was long and the toasts continued, made with tea, long after the brandy was gone. These are some positive qualities the men appreciated about women:

Women are passionate
Women are good listeners
Women are soft
Women keep life in balance
Women are gentle
Women are wise
Women are irrational
Women are spiritual
Women are fierce
Women are juicy
Women have curves
Women are erotic
Women are creators of life
Women are unpredictable
Women hold relationships
    together
Women are fascinating and
    mysterious
Women are gracious

Women are athletic
Women are patient
Women are intuitive
Women are healers
Women are creative
Women protect children
Women are sensitive
Women ask for help when
    they need it
Women are compassionate
Women provide emotional
    security
Women smell good
Women pay attention to
    details
Women are good leaders
Women walk with a lovely
    sway
Women are great teachers

Women are romantic
Women make life
    bearable
Women have breasts
Women are insightful

Women are flexible
Women are beautiful
Women create safety
Women are powerful
Women create comfort

Naturally, several women said that they were thrilled to hear that the men at last had something good to say about them.

The storm had died down to a steady rain. Everyone looked comfortable and extraordinarily happy considering the uncomfortable circumstances. We had triumphed not only over the challenges of the inclement weather but also over much of the adversity created by our emotional storms.

As I looked around the group, I thought that now, with the goodwill that had been cultivated, we were ready to do some serious work together and to consider more deeply some of the issues we had come out here to wrestle with. But that would have to wait until tomorrow.

It was late and several couples and a few singles made their way to the tents they had resurrected near the council ground. Most of us, however, unfurled our sleeping bags and pads around the fire under the lean-to and kept talking deep into the night, until we were all asleep.

CHAPTER EIGHT

PATHWAYS TO PEACE

Poles apart, I am the color of dying,
You are the color of being born.
Unless we breathe in each other, There can be no Garden
So that's why plants grow and laugh at our eyes
Which focus on distance.

— RUMI

W HEN I AWOKE, the first thing I noticed was that the storm had passed. The day was sparkling, bright, clear, and full of promise. As I looked over the camp, I felt good seeing us all together. As soon as the sun hit the water, Andy and Merle waded out and helped Jerry and Gloria fish their tent out of the lake. They spread it on the lower branches of the pines at the lake's edge. Soon others dragged out towels, tennis shoes, a wide array of soggy clothing, and even a few sleeping bags that did not survive the night very well. The varied colors of fabric in the trees gave the camp a festive air. Although the night had been challenging, spirits were high.

"I'm hungry," cried Doris. "What's for breakfast?"

Joel had made a pot of coffee, but short of that no one else had taken the initiative to get anything going.

"I want to go fishing," Liz said, looking at me expectantly.

None of the men, except Dave, seemed anxious to go out this morning. The rest of us were more interested in drying out by the fire.

"Come on, ladies," Dave cajoled, looking at Liz and others around the fire. "Let's go get 'em."

"Okay," said Liz, jumping up, "I'm game. Who else will join me?"

Susan, Lisa, Marie, and Doris all indicated that they would go. Merle and Gloria were still chilled and wanted to stay by the fire. The women borrowed gear from various men and went off with Dave. They returned in a little over an hour with more fish than we had caught on any other day.

DIFFERENT BUT EQUAL: A NEW BALANCE OF POWER

"They've been fooling us about how hard it is," said Doris. "I caught three trout all by myself. It's easy. You just toss in your line and they bite."

"Maybe fishing is not such a great male mystery after all," ventured Lisa teasingly.

Well, maybe it was the weather, or beginner's luck, or maybe the women really had better fishing magic. Who could say? What was important was that the women had claimed their hunting power. What could we men do but praise them for their skill and offer to do all the cooking. As I cleaned fish and cooked them, along with Joel, Jerry, Alan, Larry, and Andy, I found it was enjoyable to be talking around the fire and sharing a task with just the men.

Even though Dave was excused from duty, he came over and joined us at the fire. It had been the first time we reconnected as a tribe since we were at Summit Lake. For a few moments, I felt our male "gender ground" reestablished. That felt sense of male culture doesn't really have much to do with whether or not we are engaged in a traditional male activity. It is essentially connected to the experience of sharing a common task.

Once again it wasn't so important which gender did what, but rather how valued the activity was. After breakfast, when several women told us that they appreciated the preparation, cooking, and cleanup, we felt as if those tasks were just as valued as the hunting they had done. When we experience ourselves as interdependent members of the same tribe, then the way in which any particular distribution of labors may constellate around gender lines is not so important.

What is important is that each member's contribution has equal value and that the members have a choice about occupations, if they wish. That's a lot of what the gender war has been about—both women and men wanting a greater choice. They want more opportunities to enter domains that have previously been denied them through the stereotypical limits set by their culture. These days it seems that the choice women often desire is access to greater hunting-providing power and the economic benefits that go along with it, whereas more men now want the freedom to access greater nurturing-caring power and the benefits of health, longevity, and well-being that go along with it.

After breakfast we began to talk about the lists we had made the previous night—about what we love and appreciate about one another. Several things became clear. Just as our other exercises had demonstrated, some qualities we admired were shared by both genders and appreciated by both. Many traits and abilities, however, were located more on one gender's ground than the other's. Graphically represented, the differences between gender grounds would look a little like two overlapping circles, with a common ground in the center and with separate territories still remaining in the portions of the circles that did not overlap.

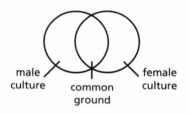

✆ THE CO-CREATED WORLD

As we continued talking, another insight emerged. In many cases what we love and admire about one another is startlingly similar to what we hate and fear. Women admire men's strength and capability, yet fear their power to control and dominate. Men love women's sensuality and effusiveness, yet fear their emotional and erotic power. Women love men's capacity for independence and self-reliance, yet hate their remoteness and inaccessibility. Men admire women's receptivity and love their gentleness, yet scorn them for being too emotional and overly sensitive. Women admire men's ability to focus, be logical, and overcome fear in the face of danger, yet scorn them for their coldness and for not being in touch with their feelings. Men respect women for their commitment to caring and their nurturing power, then resent them for being smothering and invasive.

In certain arenas one sex may be a little more blessed with one ability or another. What we most admire in the other sex is when these blessings are used in the service of others. And what we hate most is when the same attributes, like physical strength in men or emotional power in women, are used to undermine or destroy others. It is not so much the possession of power we fear, or even the unequal distribution of it, but rather the abuse of power itself.

As we discovered during our accountability council, our fears about the abuse of power are so great that both genders put energy into trying to diminish the power of the other, to render it smaller and less threatening. However, in order to meet the pressing challenges of present-day society, we need fully empowered women and men. We cannot afford to disempower or disenfranchise any woman or man of goodwill who has something to offer. Therefore, it is in our best interest to empower one another in a manner that can assuage, as much as possible, our fears about power itself.

More than fifty years ago anthropologist Margaret Mead observed,

> It takes considerable effort on the part of both men and women to reorient ourselves to thinking that this is a world made not by men alone, in which women are unwilling and helpless dupes and fools or else powerful schemers hiding their power under their ruffled petticoats, but a world made by mankind

for human beings of both sexes. In this world, male and female roles have sometimes been styled well and sometimes badly. . . . But to the degree that there have been discrepancies in the two roles, to the degree that a style of beauty that was unobtainable by most people, or a style of bravery or initiative, modesty and responsiveness, was insisted upon although the culture had inadequate devices for developing such initiative or responsiveness, then both men and women suffer. . . . A higher goal would be to assume that we live in a co-created world, sharing mutual responsibility for our problems.

It was becoming apparent to us all that the men's movement and the women's movement working singularly cannot build the bridges over the gender gap that most of us would rather travel across. Lisa pointed out that as a culture, however, just as at least two political parties are needed, separate movements must stand vigilant against injustices and discover better ways in which to heal, empower, and nurture their own gender. As we experienced in our groups, this often happens most successfully in same-sex situations. In those groups, as we also experienced, however, it is harder to perceive the "co-created" world.

"For the most part," observed Marie as we discussed this topic, "I don't feel that either gender group has been attempting to do much to right the injustices done to the other, even though in recent years increasing numbers of men have aligned with the women's movement and more women have begun to speak out on behalf of men."

"I think there's a serious limit to the vision and the ability of both women's and men's rights movements to bring about a just society for both sexes," said Larry.

Separate camps can approach only the edges of the chasm between the sexes and empower their less polarized members to build toward the middle ground. Those of us who arrive in the middle will, of necessity, surrender some of our gender "nationalism." We will stand instead on the shared ground of a new social movement that can embrace perspectives broader than the separate groups were capable of embracing.

Just as our country is moving beyond the cold war rhetoric of the past and is becoming more diplomatic with other nations, the cultures of women and men can also create more astute gender diplomats, mediators, and peacemakers to help end our divisions. During our journey we learned one thing that can cultivate an atmosphere of peacemaking: account-ability for our injustices toward one another. We had taken that step in our group. We were ready to go deeper. The next step challenged us to begin developing an ideal of gender jus-tice that went beyond the win-lose rhetoric of the women's and men's rights movements.

GENDER JUSTICE

One thing that had become clear to Aaron and me from our councils is that when one gender suffers by virtue of unfairness or inequality, the other also suffers. As our conversations in the group revealed, the nature of the suffering is almost always dif-ferent and asymmetrical. But the amount of suffering, to the degree that it is even possible to quantify pain, seemed to be generally equal in both groups.

As we discussed this topic, Alan pointed out, "Women make less money in the workplace and men get killed and injured on the job much more than women. Both situations are unjust. Both genders suffer."

Lisa acknowledged, "Many women have hit the 'glass ceiling' and are locked out of upper-level, privileged jobs, but many men are locked into lower-level dangerous jobs and passed over for promotions by affirmative action programs for women."

"Our economy is based upon a philosophy that creates a very unequal distribution of wealth and power," Joel noted. "The bulk of wealth and power in this country is held by a small majority of men and women. Last time I looked at the statistics, about one percent of women and one percent of men equally owned over one-third of the nation's wealth. I think this results in a large majority of equally disenfranchised women and men feeling they must compete with one another."

In many ways it seems that we are all fighting over crumbs. We might be better off by asking, Who owns the loaf that should be nourishing everyone? Who gains from turning issues that are more rightly about class inequalities into a gender war between women and men? If anyone does, it can be only the handful of powerful women and men who control the nation's wealth and productivity. Through the media many product manufacturers attempt to create a feeling of insufficiency in women and men, who, in turn, strive, often through consumerism, to feel sufficient and whole. Women and men are made to feel inadequate in each other's eyes unless they consume or own a certain product.

We began discussing advertisements we have seen and the messages we thought they were sending.

Larry observed, "Ads geared toward women frequently show them triumphing over a less able man by using some product to solve a household problem he couldn't deal with. They seem to say 'you'll feel superior to men if you use our cleaner.'"

Andy added, "A lot of them also show women enhancing their beauty with products that promise to help them win the wealth and power of men."

Gloria said, "I've noticed that ads appealing to men show them getting the beautiful girl through owning an expensive car or the right pair of jeans."

Lisa recalled, "Other ads simply offer men relief from the frustrations of dating if they just consume their products. 'Why say why?' they say. 'Just have another St. Pauli Girl beer and forget about her.'"

We all agreed that we were tired of being saturated daily with messages that, by treating women and men like objects, inflame the tensions between the sexes. Clearly, the process of peace between the sexes could be aided if we became more aware of both the blatant and subtle commercial messages that have been influencing us.

"Ultimately, as interesting as all this analysis is," I said, "I think the most fruitful direction to look for the loaf is in the space between us. Each of us has a piece of the recipe for societal abundance. I believe that we can successfully bake it, however, only by working in partnership for the common good.

What I'm realizing from our week together is that real gender justice involves looking at women and men as members of the same family, with some differing and some shared needs, who are equally part of both the problems and the solutions."

Aaron followed my thought, telling the group about a story he learned from mythologist Michael Meade about how in medieval France the women kept the seeds for sowing the crops and the men kept all the plows. Without the agreement of both genders about how much to plant, when to do it, and where, no planting at all could happen and everyone would suffer. This story illuminated the idea we were chewing on: that when there is no cooperation, scarcity, competition, and gender jealousy persist. So much energy gets lost in the fighting.

Our group had acknowledged to one another that we were equally responsible for creating most of the problems between us. Now was the time to discover what we wanted from each other and what we were willing to give in order to get it. We decided to probe more deeply the idea that many of our wounds were co-created, as equal combatants in a war. We wanted to look at some of these issues from both sides, with a mind toward gaining a deeper understanding rather than ascribing rightness or wrongness to either gender.

Although everyone in our group agreed that there are numerous areas of conflict between women and men, when we reviewed our week together and further discussed the concept of gender justice, a few major issues emerged as recurrent themes. We decided that our best use of the little time that remained would be to focus, in depth, on a few of them. Many of the conflicts and much of the anger are connected to how we deal with the potent forces of sex and power. Thus, an in-depth discussion about how we navigate each other's boundaries became the primary focus of our second-to-last day together.

✺ THE SILENT LANGUAGE OF MALE BOUNDARIES

"One of the things I want to know is why there is so much confusion between women and men about the difference between sex harassment and courting," said Lisa.

Unlike our former encounters, this query was not made accusingly, but rather had a tone of genuine interest and a desire for communication. The impact of tone is subtle, but tone deeply affects our ability to hear one another. It suddenly felt much easier for me as a man to respond in the new climate of empathy and openness that had developed in the group.

Doris suggested that perhaps there wasn't anything wrong with anyone. "Maybe women and men just speak different languages," she proposed, "and aren't translating them all that well."

That pointed us in the right direction. Before teaming up with Liz to do gender work, I worked with many men in a wide variety of contexts. Based on that experience and other research, I began by offering some of what I had learned about male language; the rest of the men in our group confirmed or elaborated various points as we went along.

I told the group, "In most of the cultures I've ever read about, the courting dance is very conservative. That is, regardless of its complexity, the steps of the dance are grounded in tradition and are easily recognized by both parties. Deviation or creative elaboration on the part of either party risks a breach of the courting protocols. The consequences of a breach can range from perceived insult and hurt to either party to a provocation that can create violence between families, even war between tribes."

I then shared with the group about how Peter Weir's film, *Walkabout*, had touched me deeply many years ago. It depicts a tragic situation in which an Australian aboriginal youth rescues a young European sister and brother lost in the Outback. After some weeks of feeding and protecting them, this magnificent young man performs a beautiful mating dance for the young woman, with whom he has fallen in love. She is frightened by it and runs away. She doesn't understand or respond in the manner that someone from his own culture might. Feeling that he has failed as a man, he commits suicide.

"Once upon a time," I explained, "I think the signals displayed in our culture's courting dances were, to a large degree, mutually agreed upon. Women 'dropped the handkerchief' and men had a choice whether to pick it up or not. But our society is rapidly changing. Increasingly, men and women are working together in new, noncourting contexts. Our culture is also increasingly blending together a mix of many cultures, most of which have unique mores, cues, traditions, and expectations about same-sex versus other-sex interactions.

"Just as there is a great deal of racial and cultural tension among groups attempting to coexist in our country—there are over 150 such groups in Los Angeles alone—many cross-currents are at work in male-female communications as well. One of the problems our culture faces is that there are no longer any mutually agreed-upon sets of courting signals. In most cultures some sort of sign language accompanies the development of written and spoken language, so it is not surprising that some remnants of sign language still exist in human culture. However, we are now surrounded by a babble of nonverbal cues that often mean different things to each gender group."

There are also many differences between women's and men's spoken language as described in books like Deborah Tannen's *You Just Don't Understand.* What more needs to be said about this topic, however, is that in many cases we also lack a common, nonverbal, symbolic system of communication. Men are often more attuned to the silent language of actions and women are more attuned to the silent nuances of feelings. Some theorists suggest that more than fifty percent of human communication is nonverbal, yet we rarely discuss this aspect of miscommunication between the sexes.

"When we men do physical work with women," I added, "we often feel that we have to verbally describe a series of motions, such as how to move a couch up a series of stairs, that we could easily communicate to another man just with a few nods of the head and subtle shifts in posture."

"Women, by the same token," added Liz, "feel we have to explain emotional issues in depth to men that another woman would understand just from a sigh or a look. Women say men 'just don't get it' and they are right. Many women and men don't get it in certain arenas, not because we are stupid or we don't care, but because we are often uncertain about the meanings of the subliminal signals being sent by the other sex."

"Although there is great diversity within same-sex groups," I continued, "I feel that currently there's a more common same-sex language around the ways in which boundaries, trust, power, intimacy, and friendship are negotiated. For example, I often notice that when a man consciously or inadvertently invades another man's territory, he usually receives some recognizable warning signal in response to his aggressive actions. Territory can range from physical (the space around his body); to psychological and emotional (his felt sense of self); to material (his possessions, business, hunting ground, home); to relationships with family, friends, and other people; it may even extend into abstractions like country or God.

"When we study body language we quickly learn that men generally require more territory around them than do women. If you draw an imaginary circle around women and men, men generally have a larger boundary, like a bubble, around their bodies. This line, if crossed without consent, may generate internal discomfort and the display of a usually silent signal of some sort that says, 'Back off.'

"For most of us men, the personal boundary is the space that encompasses the area that our arm, extended, would describe if we drew a circle around us." I asked Andy to stand up and help me demonstrate. "The handshake," I said reaching toward Andy, "as a traditional Western male greeting, allows us to make connection with each other without violating this instinctual boundary between us.

"When male boundaries are intruded upon, the signals are often subtle but usually very clear, man to man. They may include a widening of our eyes, arched eyebrows, a tightening of the lips, tensed shoulders or other stiffness in posture, an extended chest, a clenched hand, or, more emphatically, varying degrees of glowering, frowning, scowling, or inarticulate verbal cues." Several members of the group started laughing as Andy and I started acting like gorillas, pacing around, testing each other's boundaries.

"If none of these subtle signals are recognized by an intruder," I continued, "the signals may become more dramatic: a hand held out with a stiffened arm, shrugging off a proffered touch like a shoulder clasp or brushing away an unwanted touch, turning aside, stepping back, shoving the intruder's body away, or, even what is often a last recourse, a spoken admonition like 'Back off, motherfucker, get out of my face.'

"If these signals, ranging from subtle to increasing levels of volume are ignored, then boundaries are crossed and territory is penetrated until the core of the person feels violated. He'll consider himself challenged and up against the wall. Then the boundary violation feels like a clear and present danger rather than just an annoyance or an irritation. In this case the next response is the triggering of the fight-or-flight response. The man being violated will either completely withdraw, submit to domination in order to survive, or vigorously attack the violator."

As I stood face-to-face with Andy, well within his personal boundary, he acknowledged his discomfort and took a step backwards.

"Most of us learn these signals in adolescence. We learn the silent ballet of subtle gestures that informs us about just how close we can move toward another man or his felt sense of self—his possessions, territory, relationships, and ideology.

We learn that, rightly or wrongly, the consequence of failing to read signals properly is usually violence. A violation can be as subtle as an unwanted look or stare. Growing up as I did in urban street culture, I quickly learned that it is a violation of male protocol to watch another man with whom I was not well acquainted. 'What are you looking at, man?' may be the verbal response and challenge. If the stare persists after this warning, an attack will most likely be forthcoming."

"Although women are frequently victims of violence," Liz added, "we, unlike men, are not required by society to establish our sense of femininity through confronting or participating in violence as an initiation."

"As boys, however," I said, "we often prove our manhood through violent competitive sports, fights with one another, or training to be soldiers in war. Being a man means, in part, learning how to defend yourself and stand up for yourself in the face of aggressions ranging from the neighborhood bully to a hostile foreign power. We also learn that our role is to protect others from violence.

"So most of us feel that we must learn the language of violence in order to fulfill our roles as protectors and defenders of boundaries. There's a protocol and diplomacy of posture and nuance by which men negotiate power relationships with one another. Since traditional male culture, as I've experienced it, is often organized hierarchically, with a strong leader directing others, many of these negotiations involve dominance or submission."

"Women, on the other hand," said Liz, "have historically been exempt from the hierarchical demands of military service and also have been less involved in economic institutions that force men into submissive roles to other men. So we have more often had the opportunity to learn cooperative and egalitarian styles of communication. Consequently, most of us have more intimate friendships than men. We also have greater consent to do same-sex touching, hugging, and smiling and make other demonstrative displays of warmth and affection such as holding hands or putting our arms around each other."

"In my experience," I said, "intimate friendships between men are rare treasures. One of the reasons it is so difficult for men to establish intimacy is the complexity of this boundary language. A friendship results when we successfully negotiate our boundaries in a manner that does not require one or the other to submit or dominate, but rather allows us to forge a side-by-side relationship in which our boundaries are mutually relaxed. The basis for this relaxation is trust built on appreciation of mutual strength and a sense of alliance. Trust grows when another man shows that he will not enter your territory without your permission, that he will protect your territory in alliance with you, and that he will allow you entree to his territory.

"When we men do establish a bond, even friendly encounters, man to man, can involve displays of physical aggression. We may punch each other on the shoulder, backslap, fake a punch to the jaw or the body to elicit a flinch, slap one another's bottom, slap hands ('Give me five'), tousle each other's hair, and exhibit other nonsexual physical contacts. These acts affirm that the nature of our friendship gives us implicit permission to cross boundaries and mimic many behaviors that, without bonds of friendship, would be interpreted as hostile. We often insult one another in a good-natured way that most women find offensive or intimidating."

HARASSMENT OR COURTING

"Well, this is all very interesting," said Merle. "It gives me a lot of insight into male culture, but I don't really understand what this has to do with the issue that Lisa raised."

"I think it has a lot to do with the communication problems and perceptual differences we have," I replied. I shared my feeling that in order really to understand how women and men fail to communicate, we need to understand the cultural matrix that influences how men experience these issues, the male lens through which boundary issues are perceived. We also need to understand the cultural matrix that women find themselves in. "Let me go on a little more with this and see if I can pull it together," I said.

"The same rough behaviors that can affirm friendship and trust man to man, when exhibited by a man toward a woman can be interpreted as harassment and intimidation. So when women and men start working together, this can get very tricky. The man does not want to feel that he has to inhibit himself all the time and never be spontaneous or playful, and the woman wants to feel safe and know that she can relax without being hit on sexually or being intimidated in some way. It's no wonder that tension in the workplace is so high.

"Many men who attend our sex harassment workshops tell us that when they enter women's territory, they don't get the same sorts of boundary signals that they receive from a man. There often does not seem to be a wire on the perimeter that triggers an alarm that is clearly audible or visible to a man. So when men do not get that signal, they assume that either the boundary is open and they are welcome to advance or that they have not crossed over the boundary yet.

"In most men's experience, women often do not send a signal that is audible, to a male, until they have been violated at their core. Then men are surprised. They ask, 'Where was the subtle signal, the increase-in-volume signal, the firm drawing of limits, and the threat saying Back Off or Else? How did I get that close to your core without hearing a warning?'"

Most of the men sitting around the ashes of last night's council fire agreed that this sounded familiar.

Dave said, "If a woman laughs at a dirty joke that, in fact, was offending her, a man most likely assumes from that signal that they were having a shared and enjoyed experience of collegiality."

Alan added, "If a woman smiles at me when she's actually angry, I assume that she's enjoying whatever testing of boundaries I am engaging in and that our friendship is growing. Men rarely smile when they're angry. If a man smiles when he's angry, that may be the last thing you see. In the movies when the angry psycho killer starts to smile, it's usually just before he kills someone."

"If a woman doesn't shrug off a proffered touch," I continued, "does not physically withdraw, or doesn't attempt to limit the assertive behavior of a man, he assumes that she's accepting his sexual advances. Or, at least, when the intent is not sexual, we're led to believe that she's comfortable with his physically demonstrative way of expressing friendship. Now, this is very different from a man deliberately ignoring a woman's clear signals and advancing anyway. That is an act of aggression and domination. That *is* rape. And there is no excuse for it.

"Much of what is being called sex harassment, however, and even some cases of so-called date rape, seem to fall within this realm of missed communications. Harassment certainly exists. In all too many cases, however, what seems to be going on is not a malicious, intentionally violent, or disrespectful act, but rather a breach of courting protocol and ignorance about women's sensibilities and the mores of female culture. Men are often genuinely baffled when, at some point down the road, they're accused of violating women's boundaries. The current discussion of sexual harassment does not address the ways in which women contribute to the problem by sending double messages, mixed messages, or no message at all."

"In today's climate," added Liz, "any attempt to talk about the issue as a co-created one is usually labeled blaming the victim. But if men are not getting a clear message and then later held accountable for abusive behavior, then perhaps they're victims, too."

"Many men," I explained, "feel it's like going through a stop sign obscured by trees and getting a ticket because you should have sensed there was a sign there, even though it was not visible. The language around harassment makes the assumption that men should know what is acceptable and what isn't. But the truth is, often we really just don't know, especially in workplaces that have only recently integrated women. Men have to be told in the male mode of communication—firmly, clearly, and directly.

"To add to the confusion," I continued, "in our culture the testing of limits is frequently an integral part of the courting dance." We discussed the themes of films such as *A Room with a View, Frankie and Johnny, Groundhog Day, Green Card, Dangerous Liaisons, Crossing Delancey, Indecent Proposal*, and others that most of the men in our group felt accurately displayed a common male experience of courting. The common theme we identified is that the man persists in his pursuit until the woman eventually accepts or emphatically rejects him.

I suggested, "The no, accompanied by a smile, a posture of interest or curiosity, or a continuing visual gaze, does not read as an emphatic rejection through the male lens. That no reads as a play of the courting dance and as a test of our commitment, emotional courage, and resolve. We interpret it as a challenge to demonstrate that our self-esteem is high enough not to be crushed by rejection. Thus, we display to her our strength and capacity to succeed in an often rejecting world without succumbing to despair or fear.

"We may also persist," I continued, "in order to help her overcome guilt about being sexual by relieving her of responsibility and sweeping her away. Liz tells me that this is the predominant sexual fantasy in present-day woman's romantic literature and the secret unspoken contract in many romantic or sexual liaisons. If a man gets it right and properly responds to the sexual signals a woman puts out, then he's a hero. He's rewarded for successfully courting her. The result is consensual sex, a relationship, or marriage. If we respond the wrong way or misread the signals, then we are accused of being abusive. We are harassers, violators of women's boundaries. The result is a sexual harassment suit or, in the worst case, an accusation of date rape.

"A man who gets a mixed signal may persist in his advances," I said, bringing this talk to a close. "He doesn't know he's harassing because, in male protocol, if he had continued to violate a boundary, he would have been met with definite withdrawal or attack. Most men who've been through the courting dance have experienced the no that means yes, which is a different signal from the no that genuinely does mean no. A feminist slogan of the last decade says, What part of No! don't you understand? The male answer, while politically incorrect in the extreme, is, "the part that really does mean yes."

✒ COVERT DESIRES AND PERMEABLE BOUNDARIES

"I want to respond to that from the women's point of view, Aaron," I said. "There's another aspect to this situation that women are experiencing.

"I think it's true as you say that men are emerging out of an ancient tradition of being warriors and hunters. They've been conditioned to be vigilant around their physical boundaries. Women, however, are emerging out of a long tradition of being nurturers and gatherers. We are trained to be aware of our environment and to do what is necessary to keep it harmonious. This skill is part of a homemaker's genius as she goes about raising a family, maintaining a healthy home, and building social networks.

"This socialization is in conflict with being direct and establishing rigid boundaries. A woman may be reluctant to upset the flow. She may try to prevent rupturing a connection by giving double messages, sort of blowing smoke so she can stay under cover, without having to risk the disrupting energy that direct confrontation brings about."

It was important to me that I make the point that it is simplistic and degrading to call this type of behavior codependent, as many do these days, or to say that all women are intimidated by men's power. Certainly, these are characteristics that contribute to passivity. But what is driving this behavior from a deep archetypal and biological level is the female imperative to make human systems whole.

As we had pointed out in the group, women traditionally have had a mandate to preserve the flow in relationships and communities. In hunting and gathering societies, men frequently left for long periods of time. Often it was women who created the continuity in culture. Even in this "age of equality," many more men than women still commute to work farther from home or leave for military service and other pursuits while significantly more women still hold down the home front.

It had become clear during discussions among the women that when we are challenged to engage in direct confrontation, we're going against generations of acculturation that have trained us to be receptive and attentive to others' needs. The challenges of motherhood demand that we have flexible and permeable boundaries. To be a good mother, one has to be willing to let children access one's body for food and comfort. This is a way we women are fundamentally different from men. It's often necessary for children's survival that women put their immediate needs aside. But this maternal accessibility can be detrimental to a woman's survival when it becomes a reflex with which she engages other adults.

The more assertive women in our group were quick to point out that they run the risk of being perceived as unfeminine, just as sensitive men who express their feelings are at risk for being labeled wimps. When a woman says no, on some level she is confronting an ancient biological and cultural imperative that tells her she should say yes, even when, as in the case of child rearing, this may be at odds with her personal needs for rest, privacy, and space. You cannot tell a hungry, cold, frightened, or injured child, "I'm not in the mood to take care of you now."

I wanted everyone in the group to understand that when a man looks at a woman with yearning eyes, hoping for affection, there's a part of her that may respond, even though she may not really be sexually interested. Men frequently mistake maternal compassion about their pain or loneliness for accessibility or availability for sex. Often a woman has to take some time to distance herself from the mothering impulse in order to discover whether or not she wants to respond sexually. That's another reason why we sometimes try to stall for time, long after a man has expressed his desire to us.

"Another part of the problem for women," I elaborated, "is that, traditionally, dropping the handkerchief was done in a number of ways. In olden times, some women did exactly that. In most cases, however, dropping the handkerchief is a more subtle and complex dance. In our culture women have been socialized to convey sexual interest covertly. Open expression of sexual desire by women has historically been a violation of the social and moral codes defining courting propriety.

"We may want to date or may desire sex as much as a man, but our timing and pacing may be different. A woman may not be quite sure about proceeding with a particular man. We can feel intrigued and cautious at the same time. A man may know in ten seconds that he wants to have sex. But we may be thinking, Will this guy make a good husband or father? Do I want to risk pregnancy at this time in my life? For centuries huge numbers of women died in childbirth. For women, sex is potentially life-threatening; at the very least, it is life-transforming. There are other considerations, too, that add to the conflicts we have about our sexuality. Certainly, in this time of AIDS, these questions can all include real life-or-death concerns."

Marie added, "I've noticed that girls who give in to the stirrings of their blossoming sexuality are frequently labeled whores by boys and other girls as well. It was a real double message when boys encouraged us to have sex with them as a demonstration of our love, and then abandoned us afterward while they moved on to pursue those who held out. Most adolescent girls are instilled with a fear about their sexuality in a way that boys are not. Boys are taught that it's masculine to spread their seed. Girls are taught that it's feminine to protect their womb. Neither teaching is wrong. In fact, both are evolutionary attitudes. However, paradoxically, they're often in conflict."

"Most women I know are taught to be at war with themselves around their sexuality," I agreed. "We don't have the same cultural consent men have—to be up front about what we want. Out of the covertness training that most of us receive, a convoluted sexual response has developed within the female psyche. The yes that men hear in the no is an echo of this conflict. What we really need is for men to understand that process, to stop trying to overwhelm us, and to give us enough space to get in touch with what we really want.

"Women have, for the most part, been given little permission to express the wild, sensual, and passionate parts of themselves," I concluded. "The idealized archetype of femininity in our culture is the Virgin Mary, who is kind, compassionate, and nurturing. Her primary role is to be the Good Mother. Her pregnancy occurred through divine intervention, and it is considered blasphemous in the Catholic church to imagine Mary as a sexual being. The other half of the archetype, the Whore, was personified by Mary Magdelene, the great temptress of Jesus."

Fear of the power of female sexuality is still rampant in our collective imagination. Films like *Fatal Attraction*, *The Black Widow*, *The Hand That Rocks the Cradle*, *Body of Evidence*, and *The Crush* continue to reinforce the widely held perception that women's sexuality is dangerous, even evil. As we discussed the themes of these films, many of us realized that we felt we'd somehow lose our spiritual wholeness if we allowed our passions to become unbridled. To be feminine, in the idealized sense, is to be nonsexual, at least, not sexual on our own terms. This repression is compounded in contemporary culture by the masculinization of women in academia and the workplace, where an image of powerful women as essentially nonsexual is often promoted.

The Madonna is the good girl that many women have traditionally aspired to be. The negative side of the Madonna, however, as Marion Woodman notes in *Addiction to Perfection,* is that she is "cut off from the wisdom of her body. The virgin is frozen." As we discussed in the women's camp, many of us have felt locked out of our own bodies. An essential part of our empowerment is to reclaim our sexuality and our fierce inner beauty as an archetypal force that lies far beyond today's superficial, consumer-driven standards of beauty. It's ironic that one of the more powerful contemporary icons of women celebrating their unabashed sexual power is named Madonna. Everything about her blatantly confronts this paradox in the psyches and bodies of women.

"You would think," Doris interjected, "that with all the sexual freedom the last generation supposedly created, we wouldn't still be struggling with the dichotomy that we are either virgins or whores. There seems to be very little middle ground that encourages women of any age to explore a healthy relationship with their sensual needs. We think, 'If I don't have sex he will reject me for being a prude and if I do he will reject me for being a whore.'"

Marriage before sex was the traditional way for circumventing the problem in relations between the sexes. However, that ideal has long fallen by the wayside. In its wake, we all agreed, we need clear communications between the sexes to help direct sexual energies. Most traditional cultures contained them through ritual behaviors that guided their passions into channels that supported the growth of families and extended kinship systems, social networks, and communities.

✠ THE SECRET LANGUAGE OF WOMEN

As the day went on, the conversation moved into discussing the more subtle communications that go on between women and men. "Traditionally," I continued, "dropping the handkerchief is the way many women have conveyed their interest or availability to a man without seeming like a whore. These days dropping the handkerchief may be as simple as a side glance, a tilt of the head, a smile in response to a man's gaze, a laugh in response to a man's comment, or a gaze held longer than the usual three seconds. We may start spending more time in areas that he frequents, or sit or stand near him in the hope that he will turn his attention toward us. In most cases, these signals, even if displayed unconsciously, are deliberately ambiguous. They may mean interest or they may not. Often, only the woman really knows.

"The signals can range from the barely detectable to more obvious ones, like touching a man's hand or arm while speaking with him, picking a piece of lint off his coat or adjusting his collar or tie, standing closer to a man than usual, or giving a backward glance at him after walking past. We may feign or genuinely display some sort of helplessness that draws a man to us, on the pretext of fixing our car or the copy machine, or aiding us in some other manner.

"I've also noticed that there are various indirect, coy signals that are not broadcast directly to the man, but are also signs to convey sexual availability or interest, like when we play with our hair, sweeping it back or flipping it; adjusting our skirts to draw attention to our legs or rears; or crossing and uncrossing our legs more frequently than usual. We even might accentuate the sway of our walk."

"When I know that a man whom I want to attract is looking at me," said Susan, looking at the other women in the circle, "I tend to display more fluidity, sensuality, and grace. And I know that most women know exactly what I'm talking about. There's a subtle readjustment of the whole body and facial posture. We might hold our lips slightly parted and open our eyes wider. I think it's really disgusting that in advertising, they make conscious use of these nonverbal cues to convey a subliminal message by female models, a message that says, 'I am sexually available to you if you buy-consume-possess this product.'"

The women all agreed that we also flirt in playful ways, like commenting on a man's appearance or performance or teasing him about some personal characteristic in a way that doesn't shame him. We may make subtle innuendos. We may let a mutual friend know that we are interested so the friend can inform the man.

"One of the problems," I pointed out, "is that many of us display the same sorts of signals associated with courting simply because we want to be liked or admired. A woman may also send many of these signals as simple acts of friendliness, collegiality, and cordiality. This is natural. Most of us want to be appreciated by others. But if all the interpretation of the signals is left to the man, it is inevitable that all the blame for misreading them will also be his.

"Even more confusing, some of the same signals—downcast eyes glancing up (the Lauren Bacall look), nervousness, fussing with hair or apparel, standing with one leg bent and the hip cocked to one side, conspicuous head-nodding in agreement with a man's comments, and more—can signify a woman displaying submission to a dominating male who has power over her. We may not wish to risk offending him by displaying powerful, hard, potentially challenging signals like extended, nonsmiling direct eye contact. We may be displaying soft signals merely to ensure that we will be listened to by an otherwise uninterested male."

"I think the same issues come up in male society," Aaron added, "when a man feels that, with a more powerful male, he must demonstrate subservience in his body postures and language. The difference is that, for the most part, male submission signals do not simultaneously carry the sexual overtones that female ones do. There are cases of homosexual sexual harassment in the workplace, but they are rare. There are also cases of powerful females harassing subservient males. They, too, are in the minority."

"But Aaron," objected Dave, "one of the reasons for that is that most women are not turned on by subservient males. Most of the sensitive men I know have experienced women telling them that they now like them more in a platonic way but are not sexually interested."

"Yeah, that's true," he agreed. "Even staunch feminists, like Gloria Steinem and Jane Fonda, are more interested in millionaire businessmen than sensitive human-services workers."

"I think that many men would like to experience having a powerful woman enhance their financial status merely because she appreciated their beauty, sensitivity, or sexual performance," Dave continued. "But it seems like the women I've come across rarely date down economically. We men, however, are still conditioned to expect to marry women who are not our economic equals."

"So, where there's an inequality of power woman to man," Aaron said, "there can be a different dynamic at work than in a man-to-woman situation. The same signals often mean very different things in male culture than they do in female culture. A lot of man-to-man eye contact may be interpreted as a confrontation or a challenge by both men. The same contact woman to man may be interpreted as a flirtation by the man or an unwelcome advance by the woman. If a woman steps inside a man's personal boundary without first being invited to do so, he may regard it as flirtatious; a woman may regard the same behavior from a man as an invasion; in a man-to-man context, it is almost always regarded as a challenge.

"I've noticed that I can break eye contact with another man with whom I'm speaking, even turn my back on him while I pace around the room, but as long as the verbal communication remains collegial, the other man will usually still feel comfortable and connected. If I do this with women, however, they often see this sort of behavior as disengaged and rude. They are likely to feel insulted. Women are much more uncomfortable than men when they can't see whom they are speaking with."

"On the other hand," I added, "as women feel more connected to one another, we tend to exhibit more eye contact as a display of our growing intimacy. We're conditioned to pay close attention to the details of relationships."

"Men, however, who become closer to each other," replied Aaron, "seem to display increasingly less eye contact.

Since we're conditioned that our job is to watch the perimeter, once we feel at ease with another man, we feel free to return our attention to what we believe is our primary purpose."

As we discussed this further we realized that when gazing crosses gender lines it often takes on new meanings. Women may interpret a man looking away during conversation as being rude when, in fact, it may actually mean that he is feeling relaxed in the relationship, and men may interpret a woman's intense gaze as seductive when she is merely being attentive to the conversation.

A smile and extended eye contact from a woman may mean, "I'm dropping my handkerchief and I hope you'll pick it up—I'm sexually interested in you." Or it may say, "I'm paying attention to what you're saying or doing and am simply being polite, friendly, and cordial," or "I'm intimidated by the power dynamics of our relationship and am displaying soothing signals to you so that you will not fire-threaten-abuse me." How's a man to know?

When a man tells a woman a dirty joke, he may mean, "I'm telling you this joke because it has sexual innuendos that I'm hoping you will respond to—in my own rough way I'm telling you that I'm sexually interested in you." Or it may mean, "I respect you as an equal and regard you as a colleague or friend." And in a manner congruent with male culture and male language norms, he may be saying, "I'm attempting to break tension and deepen collegiality." Or it could mean, "I don't really trust you. I'm not sure you can handle the rough-and-tumble world of our business. I'm testing the thickness of your skin." How is a woman to know what the intent really is?

"If we women laugh or say nothing in response to a man's crude joke," I pointed out, "then what can the man do but assume that we are being collegial, like the other guys he works with? How is he supposed to know that we are feeling intimidated and sexually harassed when he is merely displaying behaviors that are acceptable in most segments of male culture? If we give a man a lot of eye contact during a conversation, how are we supposed to know that he's interpreting our behavior as a courting signal when, within the context of our female culture, we're just being polite? We need to check these things out with one another, ask questions, and keep the road clear instead of letting missed or misinterpreted cues build up to create a climate of distrust and tension."

I think men are confused because, on the one hand, they are told that women are equal in the workplace and should be treated and rewarded in exactly the same way men are, but on the other hand, they are told that women are a special category of people from a completely different culture, with a host of special sensitivities and protocols that are different from the acceptable protocols men use man to man. Men discover that women often do not clearly communicate just what those protocols are, but expect men to figure them out. If men guess wrong, then they are accused of bad behavior. A woman recently won a sixty-thousand-dollar lawsuit against a foreman because he swore at her. A similar suit by a male employee, however, would seem ludicrous.

We, on the other hand, are confused because if we exhibit the direct, confrontive, and assertive behaviors that in male culture are called "courage, leadership ability, and directness," we are labeled ballbreakers or bitches. Yet, if we are friendly and collegial, then men assume we are on the make. These double standards are driving us crazy.

"I can relate to that," said Susan. "It seems like if I'm friendly with the guys at work, they almost always interpret it as a come-on. I end up feeling like I have to be a cold bitch just to fend off the wolves."

Andy interjected, "I sympathize with you, Susan, and genuinely understand how that could be a drag for you, but just once," he said playfully, "I'd love to experience what it's like to be sexually harassed. I really do wish that someday, even just one woman would treat me like a sex object." This comment drew pained expressions from a few women and laughter from several of the men who agreed with him.

We know that most people do not really want to be degraded, treated like a sex object, or placed purposely in a shaming or hostile environment. As we questioned Andy about his comment, however, it became clear that what he really meant was that he would love to have a woman assertively communicate her desire to him without his having to guess about her intention.

In our workshops over the last few years, we have talked with thousands of women and men about this issue. Although it may happen regularly on TV, it's very rare in most men's experience, except for those men who have fame or fortune or hunk celebrity status, for women to approach them directly and announce their interest by asking for names and phone numbers, by calling first, asking them out on dates, buying them gifts, or going so far as to blatantly proposition them. So, it's not surprising that surveys indicate the majority of men regard unsolicited sexual propositions as complementary while the majority of women regard them as insulting.

 # PATHWAYS TO PEACE

Although there were potentially dozens of topics we could have raised in the light of gender justice, we spent the rest of the afternoon discussing the issue of courting versus harassment. It both embodies the essence of the gender war and reveals some of the pathways to gender peace. Toward that end, we synthesized a few ideas that expressed what it was we wanted from one another.

Joel summed up what a lot of the men felt by saying, "If women really want peace with men, then please don't flirt with us unless you really mean it. And tell us straight out when you feel we're crossing your lines, not ten years later."

Because many men have trouble translating the more silent aspects of women's feelings, they need to be told directly, "I don't like it when you talk that way," "Please take your hand off me," "I don't want to be hugged by you," "I'm absolutely sure that I'm not interested in having a sexual relationship with you."

Learning how to say no clearly, helps create gender peace. So does learning how to say yes when you want to. If women become more up front about their desires, it will be helpful. In today's climate men can no longer risk misreading a woman's covert desire to be swept away. Consequently, what we are hearing at our workshops is that more women who are unable to assert their desires are finding themselves alone. Women must say, "I'm interested in you," "I want to get to know you," or "Would you like to have dinner with me?"

Our advice to the women when this issue came up was, Don't get discouraged if he rejects you. That happens to men all the time. It's the downside of making the first moves; you have to be willing to risk rejection. On the upside, by being assertive a woman is more likely to get what she wants rather than having to choose either from whichever men blatantly indicate interest in her or staying alone because no man has approached her in an appropriate way.

Clearly, both women and men have to realize that there are different kinds of meanings behind no. The no that may really mean yes can be better understood as not now, later, maybe or maybe not. But in every case, men need to respect that any kind of no means Stop, Now!

I think all of us in the group really understood that women need men to respect their pace and that men must begin to take what women say at face value. Our whole analysis of the no that means yes is meant to breed understanding and insight and bring some honesty to the debate about harassment, something that is sorely lacking in today's climate of blame and shame. It should not be interpreted, however, as any justification for men ever to violate women's boundaries. All nos mean Stop. Period.

Being a fierce feminine warrior, however, doesn't mean that women have to wound men. A woman who wants to reject a man's advances but also wants to preserve the friendship or working relationship, can say, "I'm flattered that you find me attractive, but I just want to have a professional relationship with you. Is there any reason why that's not going to be possible?" This sort of approach lets him know that what he is doing is not wrong in and of itself, it's just not what you desire. After all, a significant percentage of marriages originate from relationships made in the workplace. So there is nothing essentially wrong with men or women displaying courting signals on the job.

Asking a question like the one above leaves an opening for discussion that can either defuse retaliation or inform you right away that the man is going to be small about it and become a problem. A woman can say, "I know you're just trying to be friendly to me, but what you're doing or saying is making me uncomfortable, it isn't what I want." If a woman rejects a man's advances in a manner that indicates she still regards him as a person with feelings of his own, then the rejection is a lot less likely to incur lingering resentment.

The men in our group sincerely wanted women to understand that they respect it when women are direct. However, not all men are so reasonable. If they don't stop coming on, then comes the time for a shaming comment, or calling others for help, or for a grievance hearing. Anytime a man persists in a boundary violation and no escape or help is available, then direct physical aggression against him may be the only recourse.

The group had faced the fact that as new gender roles evolve, more women are taking responsibility for their own physical well-being. If women feel unprepared to deal with the possibility that violence might enter their lives on some occasion and have doubts about their ability to protect themselves, they might consider taking self-defense and empowerment classes. Men represent the majority of homicide and assault victims, so clearly not even men are immune to this problem. A woman needs to learn how to defend herself so that she can meet violence head-on without becoming a victim or expecting another man to become one in her defense. And many men do not know how to protect themselves, much less another person.

From the perspective of gender justice, however, if a woman chooses not to draw her boundary clearly, for whatever reason, then it is unjust to place all the blame on men for violating it. Because men are expected to make all the assertive moves in the courting dance, they are often poor at sensing where women's boundaries really are. Women can help by displaying some understanding of the male courting paradox. They can educate other women about how to proactively establish clear boundaries, rather than reactively responding only after the boundaries have been crossed. They can also help educate men about how they would like to be approached and demonstrate to them the differences between actions that feel like sexual harassment and ones that feel like genuine, respectful admiration.

When we addressed the issue of what men can do to help the situation significantly, there was agreement that none of us should let the gray area, the ambiguous or double-message aspects of this issue, close us off to the serious and legitimate complaints women have about men who intentionally harass them. Men can be allies to women by speaking out about abuse and real harassment and by demonstrating a willingness to listen to, and act upon, women's just complaints. Also, they can help a great deal by educating other men, especially our youth, about how to approach women with respect and by discussing the real differences that may exist between male and female sensibilities. This is also fertile ground for discussion in mixed-gender groups.

So, to achieve gender justice, or even to get a sense of what it might look like, women and men must inform each other about what they really want from one another. And this communication needs to go beyond unilateral demands, proclamations, and protests. We must, women and men as partners, together renegotiate our social contracts and revise our institutions to embrace the ideals of gender justice. To achieve justice, both genders must become willing to give as well as to take. Trust between women and men will grow when we can demonstrate that we are just as concerned about the suffering of the other gender as we are our own. Out of this attitude will grow mutual respect.

The prescriptions for creating new relationships between women and men were clearly beginning to emerge from our work together. The bottom line to our discussion was that women want men to slow down, listen to them, and treat them with more respect, and men want women to be more open about what they really want and to be more direct about what they do not like.

This had been a hot topic to host in our council, yet at the end of the day, even though we did not all agree on every point, we were still together. There was still goodwill and even playfulness amongst us as we cooperated in preparing the evening meal. We took the evening off from trying to lubricate the wheels of gender justice and just enjoyed our company, taking turns telling stories around the fire and singing songs. The next day was to be our last full day together. In the time that remained, we hoped to explore new visions of partnership between the sexes.

CHAPTER NINE

The Art
of Partnership

Every breath taken in by the man who loves
and the woman who loves,
Goes to fill the water tank
Where the spirit horses drink.

— ROBERT BLY

T HE SOUND OF HOOFBEATS awoke me. Four men on
horseback rode in to the edge of camp. One horse had a
rider and what appeared to be the body of a deer, wrapped in
plastic, slung across its rear. Another horse had two riders, one
of whom was a teenage boy. I recognized a couple of the guys
as the cowboys we had seen upon our arrival.

"Morning, Miss," one cowboy said, tipping his hat. "I
didn't mean to startle you so early in the morning, but we were
wondering if you might have seen a horse wandering out this
way."

From his vantage at the edge of the camp, he could not
see the horse we had tethered in the trees at the other side of
the clearing.

"Yes," I replied as people started rousing themselves and
came over to join us. "We've got one here on the other side of

this clearing. It came running, out of control, through our camp during the storm."

"I'd sure like to see if it's the one we're missing," he said.

I nodded my assent. They climbed down from their horses and two of them walked across the clearing with me while the other two waited by their horses, looking uncomfortable.

"Yeah, this is Black Eye," he said as we arrived where the horse was secured. "I was beginning to wonder if we'd ever see her again. I'd like to thank the man who rescued my horse."

"It wasn't a man," I replied. "It was Lisa." I gestured in her direction as she walked across the camp toward us.

"Well, I'll be!" he exclaimed.

"We didn't know what to do with the horse after Lisa calmed her down, but we've been letting her graze. Lisa used her hairbrush to comb out her mud-splattered coat and pulled hundreds of burrs out of her mane."

Lisa walked up to us, patted Black Eye on the flank, and said, "That's a beautiful horse."

"Thank you," he replied. "The storm caught us by surprise. The horses spooked with all the thunder and got loose. We found them all except her."

The two men introduced themselves as Eddie and Walt. We introduced ourselves, and then Walt asked, "What are you all doing way out here? We aren't used to seeing many folks this far up. In fact, we usually see more bears than people."

I explained a little about what we had been doing as we walked together, with Black Eye in tow, across the clearing toward the others gathered around the fire. I invited them to join us for coffee. Eddie accepted and waved the other two, who were still hovering at the edge of camp, over to join us.

"This is my youngest son, Matt," Eddie told us. "And this big guy is my older boy, John. These folks are out here trying to figure out how women and men can get along with one another better," he told them, by way of introduction.

"That's simple," said John. "We never come out here with women. We come to the mountains to get away on our own for a while and everything seems to go just fine," he said, chuckling.

Matt went up to Black Eye, patted her flank, and said, "Boy, am I glad to see her. I thought I was gonna have to ride all the way back to Blue Water Creek scrunched up behind John's sweaty back," he said, wrinkling his nose at his brother. Eddie informed him that he had Lisa to thank, which he promptly did.

"Guess it was a good thing for us that these folks didn't leave their women at home, John," he said, ribbing him.

We sat down for coffee and Aaron asked them what they had been up to during the week. Walt, who was Eddie's brother, told us they were taking Matt on his first deer hunt.

"It's a family tradition," he told us. "For generations, every man in our family has gone out to kill his first deer when he was about sixteen. He learns how to ride, shoot, and hunt smaller game when he's younger, in preparation for this trip. Afterwards, we have a big venison cookout with all the family and the neighbors. After that, the boy, in our eyes, becomes a man."

It turned out that was why they had been riding through our camp our second night out. They merely wanted to get in place before dawn in an area where they have hunted for years. All the ominous projections we read into their actions were just that, projections. In reality they were doing what many men, in hundreds of cultures, had done for ages. They were introducing a young man into the world of his elders.

After coffee they got up to leave. Eddie said, "I wish you all luck with solving the problems of the world. If you all survived the storm together and caught our horse to boot, you must be doing something right. But if you've been living out of those little backpacks for a week, I bet you could use some fresh food." He unwrapped the deer carcass and carefully cut off a generous chunk of its rump. They bid us farewell. Then, as cowboys will do, I guess, they rode off into the sun, which had gloriously risen over the rim of the eastern ridge during our talk around the fire.

INITIATION AND GENDER GROUND

"Wow," said Merle, "that was very interesting. I had this basic conception about all cowboys being macho, Marlboro men. But those guys were pretty cool."

"I'm impressed by how consciously they were doing a coming-of-age ritual for that young boy," said Larry. "I would have loved to have had some kind of experience like that with my father. Most adult men give very little attention to the younger ones. I never felt like a man until I had sex for the first time. And even that was pretty unsatisfactory, as initiations go. Everything was going fine until a cop rapped on the window of my car, but that's another story."

"I knew that I should have done something for my son when he became a teenager," added Doris. "In my grandmother's days, the men would have come and taken him off into the wilderness to do a vision quest in which he would fast and pray for direction in his life. When he returned he would sit with the elder men who would interpret his experience and help give it meaning. But nothing like that exists in my family anymore. Not even amongst the full-bloods. In some tribes women still do Beauty Way blessings for the girls when they mature, but not much is happening for boys that I know about. I did the best I could as his mother, but I know it was inadequate."

"When we were with the women at Blue Water Creek," said Susan, "I felt like I was having an experience of initiation with women elders that I would have loved to have had as a young girl. Did you feel that, too?" she asked, looking at the other women.

"Definitely," answered Marie. "All that talking we did about our cycles and reweaving the Motherline felt like something that women have been doing for eons, but forgotten in recent generations. I hope Larry and I can do something worthwhile with our own daughter in the next couple of years."

"We created a ceremony for our daughter Noelani shortly after she got her first menstrual cycle," I told them. "Some of my women friends who were like her aunties and I took her into the mountains above our home in the Santa Barbara foothills. We blindfolded her and walked her through the oak forest to a spot on a creek that had been inhabited by the Chumash Indians in centuries past. Then we told her stories about our mothers and grandmothers, invited her to ask questions about being a woman, gave her lots of unsolicited advice as well, and then ritually bathed her in the water.

"We brought her back to Aaron and his men friends, who had prepared a celebration dinner for her. They welcomed her as a young woman, no longer a child, and pledged their intention to be there for her as friends, allies, and brothers. During the course of conversation, we invited her to ask the men questions she had about boys and men."

"She asked some pretty tough questions," added Aaron. "And a lively conversation ensued about dating, kissing, and how to deal with boys that don't show respect. She loved the whole experience. And it was healing for all of us as a community of women and men as well. I don't think that the form of the initiation is all that important. What was most valuable for Noelani was simply the full attention that we, as adults, gave her. It demonstrated that we regarded her life as having worth and that we were all aware that she was transforming from one phase of life to another."

In most non-industrial societies, at the onset of puberty young men and women are initiated into men's and women's lodges. In those lodges they experience a deep form of mirroring from their same-sex group. In such rites of passage, the elders transmit information to the young men and women about their emerging roles as adult men and women coexisting in community.

Even in our own culture, we can easily see that women and men have had various traditional means of meeting apart from one another. For generations women gathered over coffee, cooking, or quilting; men bonded in bars and at sporting events, and raised barns together. But in modern society, we lack workable forms of initiation that deepen our sacred sense of self within the context of our gender.

Few of us in our group have had any meaningful ritual initiation into adulthood. And that is true for most people in our culture. Consequently, we have struggled over the years to embrace our authentic gender identity and have become mature adults without the support of an intact community of elders. We are only now discovering that the developmental needs of each sex require the strength and security that come from affiliation with a bonded, same-sex group.

As we talked among ourselves, we realized that our initiation experiences, such as confirmations, bar mitzvahs, first sexual experiences, or high school graduations, did not really do it for us. Similarly, most young people today are not taught how to respect and honor their own cultural identities or, consequently, that of the other sex. They arrive at adulthood with a confused idea of gender identity and are often also mystified and distrustful about the other sex's differences.

From one perspective we can view initiation as a conservative institution that limits our freedom by conditioning us in specific, even rigid ways. That is the shadow inherent in initiation. Philosopher Sam Keen notes that one of the gifts of American culture is our "lostness." If we are not overly defined by tradition, then we have more opportunity for self-discovery and expansion into new roles and possibilities not imagined by previous generations.

It's important, however, not to let the shadow of initiation cause us to discard initiation as a workable ritual for healing, maintaining, and invigorating society. Rather, we should salvage the valuable aspects of initiation and construct our rituals so as to convey a sense of belonging, welcome, appreciation, and worth to our children without simultaneously limiting their imagination about what they can become. Healthy modern initiation rituals can awaken our imagination and stimulate our capacity to explore our further limits.

I think the need for gender community is deeply ingrained in both sexes. And, in the absence of initiation, many societal problems persist. In a desperate attempt to create gender affiliation, inner-city boys frequently form gangs in which acts of violence often become the measure of masculine courage. This happens in the absence of intact lodges of mature men who can be mentors to younger men and guide them toward using their masculine power in service to the community.

As we continued our discussion, Andy said, "This makes a lot of sense to me. I can see how useful this could be with the teenage boys I work with."

"I think it could help a lot," Aaron agreed. "When a young man is initiated into an intact, mature male community, he doesn't need to find his manhood through perpetrating violence on others. In the faces of the older men like you, and through the guidance that you provide, the young man can see the possibility for his own mature masculinity. He's empowered and entrusted with the responsible use of this masculine power."

"It's also true for girls, "I said. "I've noticed that teenage girls, in the absence of mature women who feel powerful in their own right, often end up becoming obsessed with beauty, with all its negative consequences for their physical and mental well-being. In a women's lodge, however, through the presence of women of all ages, sizes, and shapes, a young girl can discover the mysterious, multifaceted nature of femininity. I think that an initiated woman learns that her true beauty and real power are much deeper and more lasting than her external appearance. And then she can learn to use this feminine power with integrity."

As we had discovered in the time spent apart on this trip, deep masculinity and femininity are most effectively experienced by men and women meeting separately. We thereby increase our own self-esteem, and we can help each other deepen the experience of masculine and feminine soul. The absence of the other sex and the opportunity to connect meaningfully with our own gender culture help us understand the collective experience of contemporary men or women. We become both validated and empowered. It is not until we meet alone with our own sex that we realize the extent to which we may have been struggling to adapt to male or female norms.

It appears to me, however, as I do more of this work with women and men, that regular separation of the sexes does not have to create antagonism. Rather, it can create a solid ground upon which we can build harmonious relationships between women and men. Separation can then be viewed as a step toward integration. After our group had separated and had spent some time apart, both the women and men felt more able to be honest and clear about their own feelings and more willing to hear from the other sex. By standing firmly rooted in our own gender culture, we gain greater appreciation for the unique gifts the other sex holds without becoming overwhelmed by the differing points of view.

Aaron and I have noticed that when we meet separately for too long, however, we risk losing perspective and fomenting the habitual scapegoating of the other sex. When bonded groups of women and men take the next step and make a commitment to meet regularly with each other, they can create partnership and peaceful coexistence in both their personal relationships and their communities at large.

It seems that initiation is an essential step toward developing the capacity for healthy partnerships between the sexes. One of the challenges in rebuilding our fragmented communities is for us to find ways to create contemporary forms of initiation for our young people. Aaron has been working with some men to form mentoring communities that help guide young men into soulful manhood. I've been gratified that women have created Take Your Daughter to Work days in order to guide young women into the workplace and help them achieve the self-esteem that can result from economic empowerment. These efforts, and others like them emerging around the country, are hopeful attempts at giving birth to new rites of passage for our children.

In addition to creating new forms of initiation, we must become aware of the underlying belief systems that still influence our current relationships and continue to breed immature behaviors in women and men. All too frequently, I've noticed that the basic templates for relationships between women and men are based on old myths that do not mutually empower all of us. In many cases the myths do the opposite by trapping both women and men in stereotypical roles that bind our capacities for real freedom.

As I looked at the different body types of our group members, it occurred to me that metaphors are not merely abstract literary ideas. Images have a mysterious way of subtly defining us and even changing the way we look and act. I've noticed when I go to the gym that men and increasing numbers of women who are also caught in the image of the Hero pump up and stiffen their bodies in specific ways. They frequently deny their feelings, overestimate their strengths, and lose a capacity for spontaneity, flexibility, and joy in their bodies and emotional lives.

Women and some men as well who are caught in the image of the Princess soften their bodies, make themselves "small" in various ways, and tend to feign helplessness. They deny their real powers, ask others to do what they could learn to do for themselves, and rely on others to protect them and solve their problems. In these ways our abstract myths become concrete realities. The heroes and heroines of our cultural myths are frequently imprisoned by these roles because they have not been initiated into mature adulthood. Thus, they remain lost in adolescent modes of behavior.

"Are you interested in hearing an ancient story about an uninitiated man and woman?" asked Aaron as we continued discussing this topic.

"That sounds intriguing," Larry replied and got up to put some water on the fire for a second round of tea and coffee. Others nodded their agreement.

"Of course," said Aaron, teasing, "this won't be a story that any of us initiates can relate to, right?"

"Sure, Aaron," said Andy. "After a week of this we've got all this relationship stuff completely figured out."

Everybody laughed. I was glad we could keep our sense of humor in this process. Unwinding generations of old patterning gets overwhelming at times.

✤ ECHO AND NARCISSUS, THE UNINITIATED WOMAN AND MAN

The ancient story of Echo and Narcissus in many ways exemplifies the modern coupling of the so-called codependent woman and the self-involved, narcissistic man about whom so many popular psychology books have been written. For the past few days, our group had been struggling with issues around the split archetypes of Victimizer-Victim and Hero-Princess. Echo and Narcissus form another part of the old broken foundation upon which so many shaky relationships are built. By uncovering the rest of the foundation, we hoped to find fresh bedrock upon which to erect a new psychological structure that mutually empowers and supports women and men.

I related to the group that according to the Greek myth as told by Ovid, Narcissus was a son of the naiad (a water spirit) Liriope and the river god Cephissus. His mother once asked the seer Teiresias if Narcissus would live a long life, and the seer replied, "Yes, but only if he never knows himself." One day while Narcissus was hunting deer, Echo saw him and fell in love. She was a girl who liked to chatter and frequently kept Hera distracted while her husband, Zeus, went around sleeping with various nymphs. When Hera became aware of Echo's ruse, Hera cursed her and said, "The tongue that made a fool of me will shortly have shorter use." Echo thenceforth could not initiate a conversation or fail to answer others when addressed. She could respond only by repeating the last few words spoken to her.

Echo wanted to express her burning love for Narcissus, but could only reiterate his words. When she is rejected by him, "She frets and pines . . . cannot sleep . . . becomes all gaunt and haggard . . . her bones remain and then she is voice only—an echo."

Narcissus rejected many maidens who desired him and many young men as well. Eventually, one rejected youth implored the heavens to curse Narcissus with unrequited love. Nemesis (the Goddess of Vengeance) complied and cursed him with a love for himself, one that he could never win over.

Narcissus finally fell in love with his own image reflected in a still, silvery, glassy pool. When he realized that his lover was his own image, he observed that "my riches make me poor." He then, like Echo, faded away into death, where he continued to gaze forever into an Underworld pool, never finding relief from his obsession. Only a flower—the narcissus—exists where he had once been.

In the setting of this myth, Narcissus was about sixteen years old, the same age as our new cowboy friend, Matt, the Hunter of High Mountain Deer. Narcissus's role is indicative of the fate that befalls a young man who is not initiated by other adult males whose fierce presence is strong enough to overshadow his reflection in the pool of his self-absorption. He gazes at his reflection, lost in the dwelling place of his mother, a water spirit.

I believe that if the adult men in a boy's life fail to initiate him into deep masculinity, his emotional body will not mature. An immature, emotional body is too weak to meet the full-blown erotic, emotional, and psychic presence of an initiated woman. That's why uninitiated men inevitably become enmeshed with uninitiated women. In a directly parallel manner, of course, a girl who has not been initiated into deep, fierce femininity by women is also unable to meet a mature man without losing her sense of self and becoming overwhelmed by his power.

The highest calling for relationship with the other sex may be the transformation and deepening into soul that an "other" can evoke. But when we are not strongly rooted enough in our own gender ground, we become overwhelmed by the strong force of another. Rather than risk destruction, an uninitiated woman or man withdraws into the seemingly safe environs of the self (narcissism) or tries to take refuge in the identity of someone else (codependency). Ultimately, there is no safety either in living imprisoned within the boundaries of our self or in losing that self by attempting to merge with another.

Only through continual transformation can we grow into our full potential as human beings. Narcissistic behaviors— anorexia, substance addictions, and obsessions with beauty, work, wealth, and even death—are all attempts to erect defenses against the world of transformation and to fill the void that grows behind emotional gates barred against the transformative power of relationships. In men these behaviors are frequently symptoms of a male role model that is erected to serve as a defense against dependency on a woman or in reaction to fears of separation from her. In women, these behaviors frequently reinforce dependency on men and manifest themselves in fears of autonomy and resistance to female maturity.

Echo is analogous to an anorexic girl who cannot mature and thus wastes away. She is an archetypal image of a young woman with a dependent personality disorder, a victim. She is not initiated and, as such, cannot initiate a relationship. She can only repeat the words of others. She has no boundaries or independent will, indicated by the fact that she must reply when spoken to. She is the codependent woman who conspiratorially aids Zeus in his sex obsessions, just as codependent wives enable their husbands to drink and work themselves to death rather than risk the transformative combat that may arise if they lovingly confront them.

In the Echo position, it appears that women identify themselves through their association with the other person. As Liz and I have heard from many women over the years, this perspective makes women weak and encourages them to blame men for their weakness. Echo, who decomposes into a mere phantom of a person, exemplifies the dependent, modern "girl" who resists or fails to receive initiation and transformation into womanhood. At age seventy-one, Helen Gurley Brown, the editor of *Cosmopolitan*, still regarded herself as a girl. She feared the "shadows, the terrors of the night and the devils" of aging that would make her end up like "an old crumb," rather than welcoming the gifts of maturity and the depth of soul they can bring to life.

Women who cannot bear their own emotional distress often choose a thick-skinned, self-involved man into whom they think they can transfer their pain because he rarely seems to react to it. A narcissistic man inevitably attracts a dependent woman. She feeds and reinforces his self-involvement, and he reinforces her dependency. Just as the Hero's rescuing of the Victim prevents her from finding her own strength, the codependent woman enables the narcissistic man to become consumed and destroyed by his self-involvement. Echo and Narcissus are paired in this tale because they co-create each other. They are part of the same dysfunctional and split complex represented by the Knight-Princess and the Hero-Victim. In this type of relationship, as actress Shelley Winters once wryly put it, "We had a lot in common, I loved him and he loved him."

No mere compliant or complaining maid like Echo will be able to shake a narcissistic man loose from his self-involvement any more than a heroic male who is always protecting women will ever help a woman develop the skills to defend and rescue herself. Both the strident blaming and the petulant whining of the Echo-identified woman only drive a man deeper into his own self-involvement. By taking refuge in himself, a man can develop an attachment to an inner state that the onslaughts of a challenging relationship cannot penetrate. As psychologist R. D. Laing succinctly said it, "To consume oneself by one's own love prevents the possibility of being consumed by another."

Many men stop communicating with their wives and bury themselves in work, the newspaper, or TV in an unconscious attempt to regain their sense of self seemingly threatened by the emotional power of women and their capacity for evoking transformation. But isn't this the very power that makes women so attractive in the first place? When a man is not rooted in the deep masculine, he is easily toppled by a

THE ART OF PARTNERSHIP

woman's potent emotional storms. In the Narcissus position, men resist relationship because to relate is to risk losing their already weak connection to the self within; the so-called fragile male ego. The changeless image of Narcissus peering into a placid pool is a face that is truly unaffected by relationships. Yet that which does not grow in relationship to the outer world can only wither and die, as did Narcissus.

It seems unlikely that a man can deeply engage with a woman until he is properly initiated, develops the strength to heal his wounds, and can stand in a place of power, maturity, and equality with the feminine. Then a fierce and present woman, who can *lovingly* confront him, becomes a force that can genuinely transform him instead of driving him deeper into himself. Men initiate boys into manhood, women bring girls into womanhood, and then women and men further initiate one another into depth. Without surrendering to the transformations that these same- and other-sex relationships can bring us, we risk remaining barren souls locked in the prison of ourselves or "hungry ghosts" inhabiting the bodies of others with little awareness of our own potential.

TOWARD A NEW VISION OF MEN AND WOMEN IN MATURE PARTNERSHIPS

When Aaron finished his tale and accompanying discussion, I continued talking about the story rather than shifting to another topic. I believe the myth of Echo and Narcissus exemplifies one of the fundamental struggles between the sexes: the battle between desire for relatedness and needs for autonomy. Traditionally, as we previously discussed, women have primarily located self through relationship and men primarily through being autonomous. In this myth we see the dangers that come from becoming too polarized into one or the other position.

Depending too much on our relationships to define who we are can be self-destructive. But so can too much autonomy. Each gender takes a risk when it attempts to enter into the other's mode of feeling: Men fear becoming lost in relationships as they seek greater intimacy; women fear the loneliness they may experience when they seek their identity separate from a relationship. Living solely in the web of relationships can present a great obstacle to a woman's empowerment, just as a man's overzealous quest for autonomy can breed isolation and alienation from the nurturing pleasures of relationship.

The following chart describes a few of these polarities at their greatest extremes along with the alternative partnership positions that we seek on the bridge between women and men. Through practicing our council process—the art of partnership—we can eventually learn how to achieve a healthier and more integrated balance between autonomy and relatedness.

Aaron and I have come to believe that our western spiritual mythologies aggravate the social and biological differences between the sexes. The patriarchal myth of the one All Powerful God in the Sky and the matriarchal myth of the All Good Goddess of the Earth are two severely limiting cosmologies that have outlived whatever purpose they once served. We now have the opportunity to move beyond the spiritual con-

Traditional Female Identity	Co-Creating Partnership	Traditional Male Identity
Relatedness	Integration	Autonomy
Dependency	Interdependence	Independence
Codependent	Empathetic	Narcissistic
Victim	Partner	Rescuer
Covert	Diplomatic	Overt
Passive	Assertive	Aggressive
Erotic Power	Creativity	Production Power
Family	Community	State
Submissive	Interactive	Dominating
Fearful	Attentive	Unresponsive
Home	Shared Work	Career
Nurturer-Gatherer	Eclectic	Provider-Hunter
Women's Rights	Gender Justice	Men's Rights

cepts that divide contemporary women and men and to develop an understanding, common to many nonwestern cultures, of God, nature, and soul being both male and female — a co-creating partnership.

As we discussed this concept further, Doris informed us, "In Navajo mythology, there's both male and female types of rain. And many other aspects of nature as well are imagined as having feminine and masculine qualities."

Then Joel mentioned, "Most romance languages ascribe female or male suffixes to nouns, but the gender of things is imagined differently in different cultures. For example, some languages, like Spanish and French, depict the ocean as feminine, and other languages, like Italian, characterize the sea as masculine. These different characteristics seem to support the idea that both sexual essences are always present in all things. What we imagine depends on which aspect we put our attention on."

"Yes," added Jerry, "just like different cultures imagine either gods or goddesses as embodying the essence of the sea."

"I don't think there's any doubt that the religious symbols of a culture have a powerful effect on the psychology of its members," offered Liz. "What we imagine as divine also inevitably becomes the image that we most honor in our daily life."

I responded to Liz, saying, "Feminists like Charlene Spretnak observe that the dominant symbol of a male god 'keeps women in a state of psychological dependence on men and male authority.' If we, however, replace a dominant male deity with a dominant female one, as most spiritual feminists suggest we do, will this really be progress? Or will we merely create a different but similar set of problems?" A religious and symbolic system that has an exclusive gender identity presents serious problems for the excluded gender and thus ultimately for all of us.

As we talked we began to realize that the bottom line to the whole issue was that *neither women nor men have ever really enjoyed true equality and partnership in our culture.* What we seek appears to be an entirely new kind of relationship between women and men. A quest for a true equality must be based upon a deeper understanding and a new respect for our differences. This task is more connected with rediscovering a deep gender identity than merely revising our social, political, or economic roles.

It seems that at this juncture in human evolution, it is more useful to embrace religious and philosophical belief systems that honor the sacredness and inherent value of both sexes. Many images can inspire us in this new direction. For example, even in the ancient roots of monotheism the earliest Hebrew name for god was *elohim,* a plural word of obscure origins that could mean goddesses and gods and was also used to mean the spirits of the ancestors. The ideal of co-creationism has roots in many diverse cultures throughout time.

I was reminded, as we sat talking together, that numerous mythological divine couples have guided the development of human culture. The Sumerian Inanna and Dumuzi, Navajo First Man and First Woman, Babylonian Tiamat and Apsu (also known as Sweetwater and Saltwater), Egyptian Isis and Osiris, Japanese Izanami and Izanagi, and many other sacred partnership images can inspire us to create a new vision for the future.

The story of the Hindu divine couple Shiva and Parvati is one of the more ancient nonwestern tales concerned with balance and partnership between the sexes. Shiva's primary delight in life was meditating on the mountaintop, a male self-preoccupation in some ways similar to that of Narcissus. Parvati often wearied of Shiva's perpetual asceticism. In vain she, like Echo, waited patiently beside him in adoration. Plunged in meditation, Shiva did not even notice her presence. However, in this myth, instead of the couple becoming absorbed in deadly preoccupation like Echo and Narcissus, Parvati awakened her feminine fire and thus changed the outcome.

One spring day, as the story goes, the gods became concerned about Shiva's growing aloofness and said, "If he remains forever in a rocklike state of meditation, how will he be able to destroy the enemies of the earth when a renewal is necessary?" Brahma, the high god, decided to attempt tearing Shiva away from his contemplations by sending Kamadeva (Love) and his wife, Pleasure, to distract him. Choosing the moment when the great beauty Parvati was approaching Shiva to worship him, Kamadeva drew his bow. But at the very moment when he was about to loose the shaft, Shiva saw him and with a burning flash of his third eye consumed Kamadeva. While Pleasure mourned over Kamadeva, believing him lost forever, a voice spoke to her, saying, "Your husband will return. When Shiva weds Parvati, he will give back Love's body to his soul."

Parvati desired this marriage, but, unlike Echo, she quickly wearied of the god's indifference. She began meditating in a hermitage, seeking her own direct connection with the Great Mystery. It turned out that she was very good at meditation. She started having many fine visions and accumulating spiritual powers. One day she was visited by a young Brahman who praised her for her deep devotion and powerful focus, but also tried to persuade her to cease her spiritual practices and return to the world of relationships and other pleasures.

Parvati merely became angry at the young man for disturbing her meditations and sent him away. But then the man revealed himself in his true form: he was Shiva. Moved by Parvati's degree of spiritual attainment, Shiva promised her his love, which was something she still desired. She demanded, however, that first he return the body of Kamadeva to Kamadeva's wife, Pleasure. Shiva agreed, and Parvati then consented at last to meet his desire as an equally empowered being and with an equal passion of her own. It is said that their embrace made the whole world tremble.

As we started discussing this tale, Aaron said, "I think this story eloquently addresses an age-old conflict between many women and men: Shiva's need to contemplate on the mountain and Parvati's need for intimacy. Eventually, Parvati lets go of trying to be with Shiva and goes off on her own to sit in contemplation, increasing her own power. It's after this that Shiva approaches her, wanting to be in relationship. Unlike the uninitiated Echo, Parvati doesn't wait for Shiva to love her in order to feel complete. By attending to her own spiritual process, her innate need for connection becomes tempered through her willingness to seek her own autonomy."

"It's interesting that in this myth balance is restored to the world through a female moving toward the pole of independence," I added. "Since nature hates a vacuum, the masculine is then naturally drawn into relationship in a way that no amount of direct demand for intimacy could ever bring about. To gain complete fulfillment, Shiva had to step away from autonomy and Parvati had to shake herself free from the stultifying bond of relatedness.

"Often, in my experience," I reflected, "if one person in a couple persists in dwelling at the farthest edge of the autonomy-relatedness pole, it may be partially in reaction to the other partner's polarization. Rigid identification with the extreme of a traditional gender role can be an attempt to draw the other off his or her pole. This is the essence of gender war: women and men trying to change one another through unwavering commitment to their individual points of focus. Building a bridge toward the middle, where both partners have familiarity with either pole, represents real hope for balance and a soul-making relationship."

Lisa then said, "There's another old story I love that has a different angle. In a Sumerian myth about the goddess Inanna, balance between the sexes is restored through the movement of a male god, Enki, toward relatedness, compassion, and empathy. In this five-millennia-old tale, Inanna descends to the Underworld, where she is killed by the Goddess of the Underworld, Ereshkigal. Her resurrection is achieved through the intervention of Enki, the God of Wisdom and Water.

"From the dirt under his fingernails, Enki creates creatures who go down to the Underworld and assist Ereshkigal, who is groaning with the pains of birthing. They groan and moan with her in shared empathy. She's so relieved that she consents to bring Inanna back to life. Enki heals through empathy, by meeting Ereshkigal on her own ground, just as Parvati rejoins Love and Pleasure through gaining autonomy and meeting Shiva on his own territory.

"Then, Ereshkigal demands that someone be consigned to the Underworld to take Inanna's place. This is accomplished in the end through Dumuzi, Inanna's husband, and his sister Geshtinanna, each taking turns six months of the year to live in the Underworld."

"That's a great story," I told Lisa. "It seems like in the religious system that you're describing, unlike in our culture, neither gender carries all the pain or all the power. Inanna shares the throne and command of the realm with Dumuzi, and he shares in the necessary time spent in the Underworld. Both share the gifts and burdens that accompany each domain. In the new mythology of sacred partnership that we are attempting to create, neither god nor goddess is dominant. Instead, we have interdependence, mutuality, and a willingness to learn from one another."

ALCHEMICAL MARRIAGE

"Maybe the fact that we haven't had any of these juicy divine couples in our own mythologies to inspire us has affected how high the divorce rate is in this country," suggested Larry.

"Yeah, I hardly know any long-term couples anymore. And most of the people I know that are dating only go out with someone for a few months before they move on," agreed Dave.

"It does seem that, as a culture, we've been losing our capacity to sustain deep, long-term, committed relationships. I've heard that over half of all marriages now end in divorce. It makes me sad," said Merle. "Alan and I try so hard to make it work. But there's just not much support out there, on any level. Both of our parents are divorced and so are many of our friends."

"Most of the young women I know are struggling with how to be strong and independent," said Susan, thoughtfully. "We find that as soon as we get involved with someone we start losing ground. We are either in relationship and feel varying degrees of powerlessness, or we retain a sense of power and then struggle with the sorrows of being alone."

"Men feel that way, too," countered Andy. "I'm afraid that if I commit to a relationship and have a family, then I'll enter some kind of economic treadmill that I won't ever be able to escape from. As much as I yearn for a committed relationship and children as well, I'm also afraid of losing my freedom, even my soul in the process."

"I think that the loss of intimacy, authenticity, and soul in our society affects our capacity for relationship," said Joel. "The art of partnership comes from our capacity to recognize our common issues as well as our inherent differences. Perhaps through this work we can create compassionate communities that support the unique values of each gender culture. I've discovered during our week together that we don't need to become more like one another, just more deeply ourselves."

"I think that this work can lead us all toward a new understanding about the psychological ecology of gender in our communities as well as in our individual relationships," said Aaron. "Moreover, it can create a base from which to build connections between us that can be mutually empowering. The practice of the art of partnership is essential for creating the sacred marriages and soul-nurturing relationships that we're all hoping to have in our lives. And, I strongly believe that people who are in solid relationships with one another form one of the most important building blocks for creating healthy communities."

"Don't you all think," Liz queried the group, "that the deeper purpose of intimate relationships is more than procreation, mutual support, and companionship? Perhaps men and women get involved with one another for the making of soul. By acknowledging the potential for power and magic inherent in our relationships, we can use power and magic to achieve the most profound growth that we humans are capable of. The art of partnership can be viewed as a spiritual discipline, a means by which we can encourage the deepening of men's and women's souls."

She continued with enthusiasm, "There's a great book by John Welwood called *Journey of the Heart* where he says that intimate relationships have become the new wilderness that brings us face to face with all our gods and demons. The other sex can push buttons that may never be activated in same-sex associations. Since it is only when our issues are brought to awareness that they can be healed, our intimate partners can provoke an evolutionary response that is difficult, if not impossible, for us to achieve alone."

The fears that Andy and Susan shared reflect a recent trend away from surrender and "falling" in love. This may be a healthy swing of the pendulum away from dysfunctional patterns of romantic love as depicted in romantic literature and pop songs that extol the virtues of merging and "fusion"—the sentiment that states "Baby, without you I am nothing."

The archetypes of love, such as Kamadeva, Eros, and Aphrodite, can affect us through a state of possession in which we completely lose our individuality and our will. It is possible, however, to encounter Eros through communion, as did Parvati, rather than possession, as did Narcissus. In a state of communion with each other, we are not possessed by love or desire, but rather maintain a dynamic tension of separation and surrender.

Aaron then said, "From my readings in Jungian psychology I learned what is now one of my favorite dictums of alchemy, 'Separatio before Coniunctio.' The old alchemists believed that before elements could be properly joined, they must first be separated into their essences. Healthy relationships don't thrive unless we can be both separate and together. I think that autonomy and relatedness are interdependent qualities. The ability to be separate is an essential ingredient for being in equal partnership with another person. Our well-being arises from connection with our own self. If that link becomes weak or disturbed, then our capacity for relationship also suffers.

"Liz and I are inspired by couples who are in communion rather than possession, cycling in and out of connection to each other and connection to themselves; they ebb and flow. This kind of cycling is the natural rhythm of tides, heartbeats, seasons, and all life. It seems like this kind of ebb and flow are essential for Eros to continue to be present in our relationships over time. I know that it takes skill and practice to be able to do this dance. Most of us are more familiar with being either entirely merged with the other or not in connection at all."

Our old patterns are to assume that our way is the only way, "my way or the highway," as it is sometimes said. If we hold that position, just as was demonstrated in the group's anger and shadow councils, then we sit in constant judgment of our partner. A relationship that lacks a vision of partnership is often caught in an either-or awareness rather than the need for both-and. Without this vision we may unconsciously close our hearts or even create distance through anger and blame in a desperate attempt to find ourselves again.

We've noticed that people involved in intimate relationships usually have a greater proclivity for one or the other of
these polarities. We may have a greater capacity for relatedness
or autonomy. As such, we often have a need to be "initiated"
by our partner into that which we do not know well. This is
where the alchemical process of relationship begins walking
the razor's edge.

The challenge, as always, is whether or not we can
acknowledge our differences and approach each other with an
open stance to learn. Often these differences are a constant
source of wounding in relationship. It seems most helpful
when our attitude in our individual relationships, just as in the
group council, is one of honoring and investigation. When we
have a willingness to explore and even surrender to our partner while honoring and remembering our authentic self, we
create soul-making in relationships.

Sacred relationships were the main topic of our final
council together. It seemed a fitting end to our week-long discussion. We could have gone on into the night, but it was time
to close the council and to start making some preparations for
our departure.

✀ FAREWELL,
DEAR COMPANIONS

Andy carefully roasted the venison on a spit over the fire while
others gathered miner's lettuce, mountain clover, and edible
wildflowers to make a salad. This would be our last meal

together and, thanks to Eddie's generosity, there was plenty for all.

The mood during dinner vacillated between joking and recounting stories about the various foibles we had encountered to stretches of awkward silence and somberness as it dawned on us, one by one, that our time together was indeed coming to an end. We had raged at, blamed, rejected, feared, listened to, wept and laughed with, respected, loved, and deeply appreciated one another. It was a lot to feel in these last few hours for a group that would most likely never meet again, at least not in its current form with all the same participants, because we were all so far flung.

It was getting late. Because we'd moved our camps farther out than anticipated during the course of the trip, we would have a considerably longer trek back to the parking lot. Fortunately, the journey was all downhill. To facilitate getting to our homes at a reasonable hour, we would have to break camp early and hit the trail by dawn at the very latest. Ugh.

If we were going to have any meaningful good-byes, now was the time. Liz dragged out the stone, with the now-smudged but still legible partnership symbol chalked on it, from her pack and said, "Let's pass this stone around one last time and as a way of bidding farewell say something about what we have learned and what we have gained from one another during our time together."

Gloria took the stone and held it to her cheek, saying, "It was very powerful for me when the men repeated back to us what we heard us say about our issues. For over twenty years I've been trying to get men to listen. They usually either shut down, walk away and ignore me, or try to fix me, interpret me, or take care of me in some sort of condescending way. This is the first time in my life I have ever felt deeply listened to and fully heard by a group of men. That, more than anything we've done together, has restored my hope and confidence that we can move a little deeper into community with one another.

"Also, this image of the Solar Goddess has stuck with me for days. I've spent so much of my life trying to acquire male power by becoming more like men. I leave here intrigued by the idea that I can become more powerful by becoming more deeply female instead of endlessly stalking male power and the myriad wounds that accompany it."

Dave then said, "When I first arrived at camp, I glanced around and immediately dismissed all of the women except Susan as not being my type. I wasn't very interested in any of you, as a consequence," he added, looking around at the women. "But since we've all lived, cried, caught fish, and braved storms together, you all look really beautiful to me. I'm somewhat mystified why I didn't see it before.

"You know, the women I work with every day never communicate to me in the way you have, nor do we ever seem to share real life adventures with one another. It's all just shuck and jive, work and flirt, hassle and hustle. I realize from being with you all that I need something more than that. I feel much more interested after this week in being in a committed relationship with a woman. But I also know that to support that I need a community like this, where women and men can tell the truth to one another and don't have to be so uptight about how they act all the time or how they look either, for that matter," he said, grinning.

Several people broke out laughing as we looked at the scraggly crew of unshaven men and the women with smoke-smudged faces and flyaway hair. That he saw us as beautiful, with all our warts and idiosyncrasies right out in the open, felt like the biggest miracle to come along since plastic wrap.

Marie then told us, "I was blown away to hear about the depth of wounding men suffer. As an attorney I find myself always battling the consequences of their behavior. But before this trip I never really understood just why men are the way they are. This idea of gender justice is a tough one for me, though. I'm so used to thinking about things in terms of women's rights and women's wounds. But I can't deny the deeper truth I've experienced with all of you—that women and men have both been wounded and that both also have an equal capacity to create change. I don't know how this is going to affect my practice, but it occurs to me that some of my more forward-thinking colleagues are now basing their practices more on mediation than adversarial strategies.

"I'm tired of fighting gender wars where there's always a winner or a loser. Women and men are tearing each other apart over child-support laws and custody practices that are clearly often gender-biased. Even the winners seem to lose something in the process when it winds up with the children losing their relationship with one parent or another. That's not justice; that's like cutting the child in two pieces to please the state. Maybe we've created a new profession here and in the future we'll be able to flip through the yellow pages and find listings for gender mediators and gender diplomats."

Joel spoke next. "As I think back over this week's conversation and try to sum things up for myself, what stands out for me is that women are upset about men's abuse of physical, political, and economic power, and men are just as upset about women's misuse of emotional, psychic, and sexual power. We're both clearly disturbed about misuse of power, but it manifests as concern about different domains where one sex feels the other sex has an advantage. Women are troubled by men's denial of feelings and vulnerability, and men are disturbed by women's denial of power and influence in shaping the culture. Again we're both confronting duplicity in the other, but in different domains.

"As we become more aware of the ways in which we unconsciously collude to co-create society's problems, I think we'll also become more empowered to create change. I believe that change will come through us developing a fierce commitment to breaking out of old gender stereotypes and embracing new ideas that allow us to become more committed allies in all things.

"I'm excited about the possibility of a new social movement emerging that embraces the best of the women's movement and the men's movement while leaving the enmity and polarization behind. A gender-justice or gender-peace movement could be much more inclusive of the broader population of women and men who can't relate to either gender movement. This week was much more advanced and much more real than anything happening on my campus these days. I thank every one of you for your honesty and your courage," he said, whipping off his battered straw hat and bowing to the assembly.

Lisa draped her arm over Joel's shoulder as he straightened up and said, "Yeah, Joel. I want to go back and host these kinds of dialogues in the university, too. I hope we can continue to have these sorts of councils where we need them the most. Our educational systems affect all our other institutions in the way they prepare students for their professions. I feel empowered to stand up to the stifling voice of political correctness that dominates academia these days and lobby to create forums where men and women can both openly talk about their differences without fear. I'm also hopeful that at least those of us who live in the Bay Area can get together once in a while to continue this conversation."

There was resounding agreement that it would be desirable to keep meeting, whenever possible, and it was suggested that even those who lived farther away could manage occasional reunions. We agreed to mail everyone an address and phone list after we returned home.

Then Andy continued our last go-round, saying, "What sticks with me is this idea that our problems are co-created. I can see that when men go to strip shows and women cheer men on the football field, we are both saying that we admire it when women and men exploit their bodies for our entertainment. Both sexes are contributing to the gender war anytime they participate in an institution that has gender injustice at its foundation.

"In order to build gender peace, we men are going to need the help of women—not to shame us and condemn us for coming out of an unbalanced past—but to join with us in creating a society that embraces gender justice for both women and men. In order to do that, we have to become men who are neither pseudo-heroes without feelings and needs nor subservient drones solely working to serve women and children.

We must find our own authenticity, free from both the hard images of old-school men and the soft images suggested by new-school women.

"So, I see a strong necessity for men to keep meeting together in contexts where they can tell the truth about their lives. I would also like to be in a regular gender council and in a committed relationship with a woman as well. Maybe one will lead to the other. Who knows? All I know is that tonight I feel at peace and very hopeful about the future. I thank you all for your truth and the genuine affection I have felt from many of you."

Then Doris said, "As I leave this council, what seems clear to me is that equality isn't something that can simply be given to us by another person or gender. We must first feel equal within ourselves. Then that equality will be reflected in the world. I too feel hopeful that there are many ways in which we can support this task with each other and in our partnerships.

"We can clean out the cobwebs of dishonoring beliefs from our own house. We can approach the other sex with the idea that it represents a different culture with its own particular values, assumptions, and priorities. We can either make war by attempting to impose our culture on men, or we can make peace by attempting to negotiate ways for us to coexist and enrich each other. We have much to gain from holding a stance of openness and cooperation, rather than control and judgment. We're all guilty of fearing what we don't understand. And we need to find forgiveness where we can, if we're going to move forward at all."

Doris sighed, looked up at the night sky, and continued. "I know many people still imagine that nature is feminine, but tonight the bright, clear light of stars feels very masculine to me, yet the dark of the night feels more like a feminine mystery. Together they are beautiful. Apart they would be oppressive. I love this idea of both male and female elements being present in all things, and it's an image that I'm going to carry home with me."

Alan said, "Well, come Monday morning I'm going to be swinging a hammer again. And I don't know exactly how I could describe this week to the guys I work with. But what I can say is that this is the most honest group of women I've ever encountered. And even though some of you guys are a little strange," he added, grinning at the men, "I've really enjoyed being with you this week, too, in a way that I never could be with my 'buddies' back home. It's been real. And Andy, we live about ten miles from each other. I'd like it if we could get together with a couple of other guys and keep meeting once in a while, too.

"I think the most important thing that's happened to me this week is understanding how real and common many of Merle's needs are. I see that a lot of stuff I've tried to write off as her neediness is really more about my own selfishness. I realize that her need to connect is the very thing I fell in love with in the first place. I remember thinking when we met, Wow! This woman really likes being with me. It felt so great after dating all these girls who weren't so sure. So, if I don't have the energy to listen to her now, maybe there's something wrong with my life, not her. It was amazing to hear all you women share such similar experiences. I really get it that we live in different cultures. Instead of judging you so hard for being different, I'm going to start listening more. I don't want to end up like that flower guy who died in a pool that Aaron was talking about."

Susan said, "I think that discussions like these are much more valuable than the hurling of missiles across the gender gap that's so common these days. We really could use something like this at work. There're over four thousand employees in my company. It would affect our whole community if we could simply talk to one another the way we have here. These peace talks gave us an opportunity to really hear each other and discover that many of our disagreements have equally valid, even if different points of view.

"So often, through blame and condemnation, we've mutually shamed each other. What I've experienced this week, however, is that through honest communication, even though we may not agree on everything, we mutually empower one another. And mutual empowerment is really in the best interest of us all, don't you think?

"Oh, yeah. One last thing. You know, Dave," she said, looking across the fire at him, "when we started out on this trip I thought you were the biggest jerk. I was really ticked off at you that first day out. But I've really been impressed by the risks you've taken and your capacity for change. And you're not hard to look at, either," she said, smiling slyly, as she had done more than once. "I want to respond to your request for women to be more up front. I'd like to get together with you when we get back to the city. You don't have to say anything right now, but I'm going to give you my number and you call me if you'd like a date. Okay?"

The surprised smile on Dave's face seemed to indicate that this suited him just fine.

Larry said, "Well, I'm really looking forward to seeing my kids tomorrow. I feel more validated as a father now than I ever have. I'm less uneasy about the fact that Marie is the primary breadwinner and that I am the primary bread baker. It feels like a natural evolution in the big paradigm shifts we've been talking about all week. I also feel more connected to men than I have in a long time. Being in the domestic sphere so much of the time makes me kind of alienated from men. I mean, I've been at PTA meetings where I was the only father present.

"One thing I've realized this week is that we men need to take a much stronger stand against men's violence and sexual harassment of women. If we don't, we'll never have gender peace. By the same token, hearing women admit their own capacity for violence and abuse, for the first time ever, healed some deep wound in me. I'm so tired of fathers being blamed for all the problems, violence, and failure to support children. More and more men are being put in jail when they can't pay enough, but women aren't held equally accountable for how they spend the money or even for living up to their visitation agreements. It gets under my skin because I'm trying so hard to be a committed dad, and I know many other men who are as well.

"So while it gives me no real pleasure to hear women admit that they also sexually and physically abuse children, and in various ways also fail to adequately nurture or support them, it puts the issue of neglect into a more genuine perspective. Just like other forms of family violence, it feels less like a gender issue to me now and more like a societal issue that affects us all. We all need to form better alliances, stronger families, extended kinship systems, and connected communities to care for our kids. And we need to provide more healing contexts for parents of either sex who are disabled in their capacity for care."

Merle said, "I can see that the only way we can truly be equal partners is through men and women taking full responsibility for how they can both be cruel and abusive and also by offering more support and understanding. Most of us have violence within us, but it seems like men and women often act it out in different ways. I've also learned a lot this week about how I really have thought of myself as a victim. I usually blame Alan for our relationship problems. But now I understand that when I make him responsible for fixing everything, I give my power away. Men or women alone will not be able to heal the mess that this world has become. We are clearly going to have to do it together.

"I'm inspired to go home and talk to my women friends about how we, as women, are also doing things that contribute to the environmental crisis and the war machine. I just don't think there's such a thing as real power without responsibility. So on that note, I'm going to start looking for a part-time job when I get back. Instead of blaming Alan for everything, I want to shoulder some of the economic burden and have a little more direction for my own life, like Parvati. Maybe that will also allow Alan to work a little less and have more time and energy for our relationship. I'll let you know how things work out."

Jerry then stood up and exclaimed, "I've been divorced from my own male body and apologetic about my masculinity for as long as I can remember. I still feel that it's very important for men to support the major ideals of feminism. But after this week I see the damage that my anti-male beliefs and overidealized views of women have done to me. I want to say, for the first time in my life, that my cock is holy and that it appears that there really are sacred images of masculinity that can inspire us as deeply as the Goddess. I also see the promise of a gender-justice movement representing a further evolution of the women's and men's movements in partnership—where neither women nor men are lesser or greater—like your Shiva and Parvati," he said, looking toward Liz as he handed the talking stone to her.

"Thanks, Jerry," said Liz, who spent a minute looking at everyone. The flames of our last fire crackled and sparked, making flickering, rosy shadows on all our faces. "All your eyes are shining right now. You are quite a sight to behold. Everyone of you has moved and delighted me with your commitment to honesty on this trip. This idea of speaking the whole truth to each other has been a very key part of our reconciliation work.

"It's important to remember that there are layers and layers of truth. We all started with our anger and then got in touch with the fear of one another that was hiding behind the anger. As we worked our way through the blame and shame, a great deal of grief came up and then, going to an even deeper layer, we experienced the authentic wellspring of love and appreciation we have for one another. I think that in every circumstance in life all those elements are present and that if we fail to tell the whole truth to one another, not much is going to happen that is of value.

"I was so impressed with you, Gloria, for the initial part you played in helping us get in touch with our fear. You stuck to your guns and stayed with your authentic feelings. It helped us all deepen into another piece of the truth. In order to move through that hard place, you had to risk being vulnerable with all of us. And I feel we all followed that lead with more courage and fortitude than I ever hoped could come forth in one week."

Then Aaron said, "After this week, more than ever before, I believe that women and men can move away from the polarized, gender-war rhetoric that's been dividing us and our social institutions, and that we can create many more forums for communication between the sexes that have the potential to unite and heal us. And those forums can take myriad forms. Not everyone has the luxury to go into the woods for a week. And not everyone needs to.

"This week together we've become more familiar with a place where we, as women and men, can stand in our full dignity and otherness while at the same time developing compassion and understanding for the other sex. What we've learned we can share with others. Now, they may not need to break so many hard rocks in order to find fertile ground. We've laid a few planks on the bridge to gender peace from both sides of the gap. Hopefully, that will allow others to start out a little closer to the middle than we did.

"Recent studies in learning theory and speculations about the manner in which new ideas and behaviors become adopted indicate that a very small, focused group can alter the behavior of a much larger society. Just a few birds in a flock or a few fish in a school that turn can change the direction of the larger group. Some people call this the 'hundredth monkey effect,' named after a controversial study about an entire group of monkeys who reportedly started washing their food in a certain way after about one hundred of them learned the new behavior. So, I bid you, my fellow monkeys, farewell. And I hope we can share our new behaviors with a few other monkeys along the way."

We stood around the fire holding hands in silence for a while. Then Liz starting quietly singing a song. After a bit, as everyone got the words, we joined in:

We are the dance of the moon and the sun
We are the light that's in everyone
We are the turning of the tide
We are the hope that is deep inside.

As we became more familiar with the song, we started singing together in pretty decent harmonies. As it should be. When we finished singing, Andy broke open a pine cone and handed everyone a seed. He asked us to imagine that our hopes for gender peace were invested in the seed. We laid each seed on the snakeskin, still on the altar as a bridge between our sacred masculine and feminine images. Then, to our surprise, he rolled up the skin with the seeds in it, dug a small hole in the ground near the lakeshore, and buried it. We all looked in silence as this simple ritual unfolded before us. Merle walked to the lake and with her Sierra cup scooped up some water, causing the moonlight to dance and shimmer at the water's edge. Then she spilled it on the earth covering the seeds. Tears were in many eyes.

Then, breaking the silence, Doris ended our council, borrowing some words of the native American "Beauty Way" and altering it with a few words of her own:

In beauty it was begun.
In beauty we walked in one another's moccasins.
In beauty we listened to the song of our own souls.
May there be beauty all around us as we go about our
    lives.
In beauty it is finished.

We clapped and yelled, whooped and stamped our feet. The sound of our voices echoed off the granite ridges as the waning moon began to rise high over the council ground. It felt like a good beginning.

To date, neither of us has been back to Grace Lake. But perhaps today there is a small tree growing as a living symbol of the peace we pray will continue to grow between women and men. If not there, then surely this image is growing in our hearts. And we hope that a seed has been planted in your heart as well.

NATARAJ PUBLISHING

is committed to acting as a catalyst for change and
transformation in the world by providing books and tapes
on the leading edge of personal and social consciousness
growth. "Nataraj" is a Sanskrit word referring to the
creative, transformative power of the universe.
For more information on our company,
please contact us at:

Nataraj Publishing
1561 South Novato Blvd.
Novato, CA 94947
Phone: (415) 899-9666
Fax: (415) 899-9667

We feature outstanding books and tapes by bestselling
authors Shakti Gawain, Gabrielle Roth, Hal Zina Bennett,
Hal and Sidra Stone, and others. To request our
free catalog with a complete listing of our books and
tapes, please call us toll free at:

(800) 949-1091

FOR
ADDITIONAL
READING

Adler, E. "The Underside of Married Life: Power, Influence and Violence." in L. H. Bowker, ed. *Women and Crime in America*. New York: Macmillan, 1981.

Anderson, W. *Green Man: The Archetype of Our Oneness with the Earth*. London: HarperCollins, 1990.

Archer, J., and B. Lloyd, *Sex and Gender*. Cambridge, England: Cambridge University Press, 1982.

Baber, A. *Naked at Gender Gap: A Man's View of the War Between the Sexes*. New York: Birch Lane Press, 1992.

Baumli, F., ed. *Men Freeing Men*. Jersey City, NJ: New Atlantis Press, 1985.

Bernstein, J. "The Decline of Masculine Rites of Passage in Our Culture: The Impact on Masculine Individuation." in L. Mahdi, and F. and M. Little, eds. *Betwixt and Between*. La Salle, IL: Open Court Publishers, 1987.

Bliss, S. "Kokopelli: Ancient Fertility God as New Model for Men." *The Sun*, December 1991.

Bly, R. *Iron John: A Book About Men*. Reading, MA.: Addison-Wesley, 1990.

Bly, R. *Loving a Woman in Two Worlds*. New York: Harper-Collins, 1985.

Bly, R., J. Hillman, and M. Meade, eds. *The Rag and Bone Shop of the Heart*. New York: Harper Perennial, 1992.

Bolen, J. *Goddesses In Every Woman: A New Psychology of Women*. San Francisco: Harper and Row, 1984.

Bolen, J. *Gods in Every Man: A New Psychology of Men's Lives and Loves*. San Francisco: Harper and Row, 1989.

Boer, C., trans. *The Homeric Hymns*. Dallas: Spring Publications, 1970.

Brumberg, J. J. *Fasting Girls: The Emergence of Anorexia Nervosa as a Modern Disease*. Cambridge, MA: Harvard University Press, 1988.

Campbell, J. *The Way of the Animal Powers*. London: Summerfield Press, and San Francisco: Harper and Row, 1993.

Carlyon, R. *A Guide to the Gods*. New York: William Morrow, 1982.

Cavendish, R. *Mythology: An Illustrated Encyclopedia*. London: Orbes Publishing, and New York: Rizzoli International Publications, 1980.

Coleman, A. and L. *The Father: Mythology and Changing Roles*. Wilmette, IL, Chiron Publications, 1988.

Crossley-Holland, K. *The Norse Myths*. New York: Pantheon Books, 1980.

Dames, M. *The Sibury Treasure*. London: Thames and Hudson, 1976.

Diamond, J. *The Warrior's Journey Home: Healing Men Healing the Planet.* Oakland, CA: New Harbinger Publications, 1994.

Dalbey, G. *Healing the Masculine Soul: An Affirming Message for Men and the Women Who Love Them.* Waco, TX: Word Books, 1988.

Downing, C. *The Goddess: Mythological Images of the Feminine.* New York: The Crossroad Publishing Company, 1987.

Druck, K. *Secrets Men Keep.* New York: Doubleday, 1985.

Edinger, E. *Anatomy of the Psyche: Alchemical Symbolism in Psychotherapy.* La Salle, IL: Open Court Publishers, 1985.

Elgin, S. *Gender Speak: Men Women and the Gentle Art of Verbal Self Defense.* New York: John Wiley and Sons, 1993.

Evatt, C. *He and She: Sixty Significant Differences Between Men and Women.* Berkeley, CA: Conari Press, 1992.

Faludi, S. *Backlash: The Undeclared War Against American Women.* New York: Doubleday, 1991.

Farrell, W. *The Myth of Male Power.* New York: Simon & Schuster, 1992.

Farrell, W. *Why Men Are the Way They Are.* New York: McGraw-Hill, 1986.

Farrer, C. R. "Singing for Life: The Mescalero Apache Girls' Puberty Ceremony." in L. Mahdi, and F. and M. Little, eds. *Betwixt and Between.* La Salle, IL: Open Court Publishers, 1987.

Fine, R. *The Forgotten Man: Understanding the Male Psyche.* New York: Harrington Park Press, 1987.

Freedman, R. *Beauty Bound.* Lexington, MA: D.C. Heath, 1986.

Friedan, B. *The Feminine Mystique.* New York: Dell Publishing, 1974.

Funk and Wagnalls, eds. *Standard Dictionary of Folklore, Mythology and Legend.* New York: Harper and Row, 1972.

Gelles, R. *The Violent Home: A Study of Physical Aggression Between Husbands and Wives.* Beverly Hills, CA: Sage Publications, 1974.

Gerzon, M. *A Choice of Heroes.* Boston: Houghton Mifflin, 1982.

Gilligan, C. *In a Different Voice: Psychological Theory and Women's Development.* Cambridge, MA: Harvard University Press, 1982.

Gilmore, D. *Manhood in the Making: Cultural Concepts of Masculinity.* New Haven, CT: Yale University Press, 1990.

Goldberg, H. *The Hazards of Being Male.* New York: The New American Library, 1976.

Goodale, J. C. *Tiwi Wives.* Seattle: University of Washington Press, 1971.

Gray, J. *Men Are from Mars, Women Are from Venus.* New York: HarperCollins, 1992.

Guirand, F. ed. *New Larousse Encyclopedia of Mythology.* New York: Crown Publishers, 1989; originally published 1959.

Gutman, D. *Reclaimed Powers: Toward a Psychology of Men and Women in Later Life.* Evanston, IL: Northwestern University Press, 1994.

Haddon, G. P. *Body Metaphors: Releasing God-feminine in Us All.* New York: The Crossroad Publishing Company, 1988.

Harding, C. ed. *Wingspan: Inside the Men's Movement.* New York: St. Martin's Press, 1992.

Harding, E. *Women's Mysteries: Ancient and Modern.* New York: Putnam, for the C. G. Jung Foundation for Analytical Psychology, 1972.

Harrison, J. *Themis.* Cleveland and New York: Meridian Books, The World Publishing Company, 1927.

Hart, G. *A Dictionary of Egyptian Gods and Goddesses.* London: Routledge & Kegan Paul, 1986.

Hearn, J., D. L. Sheppard, P. Tancred-Sheriff, and G. Burrell, eds. *The Sexuality of Organization.* London: Sage Publications, 1989.

Hillman, J. *Re-visioning Psychology.* New York: Harper and Row, 1975.

Hillman, J. ed. *Puer Papers.* Dallas: Spring Publications, 1979.

Hillman, J. *Thought of the Heart.* Eranos Lectures No. 2. Dallas: Spring Publications, 1981.

Hochschild, A., with A. Machung. *The Second Shift: Working Parents and the Revolution at Home.* New York: Viking Penguin, 1989.

Hoeller, S. "Goddesses, Yes; Goddess, No." *Gnosis* 13:54, 1989.

Horney, K. "The Distrust Between the Sexes." in H. Kelmen, ed. *Feminine Psychology.* New York: W.W. Norton, 1967.

Hyman, I., and J. Wise, eds. *Corporal Punishment in American Education.* Philadelphia: Temple University Press, 1979.

Jacklin, C., J. DiPietry, and E. Maccoby. "Sex-typing Behavior and Sex-typing Pressure in Child/parent Interaction." *Archives of Sexual Behavior,* 1984.

Johnson, R. *Ecstasy: Understanding the Psychology of Joy.* San Francisco: Harper and Row, 1987.

Jung, C. G. *Man and His Symbols.* London: Aldus Books, 1964.

Jung, C. G. *Analytical Psychology: Its Theory and Practice.* New York: Pantheon, 1968; originally published 1935.

Jung, C. G. *Archetypes and the Collective Unconscious.* Vol. 9 Pt. I of *Collected Works.* New York: Pantheon, 1959.

Kammer, J. ed. *Good Will Toward Men.* New York: St. Martin's Press, 1994.

Keen, S. *Fire in the Belly: On Being a Man.* New York: Bantam Books, 1991.

Kerenyi, K. *Dionysos: Archetypal Image of Indestructible Life.* Princeton, NJ: Princeton University Press, 1976.

Kerenyi, K. *Goddesses of Sun and Moon.* Dallas: Spring Publications, 1979.

Kipnis, A. *Knights Without Armor: A Practical Guide for Men in Quest of Masculine Soul.* Los Angeles: Jeremy P. Tarcher, 1991; New York: Putnam and Sons, 1992.

Kipnis, A., and E. Herron. *Gender War, Gender Peace: The Quest for Love and Justice Between Women and Men.* New York: William Morrow, 1994.

Knapp, M. L. *Nonverbal Communication in Human Interaction.* New York: Holt, Rinehart, and Winston, 1972.

Kohut, H., and E. Wolf. "The Disorders of the Self and Their Treatment: An Outline." *International Journal of Psychoanalysis,* 1978.

Laing, R. D. *The Divided Self: An Existential Study in Sanity and Madness.* 2d ed. Harmondsworth, Middlesex, England: Penguin Books, 1966.

Lee, J. *Facing The Fire: Experiencing and Expressing Anger Appropriately.* New York: Bantam Books, 1993.

Lowinsky, N. R. *Stories from the Motherline: Reclaiming the Mother-Daughter Bond, Finding Our Feminine Souls.* Los Angeles: Jeremy P. Tarcher, 1992.

Maccoby, E., and C. Jacklin. *The Psychology of Sex Differences.* Stanford, CA: Stanford University Press, 1974.

Mahdi, L., and F. and M. Little, eds. *Betwixt and Between.* La Salle, IL: Open Court Publishers, 1987.

Margulis, L., and D. Sagan. *Mystery Dance: On the Evolution of Human Sexuality.* New York: Summit Books, 1991.

Mead, M. *Male and Female.* New York: William Morrow, 1949.

Meade, M. *Men and the Water of Life: Initiation and the Tempering of Men.* New York: HarperSanFrancisco, 1993.

Mitscherlich, A. *Society Without the Father: A Contribution to Social Psychology.* New York: Harper Perennial, 1993.

Moir, A., and D. Jessel. *Brain Sex: The Real Difference Between Men and Women.* New York: Carol Publishing Group, 1991.

Money, J. and A. A. Ehrhardt. *Man and Woman, Boy and Girl.* Baltimore: Johns Hopkins University Press, 1972.

Monick, E. *Phallos: Sacred Image of the Masculine.* Toronto: Inner City Books, 1987.

Montagu, A. *The Natural Superiority of Women.* New York: Collier, 1974.

Moon, S. *Changing Woman and Her Sisters.* San Francisco: Guild for Psychological Studies, 1984.

Moore, R., and D. Gillette. *The Warrior Within.* New York: William Morrow, 1992.

Moore, R., and D. Gillette. *King, Warrior, Magician, Lover: Rediscovering the Archetypes of the Mature Masculine.* San Francisco: Harper, 1990.

Moyne, J., and C. Barks, trans. *Open Secrets.* Putney, VT: Threshold Books, 1984.

Nietzsche, F. *The Birth of Tragedy and the Case of Wagner.* trans. W. Kaufman. New York: Vintage Books, 1967.

Neumann, E. *The Great Mother: An Analysis of the Archetype.* trans. R. Mannheim. Bollingen Series XLVII. Princeton, NJ: Princeton University Press, 1963.

Notman, M. T., and C. C. Nadelson. *Women and Men: New Perspectives on Gender Differences.* Washington, DC: American Psychiatric Press, 1991.

O'Brien, S. *Child Abuse: A Crying Shame.* Provo, UT: Brigham Young University Press, 1980.

Olson, C. ed. *The Book of the Goddess Past and Present.* New York: The Crossroad Publishing Co., 1983.

Osherson, S. *Finding Our Fathers: The Unfinished Business of Manhood.* New York: The Free Press, 1986.

Otto, W. F. *Dionysus: Myth and Cult.* Bloomington: University of Indiana Press, 1965.

Ovid. *The Metamorphoses of Ovid.* trans. M. M. Innes. Baltimore: Penguin Books, 1955.

Paglia, C. "Feminism and the Forgotten Power of Sex." *Harpers,* March 1990.

Paglia, C. "Image." *San Francisco Examiner,* July 7, 1991.

Paglia, C. *Sexual Personae: Art and Decadence from Nefertiti to Emily Dickinson.* New Haven, CT: Yale University Press, 1991.

Paris, G. *Pagan Meditations.* Dallas: Spring Publications, 1988.

Perera, S. *The Scapegoat Complex: Toward a Mythology of Shadow and Guilt.* Toronto: Inner City Books, 1986.

Perry, D. *Warriors of the Heart.* Cooperstown, NY: Sunstone Publications, 1991.

Reichard, G. A. *Navajo Religion: A Study of Symbolism.* Princeton, NJ: Princeton University Press, 1950.

Rilke, R. M. *The Best of Rilke.* trans. Walter Arndt. Hanover and London: University Press of New England, 1989.

Rix, S. E., ed. *The American Woman, 1988–89: A Status Report.* New York: W. W. Norton, 1988.

Rogers, C. *A Way of Being.* Boston: Houghton Mifflin, 1980.

Romberg, R. *Circumcision: The Painful Dilemma.* South Hadley, MA: Bergin and Garvey, 1985.

Rush, A. *Moon, Moon.* New York: Random House, and Berkeley, CA: Moon Books, 1976.

Sanford, L., and M. E. Donovan. *Women and Self Esteem.* New York: Penguin, 1985.

Sheldrake, R. *The Rebirth of Nature.* London: Rider, 1990.

Simons, G. L. *Sex and Superstition.* New York: Harper and Row, 1973.

Singer, K. I. "Group Work with Men Who Experienced Incest in Childhood." *American Journal of Orthopsychiatry,* July 1989.

288

Sommers, C. "Hard-Line Feminists Guilty of Ms. Representation." *The Wall Street Journal*, November 7, 1991.

Sommers, C. *Who Stole Feminism?* New York: Simon and Shuster, 1994.

Starr, T. *The Natural Inferiority of Women: Outrageous Pronouncements of Misguided Males*. New York: Poseidon Press, 1991.

Steinem, G. *The Boston Globe*, May 14, 1987.

Steinmetz, S. "Battered Husbands." in F. Baumli, ed. *Men Freeing Men*. Jersey City, NJ: New Atlantis Press, 1985.

Straus, M. A., and R. J. Gelles. *Intimate Violence*. New York: Simon & Schuster, 1988.

Straus, M. A. "Physical Assaults by Wives: A Major Social Problem." in R. J. Gelles and D. Loseke, eds. *Current Controversies on Family Violence*. Beverly Hills, CA: Sage Publications, 1993.

Sugerman, S. *Sin and Madness: Studies in Narcissism*. Philadelphia: The Westminster Press, 1976.

Tannen, D. *You Just Don't Understand: Women and Men in Conversation*. New York: William Morrow, 1990.

Tannen, D. *Talking From 9 to 5*. New York: William Morrow, 1994.

Tavris, C. *The Mismeasure of Woman*. New York: Simon & Schuster, 1992.

Taylor, J. "Don't Blame Me: The New Culture of Victimization." *This World, San Francisco Chronicle*, August 18, 1991.

Teish, L. *Jambalaya: The Natural Woman's Book*. San Francisco: Harper and Row, 1985.

Tiger, L., and J. Shepher. *Women in the Kibbutz*. London: Penguin Books, 1977.

Tingley, J. *Genderflex™:Ending the Workplace War Between the Sexes*. Phoenix: Performance Improvement Pros, 1993.

Tripp, E. *The Meridian Handbook of Classical Mythology (Crowell's Handbook of Classical Mythology)*. New York: New American Library, 1970.

U.S. Department of Commerce Bureau of the Census. "Money, Income and Poverty Status." *U.S. Current Population Reports*, Series P-60, No. 168, 1989.

U.S. Department of Health and Human Services, Public Health Service, National Centers for Disease Control. *Vital Statistics of the United States*. Vol. II: Mortality, 1987. Washington, DC: National Center for Health Statistics, 1987–88.

U.S. Department of Justice, Bureau of Justice Statistics. *Source Book of Criminal Justice Statistics*. Washington, DC: USGPO, 1990.

U.S. National Center for Health Statistics. *U.S. Department of Health Service*. Washington, DC: Health Resources Administration.

Van Over, R. *Creation Myths from Around the World*. New York, and Scarborough, Ontario: A. A. Meridan Publishers, 1980.

Welwood, J. *Journey of the Heart: Intimate Relationship and the Path of Love*. New York: Harper Perennial, 1991.

Wheeler, P. *The Sacred Scriptures of the Japanese*. New York: Henry Schuman, 1952.

290

Winnicott, D. *Through Pediatrics to Psychoanalysis*. New York: Basic Books, 1975.

Wolf, N. *The Beauty Myth: How Images of Beauty Are Used Against Women*. New York: William Morrow, 1991.

Wolf, N. *Fire With Fire: The New Female Power and How It Will Change the 21st Century*. New York: Random House, 1993.

Wolkstein, D. *The First Love Stories: From Isis and Osiris to Tristan and Iseult*. New York: HarperCollins, 1991.

Wolkstein, D., and S. Kramer. *Inanna: Queen of Heaven and Earth: Her Stories and Hymns from Sumer*. New York: Harper and Row, 1983.

Wollstonecraft, M. *A Vindication of the Rights of Women*. C. Postman, ed. New York: W. W. Norton, 1975; originally published 1792.

Woodman, M. *Addiction to Perfection: The Still Unravished Bride*. Toronto: Inner City Books, 1982.

Woodman, M. *The Ravaged Bridegroom: Masculinity in Women*. Toronto: Inner City Books, 1990.

Zweig, C., and J. Abrams. eds. *Meeting the Shadow: The Hidden Power of the Dark Side of Human Nature*. Los Angeles: Jeremy P. Tarcher, 1991.

ABOUT THE AUTHORS

Aaron Kipnis, Ph.D.

Over the last two decades Dr. Aaron Kipnis has facilitated men's and mixed-gender groups for more than twenty thousand people. He has lectured on male psychology and gender issues for various institutes and universities including Harvard Medical School, and has trained several thousand therapists, managers, and human resource personnel about how to work with gender-related issues. As the director of the National Violence Prevention Center and co-director of the Gender Relations Institute, he has been an adviser to corporations and U.S. governmental agencies as well as to foreign governments. He is also a frequent guest on radio and national television and is a contributing editor to several journals. Aaron has written many articles, has contributed chapters to half a dozen book anthologies, and is the author of the critically acclaimed book *Knights Without Armor.* (Tarcher 1991, Putnam 1992).

Elizabeth Herron, M.A.

Elizabeth Herron is a trainer, consultant, and educator with more than fifteen years of experience in gender reconciliation and women's empowerment. She has conducted numerous trainings, classes, and conferences for women and has taught Gender Diplomacy™ to thousands of women and men in universities, training institutes, corporations, and governmental agencies. She has also trained many managers and helping professionals of both sexes about how to work more effectively with members of the other sex. Elizabeth has been a guest on many radio and TV talk shows such as the "Today Show," "Donahue," and "Sonya Live," and is the author of numerous articles on gender issues. She has also contributed chapters to several book anthologies. She is co-director of the Gender Relations Institute and is the mother of two healthy, fierce, and beautiful young women.

For correspondence with the authors or their current lecture and training schedule, write to

> The Gender Relations Institute
> P.O. Box 4782
> Santa Barbara, CA 93140

Also by Aaron Kipnis

Knights Without Armor: A Practical Guide for Men in Quest of Masculine Soul. 1991 Jeremy P. Tarcher, 1992 Putnam and Sons